Aristotle's Logic
of Education

New Perspectives
in Philosophical Scholarship
Texts and Issues

James Duerlinger
General Editor

Vol. 9

PETER LANG
New York • Washington, D.C./Baltimore • Boston
Bern • Frankfurt am Main • Berlin • Vienna • Paris

Richard W. Bauman

Aristotle's Logic
of Education

PETER LANG
New York • Washington, D.C./Baltimore • Boston
Bern • Frankfurt am Main • Berlin • Vienna • Paris

Library of Congress Cataloging-in-Publication Data

Bauman, Richard W.
Aristotle's logic of education / Richard W. Bauman.
p. cm. — (New perspectives in philosophical scholarship; vol. 9)
Includes bibliographical references and index.
1. Aristotle—Contributions in education. 2. Logic. 3. Teaching. 4. Learning.
I. Title. II. Series: New perspectives in philosophical scholarship; 9.
LB85.A72B38   370'.1—dc21   97-48799
ISBN 0-8204-4007-8
ISSN 1045-4500

Die Deutsche Bibliothek-CIP-Einheitsaufnahme

Bauman, Richard W.:
Aristotle's logic of education / Richard W. Bauman.
–New York; Washington, D.C./Baltimore; Boston; Bern;
Frankfurt am Main; Berlin; Vienna; Paris: Lang.
(New perspectives in philosophical scholarship; Vol. 9)
ISBN 0-8204-4007-8

The paper in this book meets the guidelines for permanence and durability
of the Committee on Production Guidelines for Book Longevity
of the Council of Library Resources.

© 1998 Peter Lang Publishing, Inc., New York

Printed in the United States of America.

Acknowledgments

The themes of this study grew out of work originally supervised by Professor Allan T. Pearson, now Dean of Education at the University of Western Ontario, who provided thoughtful guidance, probing questions, and exemplary good cheer.

In the preparation of the final version of this book, I have enjoyed the financial generosity of Research Enhancement Fund at the University of Alberta, which provided assistance through the good offices of Dr. Ron Kratochvil, Associate Vice-President (Research) and his executive assistant, Dr. Katharine Moore.

Finally, I owe a debt of gratitude to the Faculty of Law at the University of Alberta, and its Dean, Lewis Klar, for contributing both material and moral support for the project.

Contents

Abbreviations

Titles of works by Aristotle are referred to in the text and notes in abbreviated form as follows:

An. Post.	*Posterior Analytics*
An. Pr.	*Prior Analytics*
Cat.	*Categories*
De An.	*De Anima*
N.E.	*Nicomachean Ethics*
De Int.	*De Interpretatione*
De Mem.	*On Memory and Reminiscence*
Met.	*Metaphysics*
Phys.	*Physics*
Poet.	*Poetics*
Pol.	*Politics*
Rhet.	*Rhetoric*
S.E.	*On Sophistical Refutations*
Top.	*Topics*

And in general it is a sign of the man who knows and who does not know, that the former can teach, and therefore we think art more truly knowledge than experience is; for artists can teach, and men of mere experience cannot.

Aristotle, Metaphysics A 981^b7-9

Aristotle was the first accurate critic, and the truest judge; nay, the greatest philosopher, the world ever had; for, he noted the vices of all knowledges, in all creatures, and out of men's perfections in a science, he formed still one art. So he taught us two offices together, how we ought to judge rightly of others, and what we ought to imitate especially in ourselves.

Ben Jonson, Timber: or Discoveries, ll. 3109-3117

Any explanation has its foundation in training. (Educators ought to remember this.)

Ludwig Wittgenstein, Zettel, §419

CHAPTER ONE

Introduction

In some of his work on logic, Aristotle goes beyond the formal syllogism that is one of his most original achievements, and draws a powerful portrait of the necessary and sufficient conditions by which one can judge when scientific knowledge has been attained. His arguments are not strictly about epistemology, as today we understand the concerns of that branch of philosophy. He is also interested in how this kind of knowledge can result only from teaching; and not just any teaching, but from a method that reflects the formal structure of the demonstrative syllogism. He tells us how this teaching ought to proceed and what the learner must do in order to make the teaching successful. The pedagogic enterprise is largely shaped by what Aristotle claims, with some modesty, to have discovered about valid forms of argument.

This book will investigate, first, how the demonstrative or apodeictic syllogism becomes for Aristotle the model for all teaching aimed at imparting scientific knowledge; and secondly, what implications flow from such a model. These implications are important not only for a theory of education, but they also affect the validity of some traditional views on the usefulness of all syllogistic reasoning.

The conclusion arrived at here is that, while Aristotle's programme is terminologically rigorous and philosophically ambitious, nonetheless it is inadequate for the end Aristotle envisions. His programme encompasses only a part of the knowledge that can be taught. Nor is such a programme desirable or defensible in view of our modern concepts of what science education, and other studies too, ought to achieve.

Chapter Two constitutes a brief summary of Aristotle's formal logic, including his use of variables instead of individual terms, his way of arranging series of propositions into moods and figures, the modal varieties of syllogism, and the methods he deploys to prove the validity of certain moods. This summary is limited to that degree of detail necessary to serve as a foundation for the discussion in the ensuing chapters. Chapter Two also recounts some of the historical and pedagogical background to the development of the syllogism. Out of this chapter emerges an understanding of the form of the demonstrative syllogism and the characteristics of its constituent propositions. On the teacher's ability to demonstrate, to define, and to explain scientifically rests the success of the teaching enterprise. The means by which the knowledge gained by scientific inquiry is transmitted to students is a logical method, in the strictest sense.

Chapter Three provides a lengthy account of Aristotle's theory about the teaching and learning of the sciences. His programme is chiefly set forth and explained in the *Posterior Analytics*. His discussion of this topic is studded with technical terms, compressed arguments, and references and allusions to what Aristotle has written in other works dealing with syllogism. There is also a want of examples that would undoubtedly help to illustrate some of his more obscure points. In view of these features, Chapter Three is exegetical. By keeping the pedagogic purpose of the syllogism in the foreground of the discussion, some dark places in Aristotle's treatise are illuminated, or at least made less shadowy. In particular, the contents of Aristotle's final chapter in the *Posterior Analytics*, on how the basic principles of a science are acquired by a learner, are thrown into relation against the limits to what teaching can accomplish.

How Aristotle's programme is meant to overcome the perennially vexing problem posed by Meno in Plato's eponymous dialogue is the focus of Chapter Four. Part of the general thesis defended here is that Aristotle is compelled by Meno's dilemma about learning to give an account of the acquisition of first principles. This differs from the solution offered by Plato, in the form of the doctrine of ἀνάμνησις. Although Aristotle criticizes Plato's doctrine, and attempts to provide a better solution, I shall show that Aristotle shares many presuppositions with Plato about the possibility of inquiry and learning. There is also at this stage a discussion about how Plato and Aristotle use the concept of ἀπορία or perplexity in promoting the learner's progress.

Chapter Five is devoted to a discussion of the time-honoured charge that syllogistic reasoning always involves the commission of a *petitio principii*. I argue in this chapter that such a charge cannot be maintained. Syllogism, at least in its demonstrative variety, is not intended by Aristotle to be used as a method of scientific inquiry and for the discovery of fresh knowledge. Instead, it is an organized means of imparting to students knowledge already won. That chapter considers Mill's version of the traditional critique in order to show that the syllogism, as depicted by Mill, bears little resemblance to the rational method of teaching prescribed in the *Posterior Analytics*.

Chapter Six examines the merits of Aristotle's pedagogic scheme. The assessment is mainly critical. I argue that Aristotle's attempt to escape Meno's dilemma forces him into an untenable position on the question of what previous knowledge is necessary in order for learning to occur. An alternative account of what previous knowledge can amount to is presented through examples drawn from both teaching and non-teaching contexts. Aristotle's difficulty in giving an adequate account of requisite previous knowledge is shown also to be the basis for his unsatisfying account of ἐπαγωγή or the process by which knowledge of first principles is obtained. I also consider in this context some recent misconstructions of ἐπαγωγή and I discuss the teacher's ability to disclose the αἰτία or explanation in the course of demonstration. It emerges that Aristotle's concept of explanation is largely irrelevant to modern conceptions of explanation both in the sciences and also in science teaching. Finally, I deal with and reject Aristotle's argument that there is, and can be, only a single method of teaching.

Before launching into a description of Aristotle's syllogistic scheme, I have a few remarks on how Aristotle's thoughts about a systematic pedagogy have generally been overlooked in modern discussions of educational theory. I then advance some arguments about why the study, from the perspective of educational philosophy, of such a germinal thinker in Western culture is both useful and fascinating.[1]

Aristotle has some important and interesting things to say about the concepts of teaching and learning in the arts and sciences and about the role of the state in the education of its citizens. Yet little reference is commonly made to his views among philosophers of education when they sit down to discuss such questions as: How are the sciences to be taught? What sort of knowledge is teachable? Is there a method of teaching that will infallibly help students to learn?

Where attempts have been made to illuminate or present Aristotle's thoughts on education, such treatments tend to concentrate on his political and ethical writings. For example, Burnet's translation of extensive passages from the *Politics* and the *Nicomachean Ethics* was the first attempt, early in this century, to extract from the wealth of the Aristotelian corpus what Burnet judged as likely both to interest students of educational theory and to profit them.[2] This pattern has continued to the present, as illustrated by a more modern compilation of excerpts made by Howie, and designed to give undergraduates a foothold in the study of Aristotle.[3] Studies published about an educational aspect of

---

[1]   This is not to imply that, like the poet Shelley, I think "we are all Greeks," because of some misguided sense of exclusive indebtedness to ancient Greek philosophy or culture. Rather, it is salutary to remind ourselves, in view of feminist and multicultural challenges to the educational centrality of a "Western canon," of the extent to which some modern scholars have emphasized the "strangeness" or "otherness" of ancient Greek civilization. See Bernard Knox, *The Oldest Dead White European Males and Other Reflections on the Classics* (New York: W. W. Norton, 1993), p. 31.

[2]   John Burnet (ed.), *Aristotle on Education* (Cambridge: Cambridge University Press, 1903).

[3]   George Howie (ed.), *Aristotle on Education* (London: Collier-Macmillan Limited, 1968). Note the editor's introductory words at p. 10:

This book will not have served its proper purpose unless it stimulates the student to read more extensively in Aristotle, and particularly those tremendously enriching and influential books, the *Ethics* and the *Politics*.

Aristotle's work typically have been confined to a discussion of what Aristotle has to say about the education of youth in the πόλις.[4] Those studies do not pretend to deal with the central concepts of learning and teaching and the knowledge that is obtained by theoretical science. When Aristotle is treated in histories or summaries of educational thought, the result is again that, in general, what Aristotle called the practical sciences are emphasized along with his contributions thereto. A reader might come away with little inkling that Aristotle ever deals with any problems of learning other than how people become disposed towards virtuous conduct.[5] An exception to this trend is found in the brief treatment by Brumbaugh

---

[4] See Carnes Lord, *Education and Culture in the Political Thought of Aristotle* (Ithaca, N.Y.: Cornell University Press, 1982) and, for an earlier and sketchier example, Cyril Wynn and Maurice Jacks, *Aristotle: His Thought and Its Relevance Today* (London: Methuen, 1967).

[5] See, for example, William Frankena, *Three Historical Philosophies of Education* (Chicago: Scott, Foresman and Company, 1965), pp. 15–78. For an example of Aristotle's treatment among historians of educational thought, see S. J. Curtis and M. E. A. Boultwood, *A Short History of Educational Ideas*, 5th ed. (Slough: University Tutorial Press, 1977), ch. 2. Note in particular some of the comments of the latter authors at p. 31, which on historical or philosophical grounds are difficult to justify:

> Perhaps the most important event in Aristotle's life was his appointment as tutor to the young Alexander. His teaching does not seem to have created in Alexander the power of self-control ... Alexander, when he started on his career of conquest did not forget his old tutor whom he always regarded with admiration and respect.

For a review of the ancient biographical information about Aristotle, see Anton Hermann Chroust, *Aristotle: New Light on His Life and Some of His Lost Works*, 2 vols. (Notre Dame: University of Notre Dame Press, 1973) where at pp. 131–32 it is noted:

> It should also be remembered that, according to what appears to be a well established tradition, in later years Aristotle and Alexander were not on the best of terms. It has already been shown that Alexander allegedly threatened Aristotle with dire reprisals, while Aristotle is said to have not only been mortally afraid of Alexander, but also to have played an active role in the alleged poisoning of Alexander.

and Lawrence.[6] Those authors stress that merely considering certain passages from the *Politics*, for instance, will hardly suffice to represent or indicate the full range of Aristotle's opinions on the nature, the techniques, the process, the function, and the ends of education.

The general neglect of Aristotle in educational circles differs markedly from the attention lavished on Plato, to whose work, throughout the growth of philosophy of education as a discipline, writers and commentators have continued to turn for a starting point for their own inquiries. There are several explanations for this contrast in treatment of Plato and Aristotle. First, Aristotle never collected and published in any surviving systematic treatise his views on the basic questions about education that still stimulate and perplex modern writers. Plato, on the other hand, composed both the *Republic* and the *Laws*, the first of which has been incalculably influential down the ages. There is evidence that among the early writings attributed to Aristotle's period as a member of the Academy he wrote a dialogue entitled *On Education*.[7] None of these so-called exoteric or extramural writings survives. All that remains are the judgments by ancient literary critics, who knew these dialogues well, that they were uncommonly fluent and polished. This matter of style leads to the next reason for Aristotle's relative neglect. By comparison with Plato's highly diverting dialogues, which often

---

6   Robert S. Brumbaugh and Nathaniel M. Lawrence, *Philosophers on Education: Six Essays on the Foundations of Western Thought* (Boston: Houghton Mifflin, 1963, reprinted 1986), pp. 40–75. On p. 73 they draw the reasonable conclusion that:
     . . . Aristotle's work is capable of providing us with a rather full philosophy of education when we read that work in the context of his total philosophy.

7   See Sir David Ross, *Aristotle*, 6th ed. (London: Routledge, 1995), p. 7, and Chroust, *supra* n. 5, vol. 2, ch. 2. There is also an entrenched tradition, going back to a life of Aristotle attributed to Ptolemy, that Aristotle wrote his lost *Protrepticus* in part as a criticism of Isocrates's methods of education, and that the extant *Antidosis* of Isocrates is a rejoinder to Aristotle's attack. See Chroust, *supra* n. 5, vol. 1, pp. 11 and 275, and for an outline of the views of Isocrates, James L. Jarrett, *The Educational Theories of the Sophists* (New York: Teachers College Press, 1969), pp. 94–105.

feature Socrates as the intellectual gadfly and which are easy to follow in their dramatic form, Aristotle's surviving texts at first glance appear dry, solemn, and forbiddingly technical. Yet a third explanation lies in the fate of Aristotle's work after the hegemony of Greek civilization in the West had disappeared. A loose collection of dogmas and doctrines that formed what was called Aristotelianism, and which was adopted and expounded by thinkers who were not always directly acquainted with Aristotle's writings, came into vogue in the twelfth century.[8] Especially at such leading universities as Paris and Oxford, medieval teachers promoted a scholastic curriculum that relied heavily on certain Aristotelian principles and precepts.[9] When the reaction against medieval science and intellectualism began and then gathered momentum, by as early as the fourteenth century, the perceived links between Aristotle and the so-called aridities of the Schoolmen had become so strong that Aristotle's reputation among both scientific and educational thinkers suffered.[10] Readers are not always careful or consistent in separating

---

[8] For a general account of the rise of this school of thought, see J. L. Stocks, *Aristotelianism* (London: Harrap, 1925), ch. 3.

[9] An excellent summary of the influx and study of Aristotle's Organon is contained in R. R. Bolgar, *The Classical Heritage and Its Beneficiaries* (Cambridge: Cambridge University Press, 1954), pp. 149–62. On the medieval curricula, see Gordon Leff, *Paris and Oxford Universities in the Thirteenth and Fourteenth Centuries: An Institutional and Intellectual History* (New York: John Wiley & Sons, 1968). Rashdall records some of the grumblings that the recovery of Aristotle's works caused among medieval curriculum planners (and which have a curiously modern echo):

> The humanists who wrote towards the close of the twelfth century are full of complaints at the increasing neglect of grammatical and historical training and the undisciplined rawness of the young philosophers.

This passage is drawn from Hastings Rashdall, *The Universities of Europe in the Middle Ages*, 2nd ed., edited by F. M. Powicke and A. B. Emden, 3 vols. (Oxford: Oxford University Press, 1936), vol. 1, p. 71.

[10] A good discussion of the leading pamphlets and books in the revolt against Aristotelianism can be found in Richard Foster Jones, *Ancients and Moderns*, 2nd ed. (St. Louis: Washington University Press, 1961). The uses of Aristotle's scientific work, including the treatises on biological, anatomical, meteorological, and mechanical topics are fascinatingly presented in A. C.

scientific work from philosophic work when they are both done by the same writer, and the depreciation of the former tends to obscure the continuing value of the latter.[11] Because Aristotle engaged so fruitfully in both forms of study, the occasional absurdities into which he falls as a natural philosopher have unfortunately coloured the perceptions of his work in what now is called the philosophy of science and science teaching. Some of his claims, for example, that the heart is the seat of the soul, that some animals reproduce by spontaneous generation, or that the heavens consist of fixed concentric spheres, seem outlandish today and tend to deflect some of the attention his philosophical achievements deserve.

In summary, then, because of the lack of a specific treatise by Aristotle on education, the density of his writing style and his argumentation, the revolt against Aristotelianism in the pre-modern era, and the supersession of many of his specific scientific findings, the influence of Aristotle's work on contemporary philosophy of scientific education has been slight. Reference to his work in educational journals is predominantly to his theories of ethics and politics.[12]

This consequence is the more surprising in view of the encyclopaedic range of Aristotle's interest and his unflagging curiosity. He wrote on such a variety of topics that it is hard to believe that teaching and learning do not have a place somewhere in his systematic account of how people come to know things and what

---

Crombie, *Medieval and Early Modern Science*, 2 vols. (Garden City, N.Y.: Doubleday and Co.; published in Anchor Books, 1959). Aristotle's fall from grace in the eyes of natural philosophers, which began in the Middle Ages, is recounted in Crombie, vol. 2, ch. 2, pp. 1–119.

11   See D. J. O'Connor, *An Introduction to the Philosophy of Education* (London: Routledge & Kegan Paul, 1957), pp. 21ff. For the separation of science from philosophy, and its implications for educational theory.

12   See, for example, Joseph J. Chambliss, "Aristotle's Conception of Childhood and the Poliscraft" (1982) 13 Educational Studies 33–43; Daniel Pekarsky, "The Aristotelian Principle and Education" (1980) 30 Educational Theory 281–91; Paul A. Wagner, "The Aristotelian Notion of 'Nomos' and Educational Policy Studies" (1980) 5 Review Journal of Philosophy and Social Science 219–27; and Adina Schwartz, "Aristotle on Education and Choice" (1979) 29 Educational Theory 97–107.

things they have the capacity to know. In addition, we should consider the details of his biography. After belonging to the Academy for approximately twenty years, first as a student and then as a teacher and author, he founded on his return to Athens his own school, the Lyceum or Peripatos. He was the chief administrator of that school for about a dozen years until his final departure from Athens.[13] There is also the biographical tradition, possibly apocryphal, that Aristotle was hired by Philip of Macedon to tutor the young Alexander.[14] In his *Divine Comedy*, Dante depicts a flock of philosophers, sitting as in a family, who "look to" Aristotle and "do him honor" as "the acknowledged Master of those who know." In a reversal, Aristotle is treated as Plato's teacher.[15] Averroës refers to Aristotle simply as "the Master" or the "first master of the philosophers."[16]

There are even better reasons than these for studying Aristotle from an educational standpoint. Although his conclusions, especially on some scientific matters, are antiquated, or in political theory remain largely conditioned by his time and place, his methods in conducting philosophical investigations and in reaching conclusions are still instructive. He is fond of beginning his inquiries with a review of what has previously been said upon the subject in issue, both by ordinary observers and also by those who are supposed to know, that is, the professionals. He then examines the conflicts and

---

[13]   The organization and accomplishments of the Lyceum are described in J. P. Lynch, *Aristotle's School: A Study of a Greek Educational Institution* (Berkeley: University of California Press, 1972) and, to a lesser extent, in Felix Grayeff, *Aristotle and His School* (London: Duckworth, 1974), pp. 13–88. For an amusing reconstruction of what Aristotle's own classroom and lecture-style might have been like, to judge from the evidence in the surviving treatises, see Henry Jackson, "Aristotle's Lecture-Room and Lectures" (1920) 35 Journal of Philology 191–200.

[14]   See Chroust, *supra* n. 5.

[15]   At the time Dante composed, many of Aristotle's writings had been translated, via Arabic versions, into Latin, while Plato's dialogues were still unavailable in the West: see Knox, *supra* n. 1, p. 16.

[16]   See Dante Alighieri, *The Inferno of Dante*, trans. Robert Pinsky (New York: Farrar, Straus and Giroux, 1994), p. 41 (Canto IV, 1. 131) and Averroës, *Tahafut al-Tahafut*, trans. Simon van den Bergh (London: Luzac and Co., 1954), p. 11.

inconsistencies arising out of what has been said. From this initial material he moves forward into his inquiry proper and sets forth preliminary arguments and makes subtle discriminations where he thinks they are required. He rarely loses sight of the fundamental question, but keeps circling it, trying to catch a new aspect of it. He is always willing to retrace his steps if one branch of an argument turns out to lead nowhere. He constantly measures arguments, both his own and those propounded by others, against rigorous standards of validity and soundness, even if such arguments are not framed in a deductive form. He recognizes that different subjects of inquiry must be investigated in different ways and that the principles underlying a phenomenon of nature are not always discoverable by any one simple formula. It is in view of these characteristics, not because of what later interpreters might conceive to be his final doctrines, that Aristotle serves as a salutary and instructive model for the practice of philosophy in general, and for the philosophy of education in particular. Besides these methods of doing philosophy, we should take cognizance of certain key concepts and terminology that pervade his thought, for they have a possible permanent value that goes beyond those specific conclusions Aristotle reaches. Readers should not be deterred by the apparent technicalities with which his writing abounds, made all the more formidable because ancient Greek is now a dead language. Even so studied a stylist as Mill allows that "Aristotle's literary style, though often awkward (being both prolix and elliptical) is by no means, in his best preserved works, deficient in clearness."[17]

---

[17]   John Stuart Mill, "Grote's Aristotle" in *Collected Works of John Stuart Mill*, ed. J. M. Robson, 12 vols. (Toronto: University of Toronto Press, 1978), vol. 11: *Essays on Philosophy and the Classics*, p. 510. We might also keep in mind the following words, and recognize that difficult thought cannot always be made easy:

> If, in the hands of a competent writer, prose style is the image of the mind that produces it, Aristotle's prose cannot be expected to lack force, structural strength, subtlety, or complexity . . . In translating, I have decided therefore to keep very close to the words, to add no grace, to smooth no roughness, thinking rather of Aristotle as a lecturer whose authority rests in the sustained gravity and openness of speech; a man who chooses deliberate, even angular, plainness in

This book is not intended to be an essay in the history of ideas, much less the history of Aristotle's own contributions to the educational practices of fourth-century Athens.[18] Rather, my aim here will be to discuss Aristotle's work so as to "engage him in argument as if he were a contemporary."[19] Although the focus will be primarily on his logical works, and in particular the *Analytics*, reference will also be made to works throughout the Aristotelian canon, because the technical terms and modes of argument that Aristotle uses and develops recur in his writings on quite dissimilar topics. A usage in one context often throws light on a usage in a different passage. For example, his account of how a person learns to become good in an ethical sense owes something to his account in general of the dichotomy of potentiality and actuality in nature, the principle of change, and the formation of dispositions out of repeated actions. The same general account, in turn, has some bearing on the learner's acquisition of first principles of a science. Throughout his philosophic writing Aristotle is concerned with clarifying and augmenting our understanding of many of the fundamental ideas by which subsequent philosophy has been dominated and intrigued: nature, reason, cause, number, knowledge, soul. These ideas are common to many fields of study and it would be misleading, to Aristotle's way of thinking, to characterize each of them as having a special import or meaning in one field that completely excluded, or was immune from, the meaning of that idea in another field.

Aristotle's thoughts on education are not, as with some other major philosophical figures (Kant and, more recently, Russell come to mind), a mere adjunct to his substantive philosophical work. Instead, what Aristotle has to say about instruction and the criteria

---

preference to rhetoric, stylishness, or fine and memorable phrasing. George Whalley, "On Translating Aristotle's *Poetics*" (1970) 39 University of Toronto Quarterly 77–106, pp. 86–87.

[18] On the latter topic, see such works as H. I. Marrou, *A History of Education in Antiquity*, trans. George Lamb (New York: Sheed and Ward, 1956) and Kenneth J. Freeman, *Schools of Hellas* (New York: Teachers College Press, 1969), as well as Lynch, *supra* n. 13.

[19] J. L. Ackrill, *Aristotle the Philosopher* (Oxford: Oxford University Press, 1981), p. 2.

for judging knowledge and understanding and how logic can be used to convey a certain type of knowledge form an inextricable part of the basic topics on which he exercises his genius. By contrast, in the work of Kant, it is often difficult to see how his precepts on education are derivable from, or in any way related to, the philosophical positions to which he adheres in his work on metaphysics and epistemology.[20] In form, Kant's contribution to education consists mainly in normative prescriptions about how pedagogy should proceed and at what it ought to aim. Aristotle's work on teaching and learning the sciences, although it includes many ideas that accord with common sense, does not form a pedagogy that consists of simple platitudes. The method of demonstration, which he envisions is alone capable of transmitting scientific knowledge, reflects stiff criteria by which one can judge when a person has learned something new. Aristotle does not adopt an epistemological stance and then see what this implies about teaching. Rather, his theory of teaching is interrelated with his theory of knowledge from the outset.[21] When we come to examine the *Posterior Analytics*, we shall find that we are dealing with an original thinker with a highly systematic bent. It might be said that some of the characteristics that distinguish Aristotle's customary way of approaching a philosophical problem have been revived in the field of educational theory, notably in the work of R. S. Peters and D. W. Hamlyn.[22]

---

[20]   For Kant's views, especially on what we would now call elementary schooling, see Frankena, *supra* n. 5.

[21]   Thus Aristotle's work should not be approached in the manner caricatured by Wittgenstein in the following passage:

> But the idealist will teach his children the word "chair" after all, for of course he wants to teach them to do this and that, e.g. to fetch a chair. The where will be the difference between what the idealist-educated children say and the realist ones? Won't the difference only be one of battle cry?

Ludwig Wittgenstein, *Zettel*, ed, G. E. M. Anscombe and G. H. von Wright, trans. G. E. M. Anscombe (Oxford: Basil Blackwell, 1967), §414, p. 74e.

[22]   For example, see R. S. Peters, "Reason and Habit: The Paradox of Moral Education" in W. R. Niblett (ed.), *Moral Education in a Changing Society* (London: Faber and Faber, 1963), pp. 46–65. Many of the prominent features

Throughout this book, references to the Greek text of Aristotle's writings will be to the texts contained in the Oxford Classical Series. Translations used here are generally drawn from the Revised Oxford Translation of Aristotle's works.[23] With respect to the *Posterior Analytics*, particularly where argument over the meaning of the original Greek is philosophically relevant, alternative various translations of that treatise will prove useful.

---

that mark Aristotle's philosophical method are described in Richard R. K. Sorabji, "Aristotle and Oxford Philosophy" (1969) 6 American Philosophical Quarterly 127–35. Sorabji usefully discusses also the relationship between definition and explanation in demonstrative syllogisms, as well as the notion of necessity in Aristotle's work and how it compares with some modern ideas on logical and non-logical necessity.

23   Aristotle, *The Complete Works of Aristotle*, ed. Jonathan Barnes, 2 vols. (Princeton: Princeton University Press, 1984). On occasion, I have consulted (and noted this accordingly in my text) the earlier standard Aristotle, *The Works of Aristotle Translated Into English*, eds. J. A. Smith and W. D. Ross, 12 vols. (Oxford: Clarendon Press, 1908–52).

CHAPTER TWO

Rudiments of Aristotle's Formal Logic

The value of Aristotle's effort in constructing his system of syllogistic inference (what we would nowadays call the foundations of formal logic) about what in some sense we already know is not unanimously conceded. Opinions range from Russell's scathing comment, "[a]ny person in the present day who wishes to learn logic will be wasting his time if he reads Aristotle or any of his disciples," to Jaeger's encomium of Aristotle's analytical style, which Jaeger sees as shaped by his discoveries in logic, so that:

> In his words everything is the most perfect, polished, logical art, not the rough-and-ready style of modern thinkers or scholars, who frequently confound observation with inference and are very poor in conscious nuances of logical precision.[1]

It is not necessary here to adjudicate between these two extreme points of view. The focus of this chapter is not on the syllogism in its

---

[1]   Bertrand Russell, *History of Western Philosophy* (London: George Allen and Unwin, 1961), p. 212; Werner Jaeger, *Aristotle: Fundamentals of the History of His Development*, 2nd ed., trans. Richard Robinson (London: Oxford University Press, 1950), pp. 370–71.

aspect as an analysis of all forms of judgment or in the aspect of how it relates to Aristotle's own philosophical practice as evidenced by his surviving treatises. Rather, the purpose of this chapter is to adumbrate Aristotle's system of valid inference and to introduce the argument that this system has an instructive or pedagogical side to it. Aristotle's logic is supposed to help explain the nature of the world by making intelligible those truths which can be deduced from basic premisses.[2]

This is to say more than that Aristotle's account of the syllogism can be and is used as an aid to learning elementary logic (*pace* Russell). This use is borne out by an examination of modern logic textbooks, which often contain a recapitulation and discussion of the categorical syllogism, complete with the sort of notation developed by teachers during the centuries after the rediscovery of the *Prior Analytics*, as well as exercises in class reasoning and such relatively modern devices as Venn diagrams and Euler circles.[3] The conclusion approached in this chapter is that syllogistic reasoning has, as a counterpart in Aristotle's account, syllogistic demonstration by which learners grasp principles of the highest order of generality.

It is necessary to review the salient features of Aristotle's account of the syllogism in general before we can proceed further to examine the use of the so-called apodeictic syllogism in the teaching and learning of what Aristotle refers to as scientific knowledge

---

2   See Jonathan Lear, *Aristotle: The Desire to Understand* (Cambridge: Cambridge University Press, 1988), p. 211.

3   See, for example, Herbert L. Searles, *Logic and Scientific Methods*, 3rd ed. (New York: Ronald Press, 1968), ch. 8; Morris R. Cohen and Ernest Nagel, *An Introduction to Logic* (New York: Harcourt, Brace and World, 1934, reprinted as a Harbinger paperback, 1962), ch. 4; Irving M. Copi and Carl Cohen, *Introduction to Logic*, 8th ed. (New York: Macmillan, 1990), ch. 6; Samuel Gorovitz and Ron G. Williams, *Philosophical Analysis: An Introduction to Its Language and Techniques*, 2nd ed. (New York: Random House, 1969), ch. 1; Robert H. Ennis, *Logic in Teaching* (Englewood Cliffs, N.J.: Prentice-Hall, 1969), ch. 4; Roger Simonds, *Beginning Philosophical Logic* (Washington, D.C.: University Press of America, 1978), ch. 5 *et passim*.

(ἐπιστήμη).[4] This latter topic is treated at length in the *Posterior Analytics*. Aristotle recognizes that only after he has introduced certain terminology, drawn pertinent distinctions, conducted a host of proofs and disproofs, and generally organized that branch of logic that we now call Aristotelian or traditional syllogistic, will he be able to discuss scientific demonstration. In his prefatory remarks to the *Prior Analytics* he claims:

> Syllogism should be discussed before demonstration, because syllogism is the more general: the demonstration is a sort of syllogism, but not every syllogism is a demonstration.[5]

In the text of this chapter and the notes that accompany it any reference solely to the pages, columns and lines of the Bekker edition of Aristotle's works will be to the *Prior Analytics*. Reference to other works of Aristotle will contain the relevant title as well. Unless otherwise indicated, English translations cited and quoted in this context are from Jenkinson's translation in the Revised Oxford series mentioned in the preceding chapter.[6]

---

4   Aristotle has various ways of categorizing syllogisms. Which way he chooses depends on the purpose he has in mind. The truth-value of the premisses determines the following fourfold classification of syllogisms into: (1) apodeictic, (2) dialectic, (3) rhetorical (*An. Pr.* 68ᵇ11–14), and (4) eristic or contentious (ἐριστικὸς). The last type of syllogism in this list appears to be based on generally accepted opinions but is not really so (*Top.* 100ᵇ23–26). The aforementioned classification is not to be confused with Aristotle's division of syllogism into: (1) assertoric, (2) apodeictic, and (3) problematic. Further, on occasion in the *An. Pr.* Aristotle distinguishes between ostensive and hypothetical syllogisms. These are so marked off from one another depending on whether they can be proved with or without the need for the assumption of a false premiss: see, for example, 45ᵇ8–11.

5   25ᵇ27.

6   The order of composition of the various works which together constitute the Organon (this collective noun first appears in the sixteenth century) has been subject to conjecture and dispute since early in the present century. It is unclear whether Aristotle actually wrote the bulk of the *An. Pr.* before writing the *An. Post.* I will not deal with this topic here, as no issue in my discussion turns on the answer to the problem of the relative dates of composition. The dispute and the positions taken by various scholars are summarized in J. L.

Aristotle's formal logic

The systematic exposition of what syllogism is, how each syllogism may be produced, and the proof of the validity of each syllogism occupies a significant part of the *Prior Analytics*. There are lengthy passages in that treatise devoted to methods of proof. In Book Beta, Aristotle digresses into topics of proof and refutation, the manipulation of premisses, the fallacy of *petitio principii*, the production of countersyllogisms and defences to these, and how error in judgments is possible and may be explained. A great many of these topics lie outside our scope here, for the chief purpose of this chapter is to present the background of Aristotle's discussion, in another part of the Organon, of the principles of instruction in the various sciences. In addition to an outline of the art of testing arguments by the standard of the syllogism, Aristotle is at least arguably interested in how a teacher may use a formal analysis of the process of stating premiss-pairs and forcing a fellow participant in the logical exercise to concede the truth of a conclusion. Hints and suggestive analogies about the latter use of syllogism can be found in the *Prior Analytics*, but the full working out of this position is

---

Stocks, "The Composition of Aristotle's Logical Works" (1933) 27 Classical Quarterly 114–24. Stocks agrees with Friedrich Solmsen in dating the composition of the *An. Pr.* rather late in Aristotle's career and most of the *An. Post.* rather early. These conclusions are based on such evidence as textual cross-references, the contents of one work presupposing those of another, the comparative styles of different works, internal references to historical events, and the "philosophical atmosphere" of the writing, as this last criterion is explained in W. D. Ross, *Aristotle's Prior and Posterior Analytics* (Oxford: Clarendon Press, 1949, reprinted 1957), pp. 14–19. Ross takes issue with Solmsen's position in "The Discovery of the Syllogism" (1939) 48 Philosophical Review 251–72. As often pointed out, Aristotle himself refers to the *An. Pr.* and *An. Post.* collectively by the single title τὰ ἀναλύτικα and distinguishes them only by referring to their respective contents. This issue of "logical" versus "chronological" order has been dismissed by some commentators as of "no great importance": see William Kneale and Martha Kneale, *The Development of Logic* (Oxford: Clarendon Press, 1962), p. 25. Nevertheless, the debate has been revived in such articles as Robin Smith, "The Relationship of Aristotle's Two *Analytics*" (1982) 32 Classical Quarterly 327–35.

contained in the *Posterior Analytics* and the *Topics*.

Aristotle gives us a highly schematic or formal logic (in the modern sense of the word "form," not in the Aristotelian sense) in the *Prior Analytics*. The content of individual propositions is left aside and, through the use of letter symbols, the form of such propositions is conveniently displayed. Aristotle proposes to describe how a proposition such as "All men are animals" may be formalized as "All S's are P's," where S represents the subject "man" and P represents the predicate "animal." In what may be seen as a propaedeutic to his work on ordered sequences of propositions in the *Prior Analytics*, Aristotle discusses the elements of such deductive reasoning in *On Interpretation* and the *Categories*, where he deals with the term and the proposition, respectively. His philosophical accounts of the term and proposition are not significant here, except incidentally. In general, this chapter bears only upon the series or chain of reasoning which he denominates by the technical term συλλογισμός. This term appears to derive, etymologically speaking, from the verb συλλέγω, which may be rendered as "I gather" or "I collect."[7] Ross characterizes the original meaning of the passive infinitive, συλλογίζεσθαι, as "to compute, to reckon up" and cites a passage from Herodotus in support.[8] The technical usage of συλλογισμός is adopted generally throughout Aristotle's *Analytics*, though it should be noted that when he uses συλλογισμός or a cognate thereof in other parts of the Organon he may mean by it something in the nature of deductive reasoning as a whole rather than the process or product of syllogism in particular. To express this another way, his use of συλλογισμός and related terms may expand or contract, depending on the context in question.[9] Syllogism is not restricted, in his account, to those chains of reasoning in which the premises are true and the conclusion follows necessarily. In the *Topics* he discusses at length the dialectical syllogism, which involves the use of premises that are only probable or generally accepted rather than

---

[7]   H. G. Liddell, R. Scott, and H. S. Jones, *A Greek-English Lexicon*, 9th ed. (Oxford: Clarendon Press, 1940, reprinted 1961) s.v. συλλέγω I.

[8]   Ross, *supra* n. 6, p. 291.

[9]   For example, in his introduction to the *S.E.* Aristotle seems to use συλλογισμόι in a broad sense, meaning "reasonings": 164^{a}23–24. See also *Top.* 156^{a}20–21.

true.[10]

Although we are not here concerned with *On Interpretation*, it should be made clear at the outset how that work shows his preoccupation with propositions that exhibit the following standard form. Each proposition is composed of three elements: a subject, or that which is spoken about; a predicate, or that which is spoken of the subject; and a form of the copula or the verb "to be" (εἶναι).[11] This canonical form of proposition is the foundation of Aristotle's account of syllogism. We may represent this form by substituting capital letters to serve as variables. We thus arrive at the formalization: "S is P." Aristotle in the *Prior Analytics* does not use any one way uniformly for stating the relationship between subject and predicate. In fact, he uses at least four different syntactical constructions. These are:

(a)   P belongs (ὑπάρχειν) to S;

(b)   P is predicated (κατηγορεῖσται) of S;

(c)   P falls (ὑπὸ τὸ) under S; and

(d)   P is wholly contained (ὅλῳ) in S.[12]

---

10   See *Top.* 104ª8 et seq. for a definition of a dialectical proposition. It can be that which accords with what is held either: (1) by everyone, (2) by the majority, (3) by all of the wise, or (4) by the best known of the wise. Later in this chapter the typical setting of the dialectical exercise is discussed. It is easy to imagine how two participants must each propound one side of a proposition drawn from one of the above sources.

11   *De. Int.* 17ª8–24. See also *Cat.* 2ª5–6. This triad is a traditional way of analyzing Aristotle's standard proposition, but some commentators (for example, D. J. Allan, *The Philosophy of Aristotle*, 2nd ed. [Oxford: Oxford University Press paperback, 1970], p. 103n.1) would quibble with this, claiming that the copula would have been included in the predicate, to Aristotle's way of thinking. By contrast, in Sir David Ross, *Aristotle*, 6th ed. (London: Routledge, 1996), p. 28 it is argued that by the time the *An. Pr.* was written the copula was "completely disengaged" from the predicate.

12   These four ways of representing the relation between S and P are exemplified at: (a) 25ª1, (b) 24ᵇ37–39, (c) 30ᵇ13, and 51ᵇ38, and (d) 24ᵇ26–27, respectively.

The first usage listed above is preponderant in the *Prior Analytics*, and so to be truly reflective of Aristotle's analysis of propositions that are constituents of a syllogism we should adhere to the form "P belongs to S" in describing those propositions.[13]

---

[13]   Translators have handled Aristotle's use of the verb ὑπάρχειν in different ways. So when Aristotle says at 25ᵃ15, for instance, that if οὖν μηδενὶ τῷ Β τo Α ὑπάρχει, Jenkinson renders this as "If no B is A," while Tredennick, in the Loeb edition, *The Organon: Prior Analytics*, trans. Hugh Tredennick (London: William Heinemann Ltd.; Cambridge, Mass.: Harvard University Press, 1938), gives us "If A applies to no B." Warrington, in *Prior and Posterior Analytics*, trans. and ed. John Warrington, Everyman's Library (London: Dent, 1964), follows Jenkinson's practice in general. The choice of translating the standard categorical proposition by "P belongs to S" rather than by "S is P" also emphasizes a related and important philosophic point made by Aristotle. One of the keystones of his system of metaphysics is the claim that the verb "to be" has several distinct senses or that things may be said to be in different, yet related, ways: *Phys.* 125ᵃ20–27; *Met.* Γ 1003ᵃ33–34. The *Met.*, particularly Book Z, goes deeply into the implications of the use of the copula. Aristotle's whole discussion in the *An. Pr.* of predication is transported into this larger philosophical context by his statement that "to belong to" (ὑπάρχειν) has as many senses as "to be" (εἶναι). His account is as follows:

> But we must suppose the verb "to belong" to have as many meanings as the senses in which "to be" is used, and in which the assertion that a thing "is" may be said to be true. Take for example the statement that there is a single science of contraries. Let *A* stand for "there being a single science," and *B* stand for things which are contrary to one another. Then *A* belongs to *B*, not in the sense that contraries are a single science, but in the sense that it is true to say of the contraries that there is a single science of them. (48ᵇ3–10)

Similarly, Aristotle reconciles his doctrine of categories with his preferred locution of "P belongs to S" by saying at 49ᵃ6–10 that such attribution should be understood in as many different senses as there are categories (αἱ κατηγορίαι). The relation between Aristotle's use of certain terminology in his logical works for expressing relationships between classes of things, and between individuals and classes of things, is as interesting as it is complex. Though Owen surmises that the composition of the Organon antedates Aristotle's work on the general science of τὸ ὄν ᾗ ὄν, and Owen argues that no such science was envisioned in any of Aristotle's logical works, he does not refer to the above-quoted passage from the *An. Pr.* in order to judge what evidentiary value, if any, it has for Owen's thesis. See G. E. L. Owen, "Logic and Metaphysics in Some Earlier Works of Aristotle" in *Aristotle and Plato in the Mid-Fourth Century*, eds. I. Düring and G. E. L. Owen (Göteborg: Almquist

Aristotle is interested only in certain types of propositions in respect of generality. As it is traditionally portrayed, his account embraces only universal propositions (for example, "All men are animals" or, to put this in standard form, "Animal belongs to every man") and particular propositions (for example, "Some men are wealthy" or, again to standardize this, "Wealth belongs to some men"). In his account in the *Prior Analytics*, he is not interested in singular propositions (for example, "Socrates is a man"), which he nevertheless acknowledges is a third way in which a predicate is affirmed or denied of a subject.[14] There is a fourth way, which Aristotle also recognizes but is not interested in, namely the indefinite proposition (for example, "Pleasure is not good"). Of this type of proposition Aristotle says at 24^a19–21 that there is no "mark to show whether it is universal or particular," and so it drops out of his account. Aristotle's syllogistic is concerned only with universal and particular propositions in respect of what we might call their quantity. There is no room for consideration of the singular proposition as a possible premiss, for Aristotle clearly is interested in what relationships may be said to hold between classes of S's and classes of P's. This concern, in modern logical terminology, is with class inclusion and class exclusion rather than class membership.[15] It is therefore misleading to introduce the concept of syllogism by means of the following stock example adduced to us as schoolchildren:

> All men are mortal
> Socrates is a man
> Therefore, Socrates is mortal

---

and Wiksell, 1957), pp. 163–90, p. 175.

[14] 43^a26–29.

[15]   G. E. R. Lloyd, *Aristotle: The Growth and Structure of His Thought* (Cambridge: Cambridge University Press, 1968), p. 121; Searles, *supra* n. 3, pp. 62–63. But see Ross, *supra* n. 6, p. 29, where Ross argues that it is incorrect to see in the relation "P belongs to S" class inclusion. Ross thinks it is more consistent with Aristotle's overall theory of predication, as revealed in both the *An. Pr.* And other treatises, to take the relation to be one of the necessary connection of attribute to subject and not the inclusion of one in the other.

The above example does not exhibit a form of syllogism that Aristotle includes among the valid moods, which are entirely made up of universal and particular categorical propositions.[16] Such propositions are called "categorical" to distinguish them from the hypothetical propositions used as components to create a different type of syllogistic formulated after Aristotle's time.[17]

These types of universal and particular propositions can be formalized so that the result will be a compact and useful abbreviation of the possible forms of categorical proposition. Aristotle discerns four possible syllogistic relations between a subject and a predicate in these two types of proposition. What they are and how they may be denoted symbolically are shown in the following table:

[16] This same example is used by Frederick Copleston, S.J., *A History of Philosophy*, 9 vols., rev. ed. (New York: Image Books, 1962) 1: 20–21. Such use is criticized in G. R. G. Mure, *Aristotle* (New York: Oxford University Press, 1932, reprinted with corrections as a Galaxy Book, 1964), p. 211n.3, and in Jan Łukasiewicz, *Aristotle's Syllogistic from the Standpoint of Modern Formal Logic*, 2nd ed. enlarged (Oxford: Clarendon Press, 1957), p. i . This syllogism can be represented in modern predicate calculus in the following form:

(x) (Mx → Ox)
(∃x) (Sx & Mx)

———————
(∃x) (Sx & Ox)

Note that at 47^b20 *et seq.* Aristotle produces arguments involving individuals (Aristomenes and Miccalus) in the context of showing how some argument patterns resemble syllogisms, but really are not.

[17] Kneale and Kneale, *supra* n. 6, pp. 110–11; *Encyclopedia of Philosophy*, s.v. "Logic, History of" (sub-section on ancient logic), by Czesław Lejewski.

Form of proposition	Quantity	Quality	Appropriate vowel
P belongs to every S	Universal	Affirmative	a
P belongs to no S	Universal	Negative	e
P belongs to some S	Particular	Affirmative	i
Not P belongs to some S	Particular	Negative	o

The use of different vowels for representing each relationship is part of an ingenious medieval system of mnemonics devised for students trying to recall the essential features of Aristotle's syllogistic. Logic was of course a central part of the medieval curriculum and for centuries the study of logic was synonymous with the study of the Aristotelian syllogism, including both his original work and the accretions it suffered at the hands of various commentators and translators.[18]

---

[18]   R. R. Bolgar, *The Classical Heritage and Its Beneficiaries* (Cambridge: Cambridge University Press, 1954), p. 161, where Bolgar discusses the advent and adoption into common use of the so-called *logica nova* (i.e., the *Top.*, including the *S.E.*, and the two *Analytics*). This part of the Aristotelian corpus complemented the already available "old logic"'' which included the *Cat.*, *De Int.* and the commentaries thereon of Boethius and Porphyry. This process of rediscovery occurred in the first half of the twelfth century. Bolgar's remarks at p. 162 indicate the enormous impact of the Organon during the remainder of the Middle Ages:

> It seems likely, however, that the great speculative systems of Scholasticism could not have been constructed, nor conversely could they have been criticised, without an intimate knowledge of the syllogism. It seems also likely that without the new Aristotle the zeal for definitions and deductions which by the end of the twelfth century invaded every branch of knowledge would never have appeared.

See also Gordon Leff, *Paris and Oxford Universities in the Thirteenth and Fourteenth Centuries: An Institutional and Intellectual History* (New York: John Wiley and Sons, 1968), pp. 127–37. Leff describes how Aristotle's logic

We now may represent the general form of the categorical proposition by the sentence-frame "P x S" where the "x" stands for one of the four syllogistic relationships that show the various combinations of the quantification of the terms and the affirmation or denial of the relationship of the class of S's to the class of P's. Then P a S may be expanded by replacing the variables to give us a proposition in ordinary language such as "Mortal belongs to every man"; P e S might represent, for example, "Vertebrate belongs to no worm"; P i S might represent "Wooden belongs to some tools"; and finally, P o S might represent "Not deciduous belongs to some trees."

Having covered the symbolic notation of propositions, we may proceed next to consider Aristotle's account of how categorical propositions may be arranged to form a valid piece of deductive reasoning. He defines a syllogism in the following passage:

> A syllogism is discourse [λόγος] in which, certain things being stated, something other than what is stated follows of necessity from their being so. I mean by the last phrase that they produce the consequence, and by this, that no further term is required from without in order to make the consequence necessary.[19]

Some controversy has arisen during this century about whether and in what sense the "things being stated" (the premisses) imply the conclusion that follows therefrom.[20] This issue shall only be flagged here without any elaboration. It does not affect the significance or

effectively displaced the *trivium* in the curriculum of the arts faculties of the leading medieval universities.

[19] 24^{b}18–22.

[20] For example, Łukasiewicz, *supra* n. 16, pp. 2–3 and 20–21, holds that the typical Aristotelian syllogism should be read as an implication having the conjunction of the premisses as the antecedent and the conclusion as the consequent. Thus, the syllogism in Barbara ought to be denoted as [(P a S & (M a S)] → P a S. The alternative would be to see the conclusion as an inference from two premisses using the word "therefore" as a sign of inference. Łukasiewicz bases his characterization, not on any example given in the *An. Pr.* (for Aristotle neglects to give any example of a syllogism fully fleshed out in the *An. Pr.*), but on certain examples found in the *An. Post.* There is some disagreement with Łukasiewicz on this: see, for example, Thomas F. Smiley, "What is a Syllogism?" (1973) 2 Journal of Philosophical Logic 136–54.

use of the syllogism for our purpose.

The schema for representing the possible forms of syllogistic reasoning can be further extended by introducing the capital letter "M" to stand for that term which serves as the middle term in a syllogism. Aristotle describes this as follows:

> I call that term middle [μέσον] which is itself contained in another and contains another in itself, in position also this comes in the middle.[21]

The latter way of distinguishing the middle term, that is, by its location in the premisses of the syllogism, is literally true only for syllogisms of the first figure, as hereafter described. Aristotle is attracted to the idea that these first figure syllogisms, being "perfect" in the sense he describes in the *Prior Analytics*, are the ideal type of syllogism, and in his discussion he goes on to show how all other syllogisms can be reduced to certain moods in the first figure.[22]

A "mood" is the traditional term used to refer to a combination of a pair of premisses (each of which is a categorical proposition and which together have a middle term in common) and an ostensible conclusion (in the invariable form of P x S). The conclusion will thus relate the predicate to the subject in one of four possible types of syllogistic relationship, depending on the quantification of the subject and whether the copula is affirmative or negative.

In the *Prior Analytics* Aristotle purports to discover the only possible syllogistic figures (σχήματα) that each exhibit a distinctive pattern so far as the positions of S, P and M are concerned. In particular, a figure will depend on where the middle term is placed with respect to S and P. The three figures which he discusses are:

21　25^{b}35–37.

22　In G. E. L. Owen, "The Platonism of Aristotle," 1965 Dawes Hicks Lecture in Philosophy to the British Academy reprinted in Jonathan Barnes et al. (eds.), *Articles on Aristotle: 1. Science* (London: Duckworth, 1975), p. 33n. 14, this claim is cited as an example of Aristotle's inclination to use a "favoured case" in explaining some important expressions and then to apply that expression generally. This acute observation by Owen is useful in another context, for, as we shall see, the first figure syllogism in Barbara becomes just such a favoured case for scientific demonstration.

I	II	III
P x M	M x P	P x M
M x S	M x S	S x M
———	———	———
P x S	P x S	P x S

In each case, the combinations of P, S and M above the horizontal stroke constitute two premisses (πρότασεις) and the proposition P x S in each figure constitutes the conclusion (συμπέρασμα).[23] The predicate in each conclusion is called by Aristotle the major term (τό μεῖζον) and the subject is called the minor term (τό ἔλαττον).[24] By substituting either a, e, i or o for each instance of x where it occurs in the above figures, we arrive at all the possible moods of the syllogism, of which some are valid and the bulk are invalid forms of reasoning. By expanding the universal negative proposition represented by P e M into the ordinary language statement "Mortal belongs to no animal"; then expanding the particular affirmative denoted by M i S into "Animal belongs to some man"; we derive the conclusion "Not mortal belongs to some man" which in form is particular negative and in our notation is represented by P o S. The result is a valid mood in the first figure that has come to be known as a syllogism in Ferio.[25] It may be schematized as P e M, M i S → P o S, where the arrow denotes the relationship "if P e M and M i S, then P o S."

From among the dozens of possible moods, Aristotle claims that

---

23   Aristotle appears to use the term σχῆμα in the *An. Pr.* first at 26[b]27 when he is discussing the structure of syllogisms containing a particular conclusion, either affirmative or negative. He uses πρότασις invariably for "premiss" and it is entroduced early in this role at 24[a]28. It contrasts with συμπέρασμα (conclusion) or, alternatively, ἀπόδοσις (consequent). Aristotle is primarily interested in its use as it relates to the former of these two possible contrasts.

24   26[a]21–22; 28[a]13–14.

25   So-called because of the aforementioned medieval system of *aides-mémoire*: see Thomas Gilby, *Barbara Celarent: A Description of Scholastic Dialectic* (London: Longmans, Green, 1949).

only fourteen are valid arguments and are therefore the only moods entitled to be called syllogisms.[26] A great portion of the *Prior Analytics* is taken up with Aristotle's account of how the validity of the syllogisms may be proven. For this task, he is forced to rely upon various principles of inference that hold between pairs of categorical propositions. These principles have been called by subsequent logicians "rules of immediate inference."[27] They are so called because those rules determine how we may draw an inference from a single premiss rather than from a pair of premises (thus, by comparison, a syllogism is a "mediate" inference). The rules of immediate inference that find a place in the *Prior Analytics* are described below.

The first group is composed of the rules of conversion and may be summarized as follows:[28]

---

[26]   The valid moods described by Aristotle in the *An. Pr.* are the following:

(a) First figure:	P a M, M a S → P a S	
	P e M, M a S → P e S	
	P a M, M i S → P i S	
	P e M, M i S → P o S	
(b) Second figure:	M e P, M a S → P e S	
	M a P, M e S → P e S	
	M e P, M I S → P o S	
	M a P, M o S → P o S	
(c) Third figure:	P a M, S a M → P i S	
	P e M, S a M → P o S	
	P i M, S a M → P i S	
	P a M, S i M → P i S	
	P o M, S a M → P o S	
	P e M, S i M → P o S	

For the pertinent medieval nomenclature, see Lear, *supra* n. 2, p. 226.

[27]   See, for example, J. L. Ackrill, *Aristotle the Philosopher* (Oxford: Oxford University Press, 1981), p. 86.

[28]   For the infinitive "to convert," Aristotle uses ἀντιστρέφειν: 25ᵃ6. Aristotle develops a theory of the conversion of syllogisms as well as that concerning the conversion of premises. The meaning of syllogism conversion is set forth in Book B, 59ᵇ1–3. Aristotle distinguishes contradictory from contrary conversion at 59ᵇ8–11. The contradictory converse of "P belongs to every S" is "P does not belong to every S" and the contrary converse is "P belongs to no S." On the various different uses of the notion of conversion, Ross, *supra* n. 6, p. 293 contains a useful summary.

(a) The universal affirmative converts to the particular affirmative, or P a S → S i P. Thus, "Mortal belongs to every animal" converts to "Animal belongs to some mortal." This is called conversion by limitation.[29]

(b) The universal negative converts to the universal negative with the terms transposed, or P e S → S i P. Thus, "Mortal belongs to no animal" converts to and is the converse of "Animal belongs to no mortal." This is called conversion *simpliciter*.[30]

(c) The particular affirmative converts to the particular affirmative with the terms transposed, or P i S → S i P. Thus, "Mortal belongs to some animal" converts to and is the converse of "Animal belongs to some mortal." This again is conversion *simpliciter*.[31]

It should be noted that the particular affirmative does not convert to the universal affirmative. Just because some animals are mortal does not permit us to infer that all animals are mortal. Also, it is clear that the particular negative proposition has no converse, because we are interested in class inclusion and exclusion and the particular negative has a subject term that is undistributed (since it refers to only a part of a class) while its predicate term is distributed (it refers to the entire class) or, in technical language, the predicate term is used in its widest possible extension.[32] If we tried to convert the P o S proposition, we would have to distribute the subject term and the quantification of the subject would therefore change as a result. We would lose the original meaning of the converted proposition.

The second group of rules of immediate inference are the rules respecting subalternation (not Aristotle's term again, but that of a subsequent logician). These rules warrant the following inferences:

---

29   25ª8–10.
30   25ª5–8.
31   25ª10–12.
32   25ª12–13. See Searles, *supra* n. 3, 115–16.

(a) From the universal affirmative may be inferred the particular affirmative, or P a S → S i P. Thus, "Mortal belongs to every animal" permits us to infer that "Animal belongs to some mortal."[33]

(b) From the universal negative may be inferred the particular negative, or P e S → P o S. Thus, "Mortal belongs to no animal" permits us to infer that "Not mortal belongs to some animal."[34]

In the process of proving which moods are valid and thus constitute syllogisms, Aristotle uses these rules of immediate inference along with other devices for proving validity.[35] The other methods that he uses in this regard include reduction, exposition and rejection by counter-example. These are discussed in turn below.

The doctrine of reduction (ἀναγωγή) is the validation of a mood in one figure by the construction of an equivalent syllogism in another figure. This doctrine is linked to Aristotle's view that only syllogisms in the first figure are perfect or complete (τέλειος) in the sense that they need no further argument to demonstrate their validity.[36] There are two types of reduction employed in the *Prior Analytics*.

First, the method of "direct" reduction is used so that a syllogism in the second figure, Camestres for example, may be reduced to the

---

[33] Aristotle did not coin, nor does he use, the terms "subaltern" and "superaltern" to describe the relations of universal to particular propositions of the same quality. He assumes that each universal statement entails its subaltern in *De Int.*, or this is how it is described in Kneale and Kneale, *supra* n. 6, p. 56. Presumably they are referring to Aristotle's discussion in Chapters 7 and 8 of that short treatise.

[34] The remarks in the immediately preceding note apply as well to this "assumption" on Aristotle's part.

[35] It should be recognized that, although not employing them expressly in *An. Pr.*, Aristotle is aware of the rules of obversion, whereby, for example, the terms of a universal affirmative proposition may be changed from P a S to yield its equivalent in the universal negative, Not-P e S. See 51^{b}5–10 and *De Int.* 19^{b}30–36 for evidence of an awareness of such inference.

[36] 24^{b}22–24.

first figure syllogism in Celarent.[37] The mood represented by Camestres can be determined from examining the order of vowels in the name. This gives us: M a P, M e S → P e S. We may illustrate this mood by the following premiss-pair and conclusion:

(P_1) Being unmarried belongs to every bachelor
(P_2) Being unmarried belongs to no person in the room
(C)   Being a bachelor belongs to no person in the room

The first step in direct reduction is to transpose the premisses (the letter "m" following the first vowel in Camestres stands for metathesis or transposition). Then what was originally the second premiss and is now the initial premiss (P_2) should be converted simply to its converse, P e M ("Person in the room belongs to nobody unmarried"). What is now the second premiss (P_1) can be left intact, though it is now symbolically denoted by M a S rather than M a P, owing to our premiss-juggling. Finally, the conclusion of a syllogism may be reached by converting simply the conclusion in Camestres; hence "Being a bachelor belongs to no person in the room" becomes "Person in the room belongs to no bachelor."

The second type of reduction is "indirect," in that mere rules of immediate inference will not by themselves suffice to show equivalence in order to establish validity. Indirect reduction may be illustrated by the technique *reductio ad impossibile*.[38] This logical technique assumes that, if the conclusion of a valid syllogism is false, one of its two premisses must be false. For example, if the syllogism in the third figure known as Bocardo is to be proved valid, this method involves first assuming that the conclusion is false. The mood may be shown in our schema as P o M, S a M → P o S. If the

---

[37]   Aristotle first proves the validity of Camestres by conversion to Celarent at 27ª9–12. He says in the immediately succeeding passage, 27 ª12–15, that he could also have used *reductiones ad impossibile* (τὸ ἀδύνατον ἄγοντας) to prove both Camestres and Cesare. His general conclusion, of course, is that all imperfect syllogisms are completed by means of the first figure: 29ª30–31.

[38]   An example of proof *per impossibile* is given by Aristotle at 41ª27 *et seq.*, where the desired conclusion is "the diagonal of a square is incommensurable with the sides."

conclusion is false, its contradictory, P a S, must be true. By combining this latter proposition (and re-formulating it as the major premiss) with the original minor premiss, S a M, we can construct the following syllogism: P a M, S a M → P a S. This constitutes a valid mood in Barbara in the first figure. Since P a S contradicts the original major premiss, P o M (which is true *ex hypothesi*), one of its two premisses must be false. The minor cannot be false (again, *ex hypothesi*), so it must be the major, P a M. Therefore, its contradictory, the conclusion of the original mood, must be true and the validity of the syllogism in Bocardo has thereby been established indirectly.[39]

The procedure ·of proof by exposition or ecthesis (ἔκθεσις) involves the production of an extra term beyond those given in the mood sought to be proved valid. Aristotle uses this procedure in the course of proving the validity of the syllogism in Darapti in the third figure.[40] He thinks it is possible to prove this syllogism by any one of the procedures of proof *per impossibile*, conversion or ecthesis. The mood known as Darapti exhibits the following pattern: P a M, S a M → P i S. Aristotle argues that if some of the M's, for example N and O, are "exposed," then both P and S will belong to these exposed M's and then P will belong to some S.[41]

The production and use of counter-examples is often Aristotle's reason for rejecting certain moods as asyllogistic. For instance, he cites the premiss-pair that he describes in the following excerpt from the *Prior Analytics*:

> But if the first term belongs to all the middle, but the middle to none of the last term, there will be no syllogism in respect of the extremes; for nothing necessary follows from the terms being so related; for it is possible that the first should belong either to all or to none of the last, so that neither a particular nor a universal conclusion is necessary. But if there is no necessary consequence,

---

[39] $28^{b}15$–21.

[40] $28^{a}22$–24.

[41]   On the topic of exposition see further Ross, *supra* n. 6, p. 32; Kneale and Kneale, *supra* n. 6, pp. 77–78; and Łukasiewicz, *supra* n. 16, pp. 59–67. This method of proof is vital to the validation of the two modal syllogisms denoted as □ P o M, □ S a M → □ P o S, □ M a P , and □ M o S → □ P o S at $30^{a}6$–14.

there cannot be a syllogism by means of the premisses.[42]

Translated into our notation, Aristotle's point is that the combination of the premiss-pair P a M and M e S and the conclusion P e S does not form a valid mood. It may be concretely illustrated by the following example (for which Aristotle suggests the terms):

> Animal belongs to every man
> Man belongs to no stone
> ─────────────────────────
> Animal belongs to no stone

Similarly, neither of the propositions P a S or P o S is a necessary consequence of that same premiss-pair. This type of rejection procedure, in which Aristotle produces counter-examples that show intuitively that certain moods are invalid, is used repeatedly by him throughout the *Prior Analytics*.

No space will be devoted here to the detection, after Aristotle's time, of the fourth figure. It includes five more valid moods and may be exemplified in our notation by the following pattern: M x P, S x M → P x S.[43] Nor will we be concerned here with the so-called "weaker" moods of which Aristotle himself was aware.[44]

It is by now commonplace that Aristotle's "logic of terms" is only a part of a larger logical system which includes in addition a "logic of propositions."[45] The latter type did not gain entrance into classical logic until the theory of hypothetical syllogisms of the form "if *p*, then *q*; *p*; therefore *q*" was developed in later Greek thought.[46] Aristotle's account of the proposition, whereby only the categorical form is used as the standard, leaves out the possibility that terms may be juxtaposed in another form, for example, by the relational predicate in the proposition "P is taller than S." From such

---

[42] 26^a2–8.

[43]   Ackrill, *supra* n. 27, pp. 89–90; Ross, *supra* n. 11, p. 35.

[44]   Ackrill, *supra* n. 27, p. 91.

[45]   *Encyclopedia of Philosophy*, s.v. "Logic, History of"; Ackrill, *supra* n. 27, p. 88; Łukasiewicz, *supra* n. 16, pp. 47–51.

[46]   See *supra* n. 17.

propositions, a relational syllogistic may be constructed. It can be illustrated by:

> P is taller than M
> M is taller than S
> _____
> P is taller than S

The types of propositions that have so far been discussed in this chapter have been "assertoric," in the sense that when P is said to belong to S, this relationship has not been stated to be necessary. Aristotle's account of modal syllogisms presupposes that propositions may involve either necessity (τό ἀναγκαῖον), possibility (τό δύνατον), impossibility (τό ἀδύνατον) or contingency (τό ἐνδεχομένον).[47] A proposition of the form""It is necessary that P x S" is called apodeictic; one of the form "It is possible that P x S" is called problematic; and a proposition that lacks either one of these modalities is called assertoric.[48] A modal syllogism is a valid mood in which at least one of the premisses is a modal proposition (that is, either apodeictic or problematic). From *On Interpretation*, it appears that Aristotle sees the modal operator as qualifying the entire proposition.[49] Thus, Aristotle thinks of an apodeictic proposition as "It is necessary that P x S" rather than as "P necessarily x S." He intimates as much in the above-noted account in *On Interpretation* about what is the contradictory of "It is possible that P x S." He argues that its contradictory is "It is not possible that P x S" rather than "It is possible that not-P x S." In those chapters in the *Prior Analytics* devoted to the modal syllogism, Aristotle works his way through the various combinations of assertoric, apodeictic and problematic propositions in order to discover how many valid modal

---

[47]   For necessity, see 26^{b}29–30^{a}14; for contingency, see 29^{a}37–39 and 32^{a}19–21. The relationship of possibility and contingency, sometimes as synonymous and other times as contrasting terms, is complex. See, for example, the remarks in J. L. Ackrill, *Aristotle's Categories and De Interpretatione* (Oxford: Clarendon Press, 1963), p. 149.

[48]   25^{a}1–2.

[49]   *De Int.* 21^{a}38–22^{b}33.

moods there are.[50] For this purpose, he again uses such aids to proving validity as conversion and ecthesis. His use of conversion as a method for testing moods for validity becomes extended, as he must develop one theory of conversion for apodeictic propositions, and a second, more complex theory of conversion, for problematic propositions.[51]

For our purposes, the crucial result of Aristotle's ground-breaking excursion into the topic of modal syllogistic is that he portrays the following mood as the only one that is appropriate to scientific demonstration. This is the mood composed of two apodeictic premisses followed by an apodeictic conclusion. Furthermore, the appropriate syllogistic relationship between the subject and the predicate in each constituent proposition is the universal affirmative. If we let the symbol "□" represent the modal expression "It is necessary that" when it is prefixed to a categorical proposition, then the paradigm of all scientific demonstration may be symbolically rendered as:

$$\Box P \text{ a } M, \Box M \text{ a } S \rightarrow \Box P \text{ a } S$$

This is the modal syllogism in Barbara.[52] It may be expanded, for the purpose of illustration, to read: If it is necessary that animal belongs to every human and it is necessary that human belongs to every Greek, then it is necessary that animal belongs to every Greek. It is worthwhile mentioning in this connection that Aristotle in the *Posterior Analytics* distinguishes between the proposition that is necessary and that which is universal (κατά παντός).[53] The former includes not only the notion of universal predication, but of what is essential (καθ' αὐτό) as well.[54] When he is speaking of essential predication, Aristotle appears to have in mind propositions that are definitions. With the above paradigm before us, we shall be ready in

---

[50]   This procedure occupies a large part of Book *A*, Chapters 8 to 22, inclusive.

[51]   Kneale and Kneale, *supra* n. 6, p. 87; Ross, *supra* n. 6, p. 298.

[52]   *An. Post.* 79ᵃ17–33.

[53]   *An. Post.* 73ᵇ25–28.

[54]   See also 24ᵇ28.

the following chapters to turn our attention to Aristotle's characterization of all scientific demonstration (and that means for him all teaching and learning of certain things) as being effected by means of such a modal syllogism. Before this topic is tackled, consideration must be given to what Aristotle thinks he has accomplished in the course of compiling the *Prior Analytics*.

The purposes of the formal part of Aristotle's syllogistic

This part of the present chapter is a discussion about the use to which Aristotle thinks his formal logic can be put. There are important implications in the answer to this question for education and, in particular, for the organization of a curriculum.

Logic is not among the sciences which Aristotle divides elsewhere into the theoretical, the practical, and the productive.[55] As some commentators have aptly characterized it, the study of logic and the grasping of the rules of inference constitute an ancillary study which, when mastered, enables the learner to acquire knowledge of any and all of the sciences. Logic is not one of the departmentalized sciences but is rather an important preliminary subject.[56] This role of logic is not to be confused with the teaching of stock arguments and tricky philosophical moves, which is how Aristotle describes the educational achievement of Gorgias, the famous sophist of the fifth century.[57] In the *Sophistical Refutations* Aristotle says:

> For some of them gave their pupils to learn by heart speeches which were either rhetorical or consisted of questions and answers, in which both sides thought that the rival arguments were for the most part included. Hence the teaching which they

---

[55] *Met. E*1025ᵃ25.

[56] See, for example, Ross, *supra* n. 11, p. 20. Explicit support for this view is found in *Met. Γ*1005ᵇ2–5, where Aristotle says:

> And the attempts of some of those who discuss the terms on which truth should be accepted, are due to a want of training in logic; for they should know these things already when they come to a special study, and not be inquiring into them while they are listening to lectures on it.

[57] *S.E.* 183ᵇ36–38.

gave to their pupils was rapid but unsystematic; for they conceived that they should train their pupils by imparting to them not an art but the results of an art, just as if one should claim to be about to communicate knowledge for the prevention of pain in the feet and then were not to teach the cobbler's art and the means of providing suitable footgear, but were to offer a selection of various kinds of shoes; for he has helped to supply his need but he has not imparted an art to him.[58]

Aristotle evidently sees himself in the *Prior Analytics*, the *Topics*, and the *Sophistical Refutations* as setting forth a method (ὁδός) itself, rather than just a product of that method.[59] This method consists not only in the analysis of forms of argumentation to see if they can be fitted into a valid mood, but also in our power of constructing arguments.[60] He sees one of our central problems (and on at least one occasion he interchanges "the learner" [τόν μανθάνοντα] for "we") as finding an adequate supply (εὐπορήσομεν) of syllogisms "in reference to the problem proposed."[61] It turns out, on Aristotle's account, that this problem reduces to the question of how to discover the middle term.[62] The procedure for accomplishing this is laid out in a highly compact account in the *Posterior Analytics A* 27.

The thrust of his account is as follows. Aristotle distinguishes between different sorts of predicables by stating that all things (τά ὄντα) each fall into one of three classes. First, there are individuals.

---

58   *S.E.* 183ᵇ38–184ᵃ10; translation by E. S. Forster, *On Sophistical Refutations*, Loeb Classical Library (London: William Heinemann Ltd.; Cambridge, Mass.: Harvard University Press, 1955).

59   In the *Topics* Aristotle introduces his treatise with the statement of an overarching purpose. He aims to discover a method (μέθοδος) by which learners can reason from generally accepted opinions (ἔνδοξα) about any problem (πρόβλημα) set before them.

60   43ᵃ22–24. On the way Aristotle describes how to reduce συλλογισμόι ("arguments," in the widest sense) to syllogistic form: see Book *A*, Chapter 32 of the *An. Pr.*

61   43ᵃ20–22. For the use of the terms "learner" and "we" see 50ᵃ1–4. The significance of such terminology as "the problem proposed" for how it illustrates the setting in which Aristotle wrote his logical works will become evident later in this chapter when the ancient dialectical exercise is discussed.

62   44ᵃ39–40.

These cannot be predicated universally of anything else. An example is the man Callias. He is individual (ἕκαστον) and sensible (αἰσθητόν) and can have things predicated of him, the species "human" for example.[63] Next are universals. These can be predicated of other things, but other things are not first predicated of them.[64] Thirdly, there are those things that in some sense lie between individuals and universals. These are both predicated of other things (for example, Callias) and have other things predicated of them (for example, animal). In this instance, the example of this third sort of thing would be the species "human."[65] According to Aristotle, both arguments (οἱ λόγοι) and inquiries (αἱ σκέψεις) are primarily concerned with things of this third type.[66] The method of finding premises connected with the problem proposed involves examining the subject and its definitions (τοὺς ὁρισμούς) and all of its properties (ἴδια), as well as all of the attributes or consequents (ὅσα ἔπεται) of the subject.[67] From among these consequents, we must distinguish (διαιρετέον) those that fall within the definition (τό τί ἐστι) or essence and those which are properties (ἴδια) or accidents (συμβεβηκότα).[68] It is the consequents or attributes of the whole (ὅλῳ) of the subject, for example, those that attach to every man and not just Callias, that give us the middle terms necessary for syllogistic premisses.[69] The task is to select the consequents or attributes appropriate to the subject and not to a wider term (animal instead of human, for example) or to a subordinate term (for example, Callias instead of the species human).[70] This method of investigation will apply to both apodeictic and problematic syllogisms as well as to assertoric syllogisms.[71] The method will be the same whether we are engaged in philosophy or in any art (τέχνη)

---

63   44[a]26–29.
64   43[a]29–30.
65   43[a]30 *et seq.*
66   43[a]42–43.
67   43[b]2–4.
68   43[b]6–8.
69   43[b]11–14.
70   43[b]29–30.
71   45[b]28–31.

or study (μάθημα).[72] After we have gathered up and considered the possible relationships of the attributes of both subject and predicate in the proposed conclusion or thesis and arranged these according to the possible order of the three terms in a syllogism, we will be in a position to refute (ἀνασκευάζειν) this way (μὲν ὡδί) and to establish (κατασκευάζειν) that way (δὲ ὡδί).[73]

In discussing how the above-described method is superior to the Platonic method of division (διαίρεσις) by genera, Aristotle observes that syllogism proves a proposition by means of a middle term that is always subordinate to the major term. Division, on the other hand, takes the universal as the middle term.[74] Consequently, division assumes what it ought to demonstrate and hence it can prove nothing.[75] The achievements that the method of syllogism, properly understood, makes possible are listed by Aristotle in the context of discussing the inadequacy of Platonic division. They include:

(a)   refuting a proposition;
(b)   drawing an inference about an accident or a property;
(c)   drawing an inference about a genus; and
(d)   drawing an inference where a question of fact is uncertain (and here he reverts to his favoured example of the incommensurability of the diagonal of a square with its sides).[76]

These sorts of achievements herald Aristotle's account of scientific reasoning in the *Posterior Analytics* and provide the basis for Marjorie Grene's remark that:

We may, therefore, legitimately consider Aristotelian logic not as the first adumbration of a formal system but as a discipline

---

[72]   46^{a}3–4.
[73]   46^{a}4–10.
[74]   46^{a}39–^{b}3.
[75]   46^{b}3 *et seq.*
[76]   46^{b}26–29.

enabling the student to acquire scientific knowledge.[77]

The foregoing summary of Aristotle's view about how we ordinarily use syllogistic reasoning and what may be achieved by means of it is drawn from Book *A*, Chapters 27 to 31 inclusive of the *Prior Analytics*. Those sections of his work bring into relief the pedagogical purpose of logic. As Aristotle states, he aims to portray not only how syllogisms are produced, and how they can be reduced to figures already known so that we may be assured of their validity, but also how we have the power or ability (δύναμις) of discovering (εὑρίσκειν) syllogisms.[78] Although his article is predominantly about the use of dialectic as discussed in the *Topics*, Gilbert Ryle's remarks about the "gymnastic" purpose of the dialectical exercise are equally applicable in this regard to Aristotle's work in the *Prior Analytics*.[79] By the time he wrote the *Topics* Aristotle has already separated several different functions of dialectic, for he contrasts those who argue or discuss (τούσ λόγους) for the sake of teaching and learning with those who do so in competition with each other (τοίς ἀγωνιζομένοις) as well as with those who do so for the sake of inquiry (σκέψεως).[80] What is especially worthy of note about this recognition of different purposes for dialectic is that they all presuppose two persons engaged in a public activity, in each case a sort of dialogue. This is to be contrasted with another setting where at least two persons are involved, but which calls for a "scientific monologue." This occurs when "the master, disregarding his pupil's beliefs, develops his argument from the principles proper to his science; and the pupil listens respectfully."[81] The magisterial lecture

---

[77]   Marjorie Grene, *A Portrait of Aristotle* (Chicago: University of Chicago Press, 1967), p. 69.

[78]   47ª2–5.

[79]   Gilbert Ryle, "Dialectic in the Academy" in Renford Bambrough (ed.), *New Essays on Plato and Aristotle* (London: Routledge & Kegan Paul, 1965) 39–69, p. 41.

[80]   *Top.* 159ª26–37.

[81]   E. Weil, "The Place of Logic in Aristotle's Thought," originally published as "La Place de la logique dans la pensée aristotélicienne" in (1951) 56 *Revue métaphysique et de morale* 283–315 and reprinted in Jonathan Barnes et al. (eds.),

is not within the scope of dialectic, but the debate, the discussion and the eristic moot certainly are.

From even a cursory examination of the *Topics* it is evident that Aristotle is concerned with giving practical guidance to learners who themselves have been and will be engaged in a dialectical exercise that has its roots in ancient Greek intellectual training long before Aristotle came along to systematize certain of its key principles.[82] This exercise involves two participants, one of whom chooses to defend the affirmative or negative limb of a thesis and thereby becomes the "answerer," while the interlocutor is obliged to attack that position by posing questions that call for a yes or no answer. A questioner's aim is to take advantage of the opponent's answers to manoeuvre that person into a contradiction of the original thesis, that is, to create an elenchus.[83] The picture that emerges, of arguers working not from premisses to the unknown conclusion, but instead from a known thesis backwards, so to speak, to premisses that either lead to the thesis propounded or its contradictory, is consistent with

---

Articles on Aristotle: 1. Science (London: Duckworth, 1975) 88–112, p. 98.

[82]   Ryle, *supra* n. 79, p. 45; Ernst Kapp, "Syllogistic" in Jonathan Barnes et al. (eds.), *Articles on Aristotle: 1. Science* (London: Duckworth, 1975) 35–49, p. 40.

[83]   Ryle, *supra* n. 79, p. 45; Ernst Kapp, *Greek Foundations of Traditional Logic* (New York: Columbia University Press, 1942), p. 12. The term "elenchus" was well-entrenched before Aristotle wrote the *Topics*. It has two senses: a wider one in which it means examining a person about a statement they have made by eliciting further statements that explicate and establish the truth or falsity of the original statement; and a narrower sense, in which it is the equivalent to cross-examination or refutation. See Richard Robinson, "Elenchus" in Gregory Vlastos (ed.), *The Philosophy of Socrates: A Collection of Critical Essays* (Garden City, N.Y.: Anchor Books, 1971) 78–93, p. 78. Robinson notes interestingly that passage in Plato's *Sophist*, 229E–230E, where Plato has the Eleatic Stranger divide education into two sorts. The first is an admonitory kind and the second is the process of elenchus. Of the two, elenchus is represented as the better and smoother sort. It involves showing learners that what they are saying is inconsistent with other opinions they hold. Out of this process they are "purified" in their notions and are only thus in a position to learn. Plato employs the physician-patient analogy to give point to this purification process. It is with such a background of thesis and *reductiones ad absurdum* in mind, that Aristotle compiled his *Topics* and *S.E.*, which seem to presuppose a great variety of stock theses and well-worn tracks of argumentation.

one of the major objectives set for himself by Aristotle in his *Prior Analytics*. Alongside the question of how arguments may be analyzed into their components and how these may be formalized, is the equally important purpose of clarifying how syllogisms may be discovered. The purpose of discovering them, at least at the time when Aristotle was himself active in academic teaching and engaging in philosophic debates, and the purpose of logic in general, was not for learning better how to think for ourselves, but for "when we are talking and trying to convince one another."[84] From the evidence of certain passages in the *Topics* and in the *Prior Analytics*, it becomes clear that Aristotle conceives of multiple contexts in daily conversations where syllogistic reasoning, including the ability to find syllogisms and to impart information by such means, is useful. Among those which must have been present in the setting in which he composed his logical works, there would be the situation of the questioner and the answerer in the early Academy's type of dialectical exercise; the philosophic disputation between opponents relatively equal in terms of their experience and argumentative prowess; and the discussion between persons, not for the sake of competition, but for experiment or inquiry. What Aristotle has prominently in mind when he writes the *Prior Analytics* is the setting in which a master guides a student or disciple through the contents of a science already established. The teacher does this, not in any haphazard way, but by means of an organized method of presentation that depends for its principles of organization on the nature of the objects which the science studies as well as on the relative generality of the terms used to denominate those objects. In systematizing such a procedure, Aristotle has made a large advance beyond the Socratic refutation as a method for "purifying" the learner's mind before learning can occur. He also has improved on the notion of a mere handbook of typical topics and strategies in common Academic debate.[85]

---

[84]   Kapp, *supra* n. 83, p. 19.

[85]   This characterization of the *Topics* and the *S.E.* as embodying a handbook or manual that owe their common genesis to the sort of disputations that Aristotle would have witnessed and participated in during his period in the Academy can be found in both Ryle, *supra* n. 79, p. 40 and Owen, *supra* n. 22,

With this preliminary sketch concluded, we can turn next to an elucidation and a critical scrutiny of Aristotle's claim that all teaching and learning proceed by, and can only proceed by, a certain logical method. This method does not merely reflect his formal logic, but it is a veritable part of logic as he conceives it. In this sense, too, his keen sense of the interrelatedness of seemingly disparate human activities and his passion for penetrating to the bottom of an explanation have enabled him to advance far beyond the rather shallow aims attributed by him to such predecessors as Gorgias. His theories prefigure in a remarkable degree, at least in scope if not in content, those modern researchers who are savants in several fields, such as Jean Piaget, and who once again see a connection between learning and logic.

---

p. 15. The latter article presents an illuminating argument about Aristotle's logic stemming from the discussions in the Academy, so that some of the root ideas of the doctrines of the categories and the syllogism were probably developed by Aristotle before Plato's death. This attempt to chart the gradual evolution of Aristotle's ideas on logic and scientific procedure repairs a vast gap in Jaeger's thesis. For him, the growth of logic was autonomous and owed little if anything to Aristotle's early period when he was purportedly subject to the influence of Platonism.

CHAPTER THREE

Teaching and Learning in the *Posterior Analytics*

With this chapter, we shall be fully launched on our exposition of how Aristotle conceives of the activities of a teacher imparting knowledge and of a pupil learning it. We have already gained some idea from studying other parts of Aristotle's contribution to logic that there is evidence of syllogism playing a central role in the teacher's task. In the *Posterior Analytics* Aristotle addresses this topic directly. His line of reasoning in that treatise is pre-eminently concerned with how the apodeictic syllogism becomes the means by which all of us are led to scientific knowledge about things in this world. Since the method is highly organized according to criteria of generality in principles, expertise in specialized and autonomous branches of knowledge, and the ordered and studied exposition of what is known, we should not be surprised that scientific knowledge is not, for Aristotle, just something we can learn for ourselves through the general ruck of experience; for experience is a poor teacher, or rather, no teacher at all. The best form of learning involves teachers, who have already achieved a sophisticated level of understanding in their subject, guiding students through demonstrations towards conclusions that are, in some sense, foreordained.

The exposition of the *Posterior Analytics* demands close attention, for it is one treatise by Aristotle that has been judged to exhibit the best, or the worst, features of its author's style. It depends on one's view. Anscombe simply deplores Book *A* of this treatise as Aristotle's "worst book."[1] Barnes, on the other hand, characterizes the whole work as "on any account, one of the most brilliant, original, and influential works in the history of philosophy."[2] Again, as was the case in the previous chapter, where the *Prior Analytics* was at the focus of our discussion, such disparate views should pique our curiosity and set in motion our own reading, so that we may see what value there lies in the treatise. Even if parts of it are as opaque as Anscombe suggests, the *Posterior Analytics* for better or worse had undeniably a large influence on the practice of subsequent scientific investigation and, we may suppose, subsequent science teaching.[3]

---

[1]   G. E. M. Anscombe, "Aristotle" in G. E. M. Anscombe and P. T. Geach, *Three Philosophers* (Ithaca, N.Y.: Cornell University Press, 1961), p. 6.

[2]   Jonathan Barnes, *Aristotle's Posterior Analytics*, 2nd ed. (Oxford: Clarendon Press, 1994), p. xiv. Into the balance may be tossed also the following assessment:

> I would only like to show that the *Posterior Analytics* is not the hopeless work some have found it to be, and that it may well deserve the amount of study and commentary which it received in other hermeneutic traditions. It is a work, it seems to me, which may lack some of the conceptual force and imaginative daring of the *Metaphysics* or the *Ethics*. But like so much of The Philosopher's writings, it is subtle, wholesome, and clear-headed, and reveals the obvious to us with startling clarity and ramification.

L. A. Kosman, "Understanding, Explanation, and Insight in Aristotle's *Posterior Analytics*" in E. N. Lee, A. P. D. Mourelatos, and R. M. Rorty (eds.), *Exegesis and Argument: Studies in Greek Philosophy Presented to Gregory Vlastos* (Assen: Van Gorcum, 1973) 374–92, pp. 391–92.

[3]   The story of the preservation, diffusion, and translation of Aristotle's logical works in the Roman, Syriac, Islamic, and early medieval traditions is recounted in Marshall Clagett, *Greek Science in Antiquity* (London: Collier-Macmillan, 1955). There is an irony in how delayed was the use of the *An. Post.* in a way which Aristotle might have understood and countenanced. The succession of uses to which Aristotle's formal logic was put before the rediscovery of some of its major writings has been described as follows:

> Whereas the logic of Aristotle was developed for the primary end of exhibiting the formal structure of demonstrations in the sciences of nature, and modern logic has been developed as an abstract formulation and axiomatic derivation of the principles of mathematics, medieval logic functioned as an art of language (*sermocinalis scientia*)

Even as later authors began the process of breaking away from certain Aristotelian tenets in respect of scientific method, they felt compelled to pay due deference to Aristotle by presenting their new theories as essentially presupposed by him. This is illustrated in Roger Bacon's *Opus Majus*, written in the thirteenth century:

> What Aristotle says therefore to the effect that the demonstration is a syllogism that makes us know, is to be understood if the experience of it accompanies the demonstration, and it is not to be understood of the bare demonstration.[4]

When medieval teachers dealt with general subjects such as the explanation of change, or particular subjects such as cosmology, meteorology, mechanics, chemistry or biology, they took as their beginning Aristotelian theory in relation to each one of these

---

closely associated with grammar, to be used as a means of construing authoritative texts of Sacred Scripture and of the Church Fathers and of establishing interpretations of such texts that would be logically coherent and free from constradiction. Only after it had already achieved its distinctive form of development, in almost complete isolation from scientific applications, did medieval logic encounter, in the later thirteenth century, the system of Aristotelian sciences which had been the *raison d'être* of the Aristotelian formulation of logic. The critique of Aristotelian metaphysics and physics, which occurred in the fourteenth century and prepared the way for the scientific revolution of the seventeenth century, was made possible in large measure by the independent development of logic that had taken place when Aristotle's philosophical works were unknown.
Ernest A. Moody, "The Medieval Contribution to Logic" in *Studies in Medieval Philosophy, Science, and Logic* (Berkeley: University of California Press, 1975), pp. 373–74.

4   Roger Bacon, "The *Opus Majus* (Selections)," in *Selections from Medieval Philosophers*, ed. and trans. Richard McKeon, 2 vols. (New York: Charles Scribner's Sons, 1930), 2: 73. The tendency towards adopting a servile attitude towards Aristotle (and to some extent towards some of his Arabic expositors) is reflected in the following statement by Bacon (*ibid.*, p. 32):

> If, therefore, the badly translated text be held to the letter, then it is wholly false and contrary to Aristotle elsewhere, and so great an author does not contradict himself.

subjects.[5] Gradually, by observation, experimentation and the application of mathematical and quantitative methods, the Aristotelian system became outmoded.

The motif of Aristotle's account of scientific demonstration is introduced at the very beginning of the *Posterior Analytics*, like a strong, resonant theme that will be the subject of variation, modulation and recapitulation throughout the work. To pursue this symphonic metaphor further, we may justifiably question whether the treatment of the theme does not meander a bit and whether a satisfactory resolution is reached by the end of the *Posterior Analytics*. Indeed, we may be more inclined to wonder if this work is not itself aporetic rather than apodeictic, and, unlike a good symphonic composition, and to that extent unsatisfying, if it has not left us with a host of unanswered questions. The presentation of Aristotle's material is certainly not so elegant as in the *Prior Analytics*.

In the exposition that follows, Book *A*, chapters 1 to 6 inclusive will be summarized with a liberal amount of paraphrase added; this part of his argument is especially "knotty" and "tight."[6] The purpose of examining this part carefully will be, first, to raise any difficulties that there might be in grasping the main lines of Aristotle's argument which he limns in these initial chapters, and secondly, to apply to those sections any relevant general philosophic doctrines that Aristotle develops elsewhere in his writings. Thirdly, in this part I attempt to extract and bring into full view some tacit assumptions which underlie Aristotle's enterprise.

The discussion in this chapter will be divided into two main parts. The first deals with the nature of scientific knowledge and the conditions necessary for its attainment, the organization of such knowledge into the appropriate demonstrative sciences so that it may be readily acquired by the student, the causes of error and ignorance, and how the process of demonstration is an aid and accessory in the search for definitions. These topics are covered in

---

5   See A. C. Crombie, *Medieval and Early Modern Sciences*, 2 vols. (Garden City, Anchor Books, 1959), 1: ch. 3.

6   Adjectives applied by, respectively, Marjorie Grene, *A Portrait of Aristotle* (London: Faber and Faber, 1963, reprinted as a paperback, Chicago: University of Chicago Press, 1967) p. 85, and Barnes, *supra* n. 2, p. xv.

Book *A* and a sizeable part of Book *B*. The second major part of this chapter concentrates on how definitions and first principles are acquired. This occupies, in the *Posterior Analytics*, the latter part of Book *B*.

Once Aristotle's views on the above topics are set forth, and some time-honoured and intriguing issues relating Aristotle's account to the mainstream of educational philosophy have been discussed, the scene will be set for Chapter Six, in which a full-scale critical examination of his views and programme will be conducted from the standpoint of educational theory.

As in the case of our dealing with Aristotle's formal logic, one of the Oxford translations will be the principal source of terminology and extracts from the *Posterior Analytics*.[7] The translator in this instance is G. R. G. Mure. There is an important, contemporary translation, with extensive notes and commentary, by Jonathan Barnes in the Clarendon Aristotle Series.[8] The Loeb Classical Library edition is by Hugh Tredennick and the Everyman's Library edition is by John Warrington.[9] For the Greek text, I have relied on the edition of the *Posterior Analytics* in the Oxford Classical Texts series.[10] References made in the text and footnotes of this chapter simply to line, column and page will be to the *Posterior Analytics*.

---

7 Aristotle, *The Works of Aristotle*, eds. J. A.. Smith and W. D. Ross, 12 vols. (Oxford: Clarendon Press, 1908–52), vol. 1.

8 Barnes, *supra* n. 2. In slightly amended form, the first edition of Barnes's translation appears in the Revised Oxford Translation, *The Complete Works of Aristotle*, ed. Jonathan Barnes, 2 vols. (Princeton: Princeton University Press, 1984) 1: 114–66.

9 Aristotle, *The Posterior Analytics*, trans. Hugh Tredennick, Loeb Classical Library (London: Heinemann, 1960; Cambridge, Mass.: Harvard University Press, 1960); Aristotle, *Prior and Posterior Analytics*, ed. and trans. John Warrington, Everyman's Library (London: Dent, 1964; New York: Dutton, 1964).

10 Aristoteles, *Analytica Priora et Posteriora*, ed. W. D. Ross and L. Minio-Paluello (Oxford: Clarendon Press, 1964).

The nature and use of demonstration in teaching and learning scientific knowledge

Two matters should initially be reiterated and emphasized in order to set the tone of this part. I concluded the expository section of Chapter Two with a symbolic notation that makes clear the form of the apodeictic syllogism as developed by Aristotle. It may be written as: $\Box$ P a M, $\Box$ M a S $\rightarrow$ $\Box$ P a S.[11] The two premisses are each universal affirmative propositions, and so is the conclusion. All three constituent propositions are necessary, as shown by the modal operator "$\Box$" rather than assertoric or problematic.[12] As related in the previous chapter, I have also tried to show that a pedagogical setting was in the foreground of Aristotle's vision when he developed his system of valid inference.[13] He is not interested in describing and symbolically representing the "laws of thought," as if he were engaged on a study of how we think rather than how we communicate with one another, but sees the use of his logic primarily in the context of two persons participating in a public activity. The participants are perhaps arguing with various purposes and with different rewards at stake, depending on the type of argument, or they might be engaging in a special form of question-and-answer exercise with stringent rules on what the contestants can do while trying to refute each other. Or the two parties might be a master guiding a student from one or more better-known propositions to one that is less-known.[14] That is, these propositions are better or less known as judged from the standpoint of the student.

With this background firmly fixed, we may now approach the

---

[11]   Which may have the following terms substituted for the variables, to give the argument: If it is necessary that animal belongs to every human, and it is necessary that human belongs to every Greek, then it is necessary that animal belongs to every Greek.

[12]   For the meaning of these technical terms, see *supra* Chapter Two, pp. 34–36.

[13]   See *supra* Chapter Two, pp. 40–43.

[14]   On the contrast between this aim and the professed delimitation of the province of logic by later logicians, such as Mill, see Ernst Kapp, *Greek Foundations of Traditional Logic* (New York: Columbia University Press, 1942), pp. 85–86.

opening of the *Posterior Analytics* and Aristotle's sweeping (and somewhat paradoxical) generalization. His overarching concern is with the conveyance and acquisition of knowledge. It is crucial to his enterprise how he initially frames this topic. He asserts that:

All teaching [διδασκαλία] and learning [μάθησις] that involves the use of reason [διανοητική] proceeds from pre-existent [προϋπαρχούσης] knowledge [γνώσεως].[15]

This is Tredennick's translation. Although the matter of variances in translation will generally not burden us, it is useful to compare other English versions of this key passage. Mure is less literal than Tredennick and turns "teaching and learning" into "instruction given or received." Barnes reads "intellectual" for διανοητική and places it as an adjective modifying learning, but not necessarily teaching. He, unlike Tredennick, does not render διανοητική into English in the form of a subordinate clause that is ambiguous in its operation as an adjectival clause. Is it meant to modify only learning or both teaching and learning? Mure, for some obscure reason, translates διανοητική as "by way of argument." It becomes, in his version, an adverbial phrase rather than an adjective or subordinate clause, and it too is ambiguous about whether it is meant to extend over both teaching and learning.[16] The original Greek term, διανοητικός, as used by Aristotle and Plato, primarily has to do with thinking, contemplating or conceiving; prima facie, it has little to do with arguing.[17] Perhaps Mure in this instance is anticipating some of the

---

[15]   71ª1–3. Cf. *N.E.* 1139ᵇ25–27.

[16]   In W. D. Ross, *Aristotle's Prior and Posterior Analytics* (Oxford: Clarendon Press, 1949, reprinted 1957), p. 503, this term is paraphrased as "by way of reasoning," and is meant to contrast with "by use of the senses" (see *ibid.*, p. 504).

[17]   H. G. Liddell, R. Scott, and H. S. Jones, *A Greek-English Lexicon*, 9th ed. (Oxford: Clarendon Press, 1940, reprinted 1961) s.v. διανοητικός. This term is a cognate of the verb related to νοῦς, a term which has, as we shall see, below, excited several philological hypotheses and a charting of its uses down to and including Aristotle's use of it: see James H. Lesher, "The Meaning of *Nous* in the *Posterior Analytics*" (1973) 18 Phronesis 44–69, pp. 47–51. The preposition διά added to the verbal form often marks the "completion of the

examples that Aristotle will go on to adduce in support of his opening proposition. As will be seen below, Aristotle appeals to our knowledge of the different sorts of arguments (for which he uses both λόγοι and συλλογισμόι) as well as of the different arts and sciences for illustration and justification. Mure seems so influenced by some of these examples, namely the enumerated sorts of syllogism or deductive reasoning, that he gives quite a misleading interpretation of Aristotle's starting point. A second possible explanation is that Mure finds in διανοητική some echo of Plato's use of διάνοια, by which he on occasion means something like discourse in the soul, or the discursive thinking that underlies all reasoning. This would be a rather abstruse derivation in this instance though and would not be obvious to the reader approaching Aristotle's work without a prior grounding in Plato. In either event, Mure's translation is tendentious. All three translators agree that "pre-existent" or "already existing" is the proper English translation of προϋπαρχούσης, a term which connotes something that either has gone before (in the past perfect tense) or that was (existing in the progressive aspect of the verb) when the event being talked about occurred.

The foregoing discussion, in which I have attempted to pin down what Aristotle means by learning διανοητική, is not just pyrotechnics about how a Greek phrase may be transmuted when we seek to express it in English. I am not trying to make heavy weather of it just because it is part of Aristotle's first statement in his treatise. Just as ἐπιστήμη is not simply translatable by knowledge, but means scientific knowledge in which various attendant conditions have been satisfied, so might we expect learning or coming to know to bear a similar "strong" sense in Aristotle's philosophy. His use of διανοητική would, on this view, be an important instance tending to support such an interpretation.

We should note that Aristotle does not begin the *Posterior*

---

action of the verbal idea (perfective action)." This quotation is from Herbert Weir Smyth, *Greek Grammar*, rev. Gordon M. Messing (Cambridge, Mass.: Harvard University Press, 1920, 8th reprint ed., 1973), p. 366. Thus the compound of διά and the verb νοέειν would give us something like "by way of thinking" or "succeed in thinking."

Analytics with a procedure common to other treatises composed by him on scientific subjects.[18] He does not engage on a quasi-historical survey of what previous thinkers or the run of people have thought about the topic proposed, and then, after reciting these and the defects discernible in them, make a fresh start himself. There are no competing theories of either the method of demonstration or of teaching with which he has to deal either as an historian of philosophy or as the originator of an alternative theory to those of his predecessors. At best, he mentions obliquely his teacher, Plato, in the second half of Book *A* 1. Instead of following his usual procedure, he delves straight into his subject. To this extent, the description he applies to his original and unprecedented work on formal logic at the conclusion of the *Sophistical Refutations* also applies to his theory of "material" logic, as Ross calls it, and the systematic enterprise of teaching.[19] The Socratic predilection for ἔλεγχος and the Platonic use of διαίρεσις might be supposed to be the bases of some of Aristotle's work, but they fall so short of being systematic procedures that are grounded on a theory of demonstration that they hardly qualify as the germs of Aristotle's comprehensive analysis.

Aristotle's opening statement in the *Posterior Analytics* is cast as a conclusion that he immediately attempts to justify by canvassing different situations and forming an induction. He gives two pairs of examples and one further isolated example by which to confirm the truth of his statement. First, he says that all the mathematical sciences and every other art are acquired in this way.[20] He evidently means that students learn mathematics in this way, not that mathematical discoveries, such as that of the Pythagorean theorem back in the mists of antiquity, are so made. Aristotle often

---

18   For the order of inquiry common in Aristotle's scientific works, see Richard McKeon, "Aristotle's Conception of the Development and the Nature of Scientific Method" (1947) 8 Journal of the History of Ideas 3–44, pp. 3–5 *et passim*. Aristotle is, however, truer to his usual form when he considers the relationship of demonstration to definition in Book *B* of the *An. Post.* First, he suggests some of the difficulties with which his discussion is ordinarily fraught (90ª34–92ᵇ40), then he makes a "fresh start" and reconsiders the problem by declaring his own positive views (93ª1 *et seq.*).

19   See *supra*, Chapter Two, p. 37, and Ross, *supra* n. 16, p. 51.

20   71ª3–4.

distinguishes between the spheres of art or skill (τέχνη) and of science or understanding (ἐπιστήμη or alternative Greek nouns meaning something like our "knowledge").[21] The former has to do with how things come about or are produced (for example, the medical doctor is interested in curing patients of diseases, and hence medicine is an art or technique). The latter has to do with what Aristotle calls τὸ ὄν (which Barnes translates by the phrase "what is the case" and occasionally is translated by others as "being"). It involves a knowledge of the nature of things in a fundamental sense and supplies the theoretical and general principles which the possessors of an art or skill draw from in order to go about their business (for example, the doctor would have to be familiar with some at least of the principles of physics, which, in Aristotelian terms, is the study of the forms and explanations of change in nature). Owing to the different status accorded by Aristotle to mere skill and to complete and accurate knowledge, it is impossible to read his appeal to the methods of learning the "arts and sciences" as other than an appeal to two different types of things. They share one feature though: Aristotle thinks that they are both taught and learned by means of previously existing knowledge.

The second pair of examples is made up of arguments (λόγοι), both syllogistic and inductive (ἐπαγωγός). He says that both types produce or effect (ποιοῦνται) teaching through what we have learned or understood.[22] In the case of συλλογισμός (which Barnes prefers to translate as "deductive argument," and by which Tredennick thinks Aristotle means "dialectic," as opposed to science and rhetoric), the effectiveness of such argument depends on what an audience or opponent is prepared to grant or accept as the argument's premises.[23] This presumption of a second participant as a factor in determining how an argument proceeds is part and parcel of the notion of dialectic and therefore at the root of the origins of logic. It relates back to the setting in which Aristotle develops his

---

[21]   For example, see N.E. 1139[b]18 et seq. for ἐπιστήμη, and 1140[a]6–16 for τέχνη.

[22]   71[a]5–6.

[23]   The method of ἐρώτησις, or the latching onto premises by means of questions and answers, is alluded to at 71[a]7, and this is probably the rationale for Tredennick's translation of "dialectic." See also Ross, *supra* n. 16, p. 504.

formal system of inference in the *Prior Analytics* as well as his more loosely organized handbook for the student debater, the *Topics*.[24] Those premisses, gained in the form of either assumptions or concessions, are the basis on which the conclusion will eventually be drawn and learning will be achieved. The inductive type of argument is used to prove the universal (καθόλου), what is to be taught and learned, through the particular (καθ' ἕκαστον) being clear (δῆλον) to the mind.[25] Finally, Aristotle suggests the example of rhetorical arguments (ῥητορικοί), which persuade by means of things already known.[26] In this case what are already known are examples (παραδείγματα), which may be used inductively, or enthymemes, which may be used deductively like premises in syllogism, to produce conviction.[27]

Having recited the foregoing five things in an effort to prove by example that all intellectual learning presupposes some kind of knowledge already attained by the learner (and it should be noted that a different sort of existing knowledge is presupposed, depending on the type of science, art or argument), Aristotle proceeds next to state in what senses existing knowledge is necessary (ἀναγκαῖος). First, for some things it is necessary that they be assumed beforehand; and second, for other things it is necessary to understand what it is that is being said (τὸ λεγόμενόν).[28] For yet other things, both ways of understanding are necessary. So, for example, the learner must first know something is affirmed or denied (about what that thing is—we must not forget that Aristotle thinks that all knowledge is stateable in propositions that yield a subject-predicate analysis). The second way is exemplified by knowledge of the triangle, for the learner must first know that it signifies "this" (ὅδι τοδὶ σημαίνει).[29] Moreover, with respect to the

---

24   See *supra*, Chapter Two, pp. 41–42.

25   71^{a}8–9. See also *N.E.* 1139^{b}27–29.

26   71^{a}9.

27   71^{a}10–11.

28   71^{a}12–14. Again, there is a problem in construing this passage, for it is unclear whether the first thing necessary to be grasped is to be known (Ross), believed (Barnes), or assumed (Tredennick and Mure) beforehand.

29   71^{a}14–15.

unit (μονάδ), Aristotle thinks it is necessary that the learner know beforehand both what the thing said about the unit signifies and that the unit is (to use Aristotle's own way of expressing this).[30] Some commentators have seen in these first few concrete instances of subjects of knowledge, the triangle and the unit, both drawn from mathematics, a significant clue as to the ideal model of a demonstrative science for Aristotle. The controversy that surrounds such an issue will not detain us here, though Barnes's table showing the number of examples in the *Posterior Analytics* drawn from mathematics as against the number of non-mathematical examples is an interesting contribution to the debate.[31]

Lines 71ª11-17 are difficult to penetrate. It appears that an aspiring learner must first know (προγιγνώσκειν) what individual terms mean (for example, "triangle") as well as that certain propositions are true or false (for example, that a "unit is"). Aristotle expressly maintains that we do not grasp some of these things as clearly as we grasp others.[32] He offers no further examples in this passage. On the notion of the learner's being required to know first that something is, regard should be paid to the following passage in Book *A* 10, which is embedded in a discussion of the three factors necessary for a demonstration:

> Yet some sciences may very well pass over some of these elements; e.g. we might not expressly posit the existence of the genus if its existence were obvious (for instance, the evidence of hot and cold is more evident than that of number).[33]

---

[30] 71ª15–16.

[31] Part of the controversy over whether Aristotle intended mathematics to be such a model is stimulated by his early introduction of "mathematical" sciences as an example of teaching based on existing knowledge, and the recurrent use of geometrical and arithmetic examples in the first few chapters of the *An. Post.* See, for example, 75ᵇ3, 76ª8, and 76ª35. That, taking the *An. Post.* as a whole, examples drawn from mathematics are outnumbered by other sorts of examples is shown in the table compiled in Jonathan Barnes, "Aristotle's Theory of Demonstration" (1969) 14 Phronesis 123–52, p. 129.

[32] 71ª16–17.

[33] 76ᵇ16–19.

Ordinarily, a conscientious teacher will be very careful about what to take for granted, so that nothing is unwarrantedly assumed and a necessary step omitted in the demonstration. Otherwise the learner would either lose the path to scientific knowledge or would never start on the path in the first place. This procedure seems to be what Aristotle is referring to in the above passage, which implies that some things, provided they are obvious, may be taken for granted by teachers. They may be entitled to assume, for example, that the learner will already know that the genus which is the subject of the demonstration exists, and hence the teacher may go straight into an elucidation of the essential attributes of that genus. This interpretation is a good example of how conceiving demonstration to be a living process involving several parties, each in the appropriate role, permits us to see the point of what would otherwise be a fairly dry, obscure observation on Aristotle's part.

At 71^{a}17 Aristotle introduces the possibility that in learning it sometimes happens that one categorical proposition may already be known by learners, and yet they hit upon another at the same time as acquiring knowledge expressible in yet a third proposition. So, learners may have knowledge of the universal (for example, in every triangle, the total of its interior angles equals the total of two right angles) and they may subsequently become familiar with two further propositions simultaneously; first, for example, that there is a triangle being shown to them, and second, that the total of that triangle's interior angles equals the total of two right angles.[34] The example of the triangle is used by Aristotle at 71^{a}19-24. Is such an inference as there described capable of being formalized into an apodeictic syllogism? It does not seem possible, because the minor premiss is about an individual that is not itself predicable of anything else. Aristotle anticipates such an observation, for he allows in a parenthetical remark commencing at 71^{a}21 that this is a way of learning, even though the subject of the minor premiss is not

---

[34] Note the significance of the knowledge of the universal and of the particular being stateable in subject-predicate form, so that in general we may say that a statement about a generic universal can be denoted as P a M; and a statement about a particular, which serves as the minor premiss in a scientific demonstration, can be denoted by a sentence frame as M a S.

searched for, in the sense laid down in the *Prior Analytics*, by means of its attributes or properties.[35] Rather, the individual is somehow seen without the necessity of a middle term to act as a mediating factor. Aristotle calls this process of relating something immediately apprehended to what the learner already knows, and arriving at a newly-learned proposition, the process of "relating" or "recognizing," or at least this is how the verb γνωρίζειν has been translated.[36] It leads to the learner's drawing of a συλλογισμός. Aristotle claims that the recognition of the particular as falling under the universal occurs at the same time as learning something about the particular by virtue of its so falling.[37] Barnes uses the term "induction" to denote the second process, but one must be wary about how many different processes that English word has been used to describe as they arise in Aristotle's writings.[38] In the passage in question above, the key verbs used to describe the process are ἐπαχθῆναι and γνωρίζειν, and not ἐπάγειν.

From his example of the individual triangle, Aristotle draws an important conclusion about in what sense learners in that example can be said to know (ἐπίστασθαι) before they recognized the individual and related it to the universal. It would be easy and convenient for a philosophic-minded critic to argue that learners do not know the meaning of the categorical proposition, "the sum of the interior angles of a triangle is equal to the sum of two right angles," unless and until they have first become familiar with an individual triangle and come to know that it is a triangle *simpliciter* (ἁπλῶς) or without qualification.[39] Aristotle is eager to resolve this issue because it had bedeviled his predecessors. He grants that knowing something about the universal is different from knowing something as a result

---

35   *An. Pr. A* 27.

36   71ᵃ17–18. The meaning of the verb γνωρίζειν is more precisely rendered by Barnes as "to become familiar," though "to recognize" has the advantage that it captures the nuance of learning something that was, in a sense, already known.

37   71ᵃ19–21.

38   See Ross, *supra* n. 16, pp. 486–87.

39   For the use of the adverb ἁπλῶς in relation to its use as a modifier of adjectives, see *Top.* 115ᵇ30–35.

of the process of recognizing individuals or learning definitions, and *ex hypothesi*, it is the latter sort of knowledge that is amenable to being taught.[40] This philosophic move is of vital importance for Aristotle's account, for by means of it, he manages to escape through the horns of the dilemma posed in the *Meno*.[41] Although his move appears adroit, I shall discuss the original problem as developed by Plato and Aristotle's proposed solution in depth in Chapter Four. For the moment, it is enough to point out that the key distinction that Aristotle makes in order to avoid the result in the *Meno* is that there is a sense in which learners already know what they are learning; yet there is a second sense in which they do not know it. The learner, by knowing the major premiss of a demonstration already potentially knows the conclusion that is derivable from the conjunction of that major with a minor premiss which has the middle term in common with the major. It is the two "senses" being used to describe this that are different.

In the first sense, learners have a qualified knowledge of the proposition that will be the conclusion in the demonstration. They lack knowledge *simpliciter* of it. This is also, as Aristotle later calls it, the incidental (συμβεβηκός) knowledge of the sophist. To show what this qualified sense is, Aristotle first shows the elements of unqualified knowledge, or what we have been calling knowledge *simpliciter*. Such knowledge has two jointly sufficient criteria:[42]

(1)   we think that we are aware (γιγνώσκειν) that the explanation (αἰτία) of what is known (πρᾶγμά) is indeed its explanation; and

(2)   we think that we are aware that it is impossible (ἐνδέχεσθαι) for such to be otherwise.[43]

---

[40]   71ª27–29.

[41]   As he expressly admits at 71ª29–30.

[42]   71ᵇ10.

[43]   71ᵇ10–12. Barnes gives an acute analysis of the use here of the expressions "we think" and "we are aware of" and how they relate to the clause that follows therefrom in respect of each of the two conditions of knowledge: see Barnes, *supra* n. 2, pp. 91–93.

Aristotle countenances the possibility that it may be possible to think that one has satisfied these two criteria without actually having done so. [44]

One method (Aristotle leaves it open that there might be another method) of coming to know, and hence of satisfying both conditions mentioned above, is through demonstration (δι' ἀποδείξεως).[45] He defines the method of demonstration as follows:

> By demonstration I mean a syllogism productive of scientific knowledge [ἐπιστημονικόν], a syllogism, that is, the grasp of which is *eo ipso* such knowledge.[46]

Aristotle nowhere expands on the notion of what it means to grasp (ἔχειν) a syllogism. About the closest we can come to seeing what he means by this oft-repeated locution in the *Posterior Analytics* is Aristotle's contention that merely by grasping a syllogism we understand (ἐπιστάμεθα) something.[47] Whether a syllogism has been grasped by students will presumably be tested by whether they have understood it. It will then be up to the teacher to devise the test of understanding, for example, by rearranging the propositions and having students put them into a significant order, and not just a jumble.

Aristotle turns next to establish the requirements of what he calls demonstrative knowledge (ἀποδεικτικὴν ἐπιστήμην).[48] This is the sort of knowledge that can be disclosed by demonstration, provided that what precedes the drawing of the conclusion is capable of rendering the desired result. Demonstrative knowledge requires (or "must proceed from," in Tredennick's translation) premises made up of propositions which are marked by the following characteristics. They must be:

(1)   true (ἀληθῶν);

---

[44]   71ª14.

[45]   71ª16–17.

[46]   71ª17–19.

[47]   Barnes uses the neutral phrase "by having it."

[48]   71ᵇ20 *et seq.*

(2) primary or primitive (πρώτων);

(3) immediate (ἀμέσων);

(4) better known than (γνωριμωτέρων) the conclusion (συμπεράσματος);

(5) prior to (προτέρων) the conclusion; and

(6) causative or explanatory of (αἰτίων) the conclusion.[49]

All six characteristics are necessary for demonstration to be achieved, though deduction that does not lead to knowledge may take place without all of them being present.[50] Aristotle discusses each necessary condition individually, though they are in a sense interrelated. This discussion takes up the bulk of Book *A* 2. In his explanation in that chapter, he does not distinguish between whether the six criteria are meant to apply only to axioms (the ultimate and primitive propositions from which a conclusion can be said to be derived), or whether they are also meant to apply to propositions that serve as premises immediately leading to the drawing of a particular conclusion. The sixth feature enumerated above, the requirement of explanatory force, recalls the first criterion for knowledge *simpliciter* mentioned by Aristotle at 71[b]12. Cause or explanation (αἰτία) plays an important role throughout Aristotle's attempts to account for natural and artificial objects and our knowledge about them. Attention should be paid to his treatment of this term in the philosophical lexicon that is contained in *Metaphysics Δ* 2.[51] Tredennick uses the traditional adjective "causative" in relation to the sixth criterion. This is not as good as Barnes's use of "explanatory" in the same context, but both are to be preferred to Mure's clause, "which is further related to them as effect to cause." This is a palpable instance of overtranslation. In our understanding how the premises in a demonstration must include an account that explains the "why" of our subject, the language of "cause and effect" is potentially misleading. It would be a signal and unfortunate mistake to foist on Aristotle's account an interpretation based on a

---

[49] 71[b]19–23.

[50] 71[b]23–25.

[51] *Met. Δ* 1013[a]24 *et seq.*

philosophical notion that gained currency long after Aristotle was active and that suggests a metaphysical dispute with which his philosophy is untrammelled. His use of αἰτία should not be treated anachronistically. Otherwise the point of Aristotle's argument about the necessary content of demonstrative premises will be distorted. The idea of understanding or knowledge as being inextricably involved with the ability to give a relevant and accurate explanation when called upon is a subtle doctrine that suffuses Aristotle's work. It is safest not to approach it with any preconceptions based on a misleading translation.

Further important technical terminology is introduced by Aristotle when he turns to an explication of each of the necessary features of demonstrative premises. One of the basic pairs of opposites that runs throughout his epistemology involves that which is prior in nature (τῇ φύσει) as against that which is prior in relation to us (πρὸς ἡμᾶς).[52] Corresponding to this distinction is that by which something that is more knowable (γνωριμώτερον) in nature is different from that which is more knowable by us. Particulars, or those things which are not predicable of something else, are prior and more knowable in relation to us, whereas universals are prior and more knowable in nature and hence prior and more knowable *simpliciter*.[53] As Barnes translates 72ª4-5, Aristotle states that the upshot of this is:

> What is most universal [τὰ καθόλου μάλιστα] is furthest away [πορρωτάτω], and the particulars are nearest [εγγυτατω].[54]

---

[52]   71ᵇ34-72ª4.

[53]   Cf. *Met*. Z 1029ᵇ3–5, which reads, in the translation by Mure in the Oxford Translation referred to *supra* n. 7: "[f]or learning proceeds for all in this way— through that which is less knowable by nature to that which is more knowable."

[54]   Barnes's translation is preferable to some of the others which positively mislead. Mure gives the same passage as: "Now the most universal causes are furthest from sense and particular causes are nearest to sense." For the interpolation of the notion of causes, Mure seems to credit Zabarella's commentary, judging from Mure's notes to the sentence in question. Tredennick gives us: "The most universal concepts are furthest from our perception, and particulars are nearest to it." This language of "causes" and

Aristotle returns to the issue of how demonstration is achieved by pointing out how it may be started. What is required are appropriate (οἰκείως) first principles (ἀρχαί). A first principle is the same thing as a primary or primitive (πρῶτος) premiss (πρότασις).[55] In discussing the notion of primary premisses Aristotle distinguishes between axioms and theses. An axiom (ἀξίωμα) must be grasped by a learner in order for him to learn anything (τὸν ὁτιοῦν).[56] By contrast, Aristotle means by a thesis (θέσις) that which is an immediate (ἄμεσον) deductive (συλλογιστικός) principle (ἀρχή), but which need not be grasped (ἔχειν) for someone to learn something.[57] The context of Aristotle's discussion, in which he indicates the grounds of the distinction between an axiom and a thesis, is crucial to our understanding of the pedagogic purpose of demonstration. If teachers were interested merely in illustrating to their charges how to argue on either side of a question posed, for the purpose let us say of strengthening their skills in using argument, then it might be useful to assume a proposition without regard to its truth value. This would be a thesis, and the ensuing exercise would, in Aristotle's language, be properly classifiable as διαλεκτική, since the proposition that serves as the starting point assumes (λαμβάνειν) one part of a contradiction (ἀντίφασις) indifferently (ὁποτερονοῦν).[58] A demonstration is a different sort of teaching altogether, with a different kind of starting point and a different kind of conclusion. If scientific knowledge, which depends on premisses that satisfy the conditions set down by Aristotle, has a "strong" sense, in so far as anything less is not knowledge in the strict sense of the word, then anything short of demonstration will not conduce to learning in a correspondingly strong sense.

Aristotle goes further and divides theses into two types: the

---

"concepts" can be quite confusing, since it may tend to smuggle into the passage in question some philosophical interpretation that Aristotle could never have meant.

55   72ᵃ5–8.

56   72ᵃ16–17.

57   72ᵃ14–16.

58   Following Barnes, ἀντίφασις is read for ἀντφάσεως in the Oxford Classical Text.

hypothesis (ὑπόθεσις) and the definition (ὁρισμός). By hypothesis he means a thesis that assumes something either is (τὸ εἶναί τι) or is not (μὴ εἶναί τι).[59] Definition does not make such an assumption; rather, it concerns what something, for example, a unit, is and not whether there is a unit. Aristotle's theory of definition will be elaborated later in the *Posterior Analytics*, notably at 90^{b}4 *et seq.*[60]

The notion that there are degrees of knowability receives further treatment from Aristotle. Beginning at 72^{a}25, he argues as follows. He first assumes that one's believing (πιστεύειν) or knowing (εἰδέναι) a fact (πρᾶγμα) consists in grasping (ἔχειν) a syllogism that is in the nature of a demonstration, and this can only be so when the premisses are true. From this he concludes that the learner must necessarily know the primary premisses (τὰ πρῶτα) beforehand better than (μᾶλλον) the conclusion.[61] At this point Aristotle engages in some sort of circular reinforcement of his argument by saying that, in Barnes's translation:

> For a this always belongs better to that thing because of which it belongs—e.g. that because of which we love is better loved.[62]

This attempted justification rings strangely on our ears. It gives us a principle of wide, and somewhat dark, import. It seems that Aristotle is trying to show that if a learner grasps a demonstrandum, D (letting this capital letter stand for the sentence frame □ P a S), then the learner will understand the premisses leading to D better than D itself.[63] What does it mean to say that some things are not just better known, but by their nature are more knowable, than other things?[64] It is worth noting that in the *Categories* Aristotle argues that those branches of knowledge (for example, grammar) by which a person is described as knowledgeable (for example, grammatical)

---

[59]   72^{a}18–20.

[60]   72^{a}20–24.

[61]   72^{a}25–29.

[62]   72^{a}29–30.

[63]   Note that at *Met.* A 982^{b}2 Aristotle says that the first principles and causes are the most knowable.

[64]   71^{b}12.

themselves are classifiable under the category of quality (ποῖος), and not of relation (πρός τι).[65] Moreover, in a preceding passage in the *Categories*, he states expressly that qualities admit of being more or less (τὸ μᾶλλον καὶ τὸ ἔττων).[66] He also contends that grammatical knowledge (γραμματική) can be possessed by different persons in varying degrees. This raises the interesting result that one and the same person may know perfectly well something such as that which may be denoted by □ P a S, and yet know even better a premiss, say □ S a M, that is part of the proof from which □ P a S follows. Aristotle goes further than this and maintains that not only will learners in such a case grasp the first principles of a science as inherently more knowable, but they will also believe (πιστεύειν) in those principles more than they will in the conclusion.[67] This kind of argumentation, in which the criterion of belief is conjoined with the concept of knowledge, has held an attraction for philosophers down the ages.[68]

Aristotle takes up and considers various arguments that might be brought against the notion of a system of primary axioms that is the keystone of his account of demonstration. The first sort of objection is that this kind of scientific knowledge, dependent on prior and better known and stronger held premisses, leads to an infinite (ἄπειρος) regress, and hence that knowledge is impossible.[69] If the learner believes and knows that D has such a premiss as □ P x M, then there must be some major premiss concerning the term P, in turn, that must be prior to □ P x M and better known by the learner. The process would then continue indefinitely backwards so that there is no premiss which is itself not a D. Aristotle handles this skeptical argument in much the same fashion that he tries in the *Metaphysics* to refute the claim that the causes of things may be an infinite series.[70] The process of demonstration, he says, cannot

---

65   *Cat.* 11^b35.

66   *Cat.* 10^b26.

67   72^a36–37.

68   See, for example, Plato, *Theaetetus* 200D *et seq.*, and D. W. Hamlyn, *The Theory of Knowledge* (Garden City, N.Y.: Anchor Books, 1970), pp. 78–103.

69   72^b7–11.

70   *Met. B* 994^a1.

continue *ad infinitum* because not all knowledge is demonstrative. He thus denies the skeptic's premiss that all knowledge is acquired by the learner in the same way. The learner, according to Aristotle, knows some immediate (ἄμεσων) categorical propositions. That is, they are "unmiddled." That this is necessary is evident (φανερόν).[71]

Aristotle's second response to the imputation of an infinite regress is that there is a first principle (ἀρχή) of knowledge that enables the learner to recognize (γνωρίζειν) definitions (ὅροι).[72] What is this so-called first principle of knowledge? Much later in the *Posterior Analytics* it is placed in apposition to the thing which Aristotle calls νοῦς, and appears to be identified with it.[73] The nature of νοῦς is a pit that has been much quarried by Aristotelian commentators. We shall leave it aside for the time being, though we might note that the Greek term has been variously translated in the above-cited passage as "comprehension" (Barnes), "intuition" (Tredennick), "rational intuition" (Mure), and "intuitive reason" (both Ross and Warrington).

The argument from what is necessary and the argument from the first principle of knowledge converge at this point, because they both depend on Aristotle's thesis that some knowledge is not demonstrable and cannot be learned. Neither argument is really an argument in that it shows the fallacy of the infinite regress as applied to demonstration. Skeptics might entirely enlist our sympathy if they were to rejoin to Aristotle that the possibility there is a first principle

---

[71]   72[b]20.

[72]   72[b]23–25. The Greek expression rendered as "definitions" is τοὺς ὅρους. Ordinarily, the nominal form, ὅρος, in Aristotle's logic is translated as "term," and "definition" is reserved for ὁρισμός. It seems that the translators are on sure ground in using "definition" rather than "term" in this passage, in view of Aristotle's contention that one's search for definitions is a search for those items included in one's stock of knowledge that will serve as middle terms as the demonstrations proceed. Tredennick would dispute such a justification, as his note to this passage suggests. He prefers to translate ὅρους as the "ultimate truths." In support he cites Aristotle's choice of words at *N.E.* 1142[a]26, and claims that ὅρος here must be equivalent to ἀρχή. The problem with that is that again ὅρος in this context in the *N.E.* might equally well be interpreted as "definition" or "limiting term."

[73]   100[b]15.

of knowledge is no more likely than that there is no such thing. In Aristotle's defence, it should be pointed out that his theory should be considered as a whole, and his claim that some knowledge is non-demonstrable may just rest on the evidence that learning does in fact occur and this by itself undercuts the skeptic's position. Aristotle is in the main concerned with how we learn different types of things, and how the content of different sciences may differ, although the method of learning each science may be the same. He is not bothered unduly about any doubt over whether we can ever be said to learn. To an important degree, fundamental queries about the axioms, upon which the possibility of learning depends, are throughout Book *A* of the *Posterior Analytics* postponed to Book *B* for consideration. Those axioms are not learned through demonstration, but they are acquired by other means.

The next objection to his view, and again one that is anticipated by Aristotle himself, is that there can be demonstration of everything (πάντων), since the demonstration may be circular (κύκλῳ) or reciprocal (αλλήλων).[74] Aristotle meets this objection by arguing that, if demonstration were circular, then some propositions would be both prior to and posterior to the same other propositions. This is logically impossible, although Aristotle thinks it may be said to happen when we say that one proposition is prior to another *simpliciter*, while the former appears to us posterior to the latter. This is his argument that the same thing may be viewed from different angles, and the resultant different aspects may be expressed in language by our using different "senses" of the same term.[75] It may appear so in this instance because the latter is to us more familiar.

At the end of Book *A* 3, Aristotle raises two further arguments against the preceding objection, both of which are designed to show that there can be no demonstration of everything.[76] The second argument is particularly curious because it uses the notion that all propositions subject to circular demonstration must be convertible, so that $\Box$ P x S $\leftrightarrow$ $\Box$ S x P. As Aristotle himself shows in the *Prior*

---

[74] $72^{b}15$–18.

[75] $72^{b}25$–32.

[76]   Beginning at $72^{b}33$ and $73^{b}7$, respectively.

Analytics, conversion will be impossible where one of the propositions of which the syllogism is composed will be undemonstrated (ἀναποδείκτου); and circular and reciprocal demonstrations can only be achieved where conversion among all of the terms is possible.[77] He argues that such convertible terms rarely occur together in demonstrations.[78]

Book *A* 4 of the *Posterior Analytics* contains an expansion of Aristotle's position that demonstration, and therefore all learning, invariably involve deduction from propositions that are necessary. This modal criterion harkens back to the second criterion laid down at 71[b]10. Book *A* 6 carries this argument forward. In both of these chapters Aristotle commits himself to the view that, since that of which we have knowledge *simpliciter* cannot be otherwise, what is known by demonstration must be necessary (ἀναγκαῖος).

In discussing what must compose the premises of a demonstration Aristotle first examines three different sorts of attributes, as they may be applied to subjects. Aristotle does not actually call them attributes; this is the gloss employed by both Mure and Tredennick. These attributes are:

(1) true in every instance of its subject (τὸ καθὰ παντὸς);
(2) essential or belonging *per se* to the subject (καθ' αὐτὰ δ' ὅσα ὑπάρχει τε ἐν τῳ τὶ ἐστιν); and
(3) universal (τί τὸ καθόλου).[79]

The first is exemplified by the predicate "animal," which is true of every person at every time and place. If something is human, it will always be true to say that that person is an animal.[80] The second of the above triad is what "belongs to something in itself," such as line to triangle and point to line; it is also said to be so if what it belongs to itself belongs in the statement or formula (λόγος) that

---

[77] *An. Pr.* 57[b]33.

[78] 73[a]18.

[79] These three criteria are elucidated starting at 73[a]26, 73[a]34, and 73[b]27, respectively.

[80] 73[a]30.

makes clear what it is (τί ἐστι).[81] For example, straight (εὐθύ) belongs to line (γραμμή) and so does curved (περιφερές).[82] The third is a combination of the preceding two, for it is both that which belongs in every instance of its subject, and also is true of itself or essential.[83] The premises of a demonstration will be necessarily true in each of these aspects, or, stated another way, the attribute or predicate which is stated to belong to the subject must be universally and primarily applicable in the sense defined by Aristotle in Book *A* 4 at 73^{b}26-74^{a}2.[84]

This account of universality and primitiveness as hallmarks of the terms in demonstrative premises is further filled out by Aristotle's account of how our procedure may go wrong. It is a mistake to try to prove something which is not universal and primitive.[85] This may happen, for example, when a particular is the subject and there is no universal higher than (ἀνώτερον) it; or when there is such a higher universal but it does not distinguish between particulars of different sorts for our purposes; or when that which is to be demonstrated is part of a larger whole. In the last case, the demonstration will not be true universally and primarily.[86]

Aristotle claims that the necessary first principles involve essential or *per se* predications as defined in Book *A* 5. One must always ask, "Does the predicate belong to the subject *qua* subject or *qua* property?"[87] The predicate "has interior angles equal to the sum of two right angles,'" belongs to the triangle *qua* triangle and not just *qua* isosceles triangle.[88] Contrasted with these are accidental (συμβεβηκοτα) predications, which are not necessary, such as saying

---

81   73^{a}28.

82   73^{a}37.

83   73^{b}26–27.

84   The foregoing discussion of what sorts of things can be predicated of subjects should be linked with his discussion in *An. Pr. A* 27, which is concerned with how τὰ ὄντα (all things) naturally fall into three exhaustive classes.

85   74^{a}4–6.

86   74^{a}8–12.

87   74^{a}6–37.

88   74^{a}38–^{b}1.

of a triangle that it is isosceles or bronze.[89] Aristotle tries to clinch this point by presenting certain sorts of evidence in its favour. He says first that objections to purported demonstrations will be in the form of a challenge as to whether something is necessary, because the situation may be otherwise.[90] Secondly, the starting point in a demonstration cannot be just what is generally accepted, but it must be primarily true of the genus or kind (γένος) about which the demonstration is being made.[91] On this note of showing how demonstration must involve premisses in which one term belongs to the other necessarily and the middle term applies necessarily to the major, and the minor term applies necessarily to the middle, and to know the why or wherefore or reason (διότι) of something is to know it through its cause or explanation (αἰτία), Aristotle concludes Book *A* 6 and his account in the first six chapters of the *Posterior Analytics* of the necessary and sufficient conditions of demonstration.[92]

The remaining parts of Book *A* treat a variety of incidental questions that arise out of Aristotle's fundamental picture of a science. He summarizes the three elements in every demonstration by saying that there must be included the following:

(1) a conclusion to be proved (i.e., that some thing belongs to some genus essentially or *per se*);
(2) the axioms; and
(3) the underlying (ὑποκείμενον) genus or kind, of which the demonstration discloses what is essential and what is accidental.[93]

Aristotle also makes the point that, because the genera are science-specific, in general a proposition of one science cannot be proved by any other science. There is an exception to this when one

---

[89]   74^b11–12.

[90]   74^b18–21.

[91]   74^b21–26.

[92]   That the middle term must be necessary, see 75^a12–17; and that knowing the αἰτία is knowing the τὸ διότι, see 75^a34–37.

[93]   75^a39–^b2

science is a subordinate to another, as optics is to geometry.[94] His other conclusions include the following. The propositions used in a demonstration must be appropriate or proper to the science in question.[95] The first principles of each science cannot themselves be demonstrated. Aristotle divides these first principles into special (ἴδια) principles and common (κοινά) principles. In each case they are assumed (λαμβάνεται) for each science.[96] Aristotle is careful to qualify the notion of a common principle by stating that it is common only "analogically." The self-sufficiency of the specialized sciences is thereby not compromised.

Into his account, dispassionate and methodical for the most part, there creeps into Book *A* 9 the following sign of tentativeness on Aristotle's part at 76ª26–28:

> It is hard to be sure whether one knows or not; for it is hard to be sure whether one's knowledge is based on the basic truths [ἀρχαί] appropriate to each attribute—the differentia of true knowledge.

Notwithstanding the virtues of certainty and a sublime organization that a properly conducted demonstration offers to us, much thinking and perhaps discussion must be expended on making sure that the very starting points are correctly chosen. Teaching will

---

94   75ᵇ14–17.

95   75ᵇ37–40; cf. 71ᵇ23. Aristotle emphatically rejects the Platonic notion that there can be one supreme science consisting of principles from which all subordinate sciences derive: see 76ª16–17. He contends however that there is a first philosophy, subsequently called metaphysics, which is very general in scope: see *Met. B* 2 and 3. Also, there might be a problem of consistency raised by 77ª29–31 and the remark there that dialectic has "communion" with all the sciences; but Aristotle's statement following immediately thereafter and at 77ᵇ7 should dispel any suggestion that dialectic is being assigned a broad, Platonic scope.

96   An example of a special principle is: a line or straightness is such and such. This principle would be proper to geometry. An example of a common principle is: when equals are taken from equals the remainders are equals. This principle may be used in demonstrations in several different sciences, depending on the kind or genus that is the subject of the demonstration: see 76ª40–41.

only be as effective and sure-footed as the premisses will allow. Though Aristotle does not say so directly, the guarantee, in so far as there can be one, that the principles will be appropriate to the science, is that the person who does the choosing will be an ἐπιστήμονος (expert) in that particular science. This point may be further related to what Aristotle has to say in general terms about who shall be the teachers among us in his discussion of σοφία (conventionally translated as "wisdom") and the σοφός (wise man) in the *Metaphysics* B 982ᵃ8–19. There might seem to be a circularity in all this, for how can one learn enough in a science to be an expert without it first being decided what are the ultimate principles at the foundation of that science. Aristotle would probably give the same kind of answer to this problem as he would to the question about how a φρόνιμος (who is wise in practical matters as opposed to someone who is wise in the theoretical sciences) is possible in our ethical experience. This conjecture that the first principles would best be selected by the ἐπιστήμονος is stimulated in part by Aristotle's discussion at 77ᵇ6, which is summarized in due course below.

At 76ᵇ23 begins a murky passage that initially relates the difference between a hypothesis or a postulate and some third thing, which both Barnes and Ross take to be axioms (for these satisfy the description of being both necessary in themselves [δι' αὐτὸ] and are thought [δοξεῖν] to be necessary).[97] Aristotle then goes on to claim, in Tredennick's translation:

> . . . for demonstration, like syllogism, is concerned not with external but with internal discourse [τὸν ἔξω λόγον . . . ἀλλὰ πρὸς τὸν ἐν τῇ ψυχῇ]; and it is always possible to object to the former, but not always possible to do so to the latter.[98]

From the words immediately following those quoted above, Aristotle makes it clear that he has the teacher in mind and in what way the teacher may present to a learner unproved, and only assumed, propositions. Such an assumption is an hypothesis, if the student accepts or believes it, but it is an assumption if the student

---

97   Barnes, *supra* n. 2, p. 136, and Ross, *supra* n. 16, p. 540.
98   76ᵇ24–25.

either has no opinion (δόξα) about what is said in the proposition or holds no opinion about it. The remark about demonstration being "internal" may seem strange and unexpected after the attempts made in Chapter Two to show that Aristotle's notion of demonstration rests upon a "public" activity, specifically in a classroom. Barnes and Ross have each tried to rehabilitate this original interpretation from any damage that the above passage may tend to do to it. The key is that teaching and learning and (and, *a fortiori*, demonstration) are concerned with truth, and in this they differ from other types of discussion. In the *Topics* Aristotle notes that:

> . . . for those who teach or learn and those who compete with one another have not the same aim, and the aim of the latter differs from that of those who discuss for the sake of inquiry; for he who is learning must always state what he thinks, since no one even attempts to teach a lie; on the other hand, when men are competing with one another, the questions must by some means or other appear to be producing some effect, while the answerer must appear to be unaffected.[99]

From this passage emerges the idea that in some sense the learner's beliefs and her expressions of them are important in order for the demonstration to achieve its proper effect in the learner's soul. The demonstration is surely carried on through "external" discourse, but teaching has only become successful when, in some sense, the learner's soul is genuinely in assent to what has been proved. The notion of discourse within the soul is a highly metaphorical way of referring to something like this.

In Book *A* 11 Aristotle discusses the function of axioms which, it turns out, are used not only in demonstration but in dialectic as well.[100] He notes how dialectic proceeds by the method of questioning (ἠρώτα).[101] For this reason dialectic is not a science. It is also not a science because it is not limited to any single sort of objects

---

[99] *Top.* 159ª27–33.

[100] 77ª27.

[101] 77ª32.

(τινὸς ἑνός).[102] A demonstration in any science will consist of premisses peculiar to the science in question. Dialectic, by comparison, is promiscuous in its selection of premisses by which to proceed. This general point leads to Aristotle's conclusion that:

> There is a limit, then, to the questions which we may put to each man of science [ἐπιστήμονος]; nor is each man of science bound to answer all inquiries on each several subject, but only such as fall within the defined field of his own science . . . One should therefore not discuss geometry among those who are not geometers, for in such company an unsound argument will pass unnoticed. This is correspondingly true in the other sciences.[103]

The possibility of an erotetic syllogism has troubled Barnes. He does not see how the learner's freedom to raise questions that are demonstrative premisses rearranged in interrogatory form is consistent with Aristotle's use of demonstration as the model for teaching.[104] Barnes's supposition that all Aristotelian teaching will be in the form of a lecture *ex cathedra* will be examined in Chapter Six.

Aristotle distinguishes between knowing the fact (τὸ ὅδι) of something and knowing the reason (τὸ διότι) for it, because the latter depends on knowing the primary (πρῶτον) explanation (αἴτιον).[105] Syllogism can be used to prove the explanation in the following example given by Aristotle and starting at 78ª31:

> Being near belongs to planets.
> Not twinkling belongs to being near.
> Not twinkling belongs to planets.

This is the correct order of exposition, because it is, according to Aristotle, the nearness of the planets that scientifically explains why they do not twinkle. This is, in Ackrill's felicitous phrase, a syllogism

---

102   77ª30–31.

103   77ᵇ6–15.

104   Barnes, *supra* n. 31, pp. 141–42.

105   78ª22–26. This knowledge of the explanation or the "because" is the final criterion of scientific knowledge enumerated at 71ᵇ19–23.

of the "because."[106] If we reverse the order of the premisses, we still obtain a valid deduction, but one that does not have explanatory force. We might rearrange the premisses thus:

> Not twinkling belongs to planets.
> Being near belongs to not twinkling.
> Being near belongs to planets.

This is, in Ackrill's words, a syllogism of the "that." It does not prove that the planets are near because they do not twinkle; that will be part of proving the explanation rather than the fact. In order to achieve demonstration, the teacher must first be equipped with the knowledge of what are the real explanations of things, and not just what Aristotle would call the fact of the conclusion.

This distinction between knowledge of the reason of, or explanation for, the fact and knowledge of the fact is crucial, because "grasp [θεωρεῖν] of a reasoned conclusion is the primary condition of knowledge."[107] For this purpose, the syllogism in the first figure, denominated by later tradition as Barbara, is the most scientific (ἐπιστημονικός).[108] Book *A* 14 gives four reasons justifying this conclusion. The primary one is that it is only through the argument pattern, □ P a M, □ M a S → □ P a S, that the explanation of the conclusion is proved and displayed in universal affirmative propositions.[109]

Book *A* chapters 16 to 18, contain a discussion of the possible causes of error and ignorance. Chapters 19 to 22 concern whether there can be an infinite series of attributes extending upwards (ἄνω) from some primary subject (for example, man is biped, biped is animal, animal is something else and so forth) or, alternatively, whether there can be an infinite series of subjects extending downwards (κάτω) from some fixed attribute (for example, animal is predicated of man, man of Callias, Callias of something else that

---

[106]   J. L. Ackrill, *Aristotle the Philosopher* (Oxford: Oxford University Press, 1981), p. 95.

[107]   79ª23–24.

[108]   79ª17 *et seq.*

[109]   79ª23–30.

is part of the essence, and so on).[110] Also, Aristotle asks whether there can be an infinite number of intermediate terms between the foregoing two extremes. He argues that if there can be neither an infinite series extending either upwards or downwards as understood above, then there cannot be an infinite number of intermediate terms either.[111] In Chapter 22 he makes the significant point that where the predicates state the essence (τί ἐστι) of the subjects there must be a limit on the number of predicates. Otherwise, definition would be impossible.[112] He states again in this context the difference between essential predication and accidental predication. In fact, only essential predication turns out (as we might expect, given Aristotle's propensity for reduction in this way) to be predication *simpliciter*, while accidental predication is only predication in a qualified sense.[113] It is by essential predication that demonstrations are conducted.[114] The subject and predicate are so tied together in essential predication that:

> Predicates which signify substance [οὐσία] signify that the subject is identical with the predicate or with a species of the predicate.[115]

In this sense, essential predicates are convertible with their subjects. By contrast, accidental predicates cannot be predicated of one another (for example, a quality of a quality).[116] As there is a limit to the series of predicates that can be applied to a subject, Aristotle infers from this that there must be some term which is not predicated of anything prior to it (the individual substance, such as Callias) as well as some term of which no prior term is predicated (the highest genus).[117] Therefore, the answer to all three questions posed in

---

[110]   82ᵃ21–24. The example of the triad, man-biped-animal, is drawn from 83ᵇ3.
[111]   82ᵃ30.
[112]   82ᵇ37–83ᵃ1.
[113]   83ᵃ14–17.
[114]   83ᵃ20–21.
[115]   83ᵃ24–26.
[116]   83ᵃ36–39.
[117]   83ᵇ3–7, 28–31.

Chapter 20 is in the negative.

Chapter 22 also reveals how demonstration is concerned with essential attributes of things or, literally, "demonstration is of what belongs to the things in themselves [ἀπόδειξίς ἐστι τῶν ὅσα ὑπάρχει καθ' αὑτὰ τοῖς πράγμασιν]."[118] This leads once more to Aristotle's repeated conclusion that not everything that is known is demonstrable, nor can there be a demonstration of an infinite series of middles between two terms.[119] He tries to show two sorts of justification for these conclusions: first, by way of "principles that apply to all reasoning" (λογικῶς), and second, by an analytical method (ἀναλυτικῶς). The first way is translated by Ross's scrupulous paraphrase.[120]

When an essential attribute applies in common to two different subjects, this is so because the middle terms belong to the same genus and the premisses are derived from the same immediate premisses. This is the gist of Book *A* 23.

Aristotle argues that universal (καθόλου) demonstration is superior to particular (κατὰ μέρος) demonstration. In Book *A* 24 he is not dealing with scientific demonstration, because he has already, in his definition of that sort of demonstration, stated that it is concerned with universal and particular propositions and not with singular propositions. His example of "cultured Coriscus" at 85ª25 should be understood with this distinction in mind. He gives two arguments to refute the claim that universal demonstration is inferior as a source of knowledge. He argues that the person who knows the universal has more knowledge than the person who knows only the particular.[121] In all, he gives seven arguments in Chapter 24 in support of his position. Each of the seven is constructed on his ideas about the nature of scientific demonstration, the intelligibility and imperishability of genera and species, the use of demonstration to reach the reasoned fact or explanation, and the proximity of demonstrative premisses to first principles. He contends that the best

---

[118] 84ª11–12.

[119] 84ª32–34.

[120] 84ᵇ1–2. Ross, *supra* n. 16, p. 573. See other references to, and uses of, these two methods at 84ª7, 82ᵇ35–36, 86ª22, and 88ª32–33.

[121] 85ᵇ13–15.

argument for showing that universal demonstration is more authoritative (κυριώτηρας) is that the learner who knows that the attribute, "the sum of its interior angles equals the sum of two right angles," belongs to the genus, triangle, also knows, in a different sense, that the same attribute will belong to an isosceles triangle. This latter proposition is grasped potentially (δύναμει) even if the learner has never come across an isosceles triangle. A learner, on the other hand, who has knowledge only of the latter proposition will have no knowledge of the universal proposition, either potentially or actually.[122]

In Book *A* 25 Aristotle is concerned with showing that affirmative demonstration is superior to negative demonstration. By parity of reasoning, both affirmative and negative demonstration are shown to be superior to demonstration by *reductio ad impossibile*.[123] This is covered in Chapter 26. In Chapter 27 Aristotle shows how it is possible to rank the sciences according to whether they attain knowledge both of the fact and of the reasoned fact, or of one of these only, and also according to the objects of the science.[124] The unity of a science depends on its being concerned with a single kind (γένος) or class (σύγκειται) of object.[125] These objects are the species (the primary elements of the kind) and the essential attributes of the kind.

In Book *A* 29 Aristotle illustrates how it is possible to have more than one demonstration of the same conclusion. This may be accomplished by selecting a different middle term from the same series. Since syllogism is concerned with what is necessary or usual, Aristotle argues that there can be scientific demonstration of chance conjunctions (δ' ἀπὸ τύχης).[126]

In an important discussion in Book *A* 31, Aristotle attempts to show that scientific knowledge (ἐπίστασθαι) cannot be acquired through perception (δι' αἰσθήσεως).[127] Perception does not give us

---

[122]   86ᵃ22–29.

[123]   87ᵃ1 *et seq.*

[124]   87ᵃ31–37.

[125]   87ᵃ38–39.

[126]   87ᵇ19.

[127]   87ᵇ28 *et seq.*

a universal, but it only is of a particular thing at a particular time and place. Universals are not perceived but are recognized (γνωρίιζειν) in the process of gaining scientific knowledge. With the recognition of the universal comes a knowledge of the explanation (αἰτία).[128] Perception of the particular does not involve any recognition of the explanation, so knowledge of the universal is clearly superior. This discussion in Chapter 31 foreshadows the account Aristotle will give in the last chapter of Book *B*. Aristotle next considers the question of whether all syllogisms can have the same first principles (ἀρχαί). In Book *A* 32 he gives a variety of arguments to show that this cannot be so.

In Book *A* 33 Aristotle contrasts scientific knowledge with opinion (δόξα) and with the object of opinion. The difference in each case lies again in the fact that scientific knowledge is of the universal and is stateable in necessary propositions. Opinion is, like knowledge *simpliciter*, concerned with what can be stated to be true or false, but it embraces those things which could possibly be otherwise than what they are.[129] Something can be the object of both opinion and knowledge at the same time, but if the middle term is apprehended in the same way as a definition achieved through demonstration, this will be a mark of knowledge. An opinion will merely involve seeing those attributes as true (for example, "animal" of "human") rather than as essential. Opinion, unlike knowledge, can also be false. A logical conclusion that Aristotle derives from his discussion is that the same person cannot have both knowledge and opinion about the same object at the same time.[130]

Book *A* 34 consists of a very brief discussion about the difference between scientific knowledge and quick wit (ἀγχίνοιά). The latter is defined as "a faculty of hitting upon the middle term instantaneously."[131] The phrase translated as "instantaneously," ἀσκέπτῳ χρόνῳ, literally means "in an imperceptible time." As an example, Aristotle gives the following premiss-pair:

---

128   87^{b}37–39; 88^{a}5–6.

129   89^{a}2–3.

130   89^{a}38–^{b}6.

131   89^{b}10–11.

P (Its bright side being towards its source of light) belongs to M (lighted from the sun).

M (Lighted from the sun) belongs to S (the moon).

The conclusion is in the form of P x S or "Its bright side being towards its source of light belongs to the moon." The αἰτία or explanation of this conclusion lies in the middle term, M. The quick-witted person will appear to grasp the major and minor terms and immediately relate them by spotting the proper explanation. In a passage in the *Nicomachean Ethics* Aristotle contrasts quickness of wit with deliberation. He describes the former as a sort of shrewd guessing.[132]

In Book *B* of the *Posterior Analytics* Aristotle is concerned with three chief problems: first, how demonstration, as he has outlined it in Book *A*, is related to definition; second, how his doctrine of causes or explanation may be applied to the discovery of definitions; and finally, how we grasp the first principles that are appropriate to each science and that serve as the starting points of all demonstration. His treatment of the first two topics will be summarized in the remainder of this part; the third topic will be the subject of the next and final part of this chapter.

Aristotle's programme in Book *B* is, as was that in Book *A*, constructed with teaching and learning at the forefront of the discussion. We should again be careful to see Aristotle's philosophizing in the context of how a teacher may lay out for presentation to a learner the scientific propositions that have been won by research. When he speaks, as we shall shortly see, of demonstration as an aid to definition, he has in mind a rather complex notion of the interrelatedness of these two processes. Definition is disclosed in the demonstrative premisses, and correspondingly, in putting together our demonstration for the edification of students, we are led to tie together the appropriate terms in the most meaningful way.[133]

---

[132] *N.E.* 1142^{b}5–6.

[133] See Grene, *supra* n. 6, pp. 80–85, and Alfonso Gomez-Lobo, "Definitions in

Aristotle commences Book *B* 1 with his description of the four types of questions that we can ask in preparing to teach. Each question corresponds to what, for Aristotle, is a different sort of knowledge about the thing. These types are:

(1) whether the connection of an attribute with the thing is a fact (τὸ ὅτι);

(2) what is the reason of the connection (τὸ διότι);

(3) whether the thing exists (εἰ ἔστιν); and

(4) what is the nature of the thing (τί ἐστιν).[134]

On Tredennick's suggestion these four questions may be compressed into the following form:

(1) Does P belong to S?

(2) Why does P belong to S?

(3) Does S exist?

(4) What is (the definition of) S?[135]

Aristotle's discussion in Book *B* 2 is stimulated primarily by the last two of the above questions. The hunt for the middle term that can explain the subject is the proper sphere of anyone who wishes to know about science. Aristotle goes further and conflates the question of the explanation (αἰτία) with the question of the essence (τί ἐστι) of the thing.[136]

Aristotle devotes Book *B* 3 to 7 to a provisional discussion of the difficulties encountered in trying to ascertain how essences can be

---

Aristotle's *Posterior Analytics*" in Dominic J. O'Meara (ed.), *Studies in Aristotle* (Washington, D.C.: Catholic University of America Press, 1981), pp. 25–46.

[134] 89^{b}24–25.

[135] But Tredennick states that even this reduction raises problems, because Aristotle's discussion in Book *B* 2 is concerned more with causes and attributes of S, and less with such questions as 3 and 4 in the suggested list. Barnes also concludes that these questions are left aside so that Aristotle can investigate the following basic two, namely: Is there an explanatory middle term? And what is it? (90^{a}6 *et seq.*) See Tredennick, *supra* n. 9, pp. 174–75 and Barnes, *supra* n. 2, pp. 202 and 204.

[136] 90^{a}14–15.

discovered and how the methods of demonstration and definition bear on this. He raises a host of arguments refuting the claim that definition and demonstration are the same.[137] That to define and to demonstrate are different procedures is shown by Aristotle's argument that not everything that can be demonstrated can be defined; nor can everything definable be demonstrated. The purpose of a definition is to disclose or make clear (δηλοῖ) what a thing is, in the sense of revealing its essence, while the purpose of demonstration is to exhibit or prove that something is or is not true of something else through the use of a middle term.[138] In Book *B* 4 Aristotle regards the attempt to demonstrate a definition as involving a *petitio principii*.[139] This is unavoidable because in the definition the subject and predicate will be convertible, and hence the middle term will be co-extensive with both the major and the minor terms. As both premises then state the essence of the subject, so will the conclusion. The example Aristotle gives involves the terms "man" and "two-footed animal." The conclusion proving the essence of man will depend on premises that already state such essence, since the middle term will be co-extensive with the major. The conclusion in respect of humans' bipedalism will not therefore have been proved.

Aristotle considers the Platonic method of division as a candidate for finding definitions, and in Book *B* 5 he sets forth the arguments why this method is inadequate for such a purpose.[140] In particular, it is not a method (ὁδός) of deduction (συλλογίζεται), since there is no logical necessity involved in passing from one proposition to another.[141] He returns to such a method in Book *B* 13 and 14, where he finds some virtue in it, for he points out how it may be used to help establish a definition, providing certain rules are observed in its employment.

In Book *B* 8 Aristotle embarks on a positive discussion of the role

---

[137]   90^{b}14–15; 90^{b}19–91^{a}11.

[138]   91^{a}1–2.

[139]   91^{a}35 *et seq.*

[140]   Book *B* 5. He has discussed division (διαίρεσις) in the *An. Pr. A* 31.

[141]   91^{b}14–15.

of demonstration in discovering essences. Aristotle makes it plain that, in order for an inquiry to begin about what a thing is, we must first know that it is.[142] He gives several examples of searching for an explanation for the purpose of showing what syllogism or demonstration does. It will not reveal the essence of something in the conclusion and thereby *prove* that essence, but rather the syllogism or demonstration will *disclose* the essence by showing it as the middle term in the premises. In this sense, it is through (διά) syllogism or demonstration that the essence becomes clear to us (δῆλον μέντοι).[143] Demonstration will indeed be necessary in order to show the essence of something that has an essence other than itself.[144]

First principles do not have an explanation outside themselves that can serve as a middle term in revealing some essence. They are immediate (ἄμεσον) and both what they are and that they exist have to be assumed.[145] This relates to Aristotle's discussion at the start of the *Posterior Analytics* about the mathematician's assumptions about the unit.[146] To conclude, a demonstration succeeds in disclosing or making clear the essence of something without actually demonstrating this in the conclusion. But it must be remembered that only some kinds of essence are capable of being made clear in this way. Aristotle says in Book *B* 9 that immediate essences, that is, first principles, cannot be shown or exhibited by demonstration.

The several kinds of definition that Aristotle analyzes in Book *B* 10 can be summarized as follows:

(1) a statement or account (λόγος) of the meaning (σημαίνει)

---

142 93ᵃ27 *et seq.* He wishes, in a familiar pattern, to make a fresh start or, as he says, let us "speak [εἰπόντες] again [πάλιν] from the beginning [ἐξ ἀρχῆς]": 93ᵃ16.

143 93ᵇ15–18.

144 93ᵇ18–20, and see 93ᵃ5. On the meaning of the phrase, "explanation other than itself," see Book *B* 9. Those things which do not have an explanation other than themselves are, in traditional Aristotelian terminology, substances, each of which has its distinctive form. Those things which are called "attributes" in the translations by Tredennick and Mure are what Aristotle is speaking of in chapters 8 through 11.

145 93ᵇ21–24.

146 71ᵃ16–17.

of the name or word (ὄνομα);

(2) a form of words or formula (λόγος) exhibiting the cause or explanation of a thing's existence; and

(3) a definition of immediate terms (ἀμέσωιν ὁρισμὸς) positing (ἀναπόδεικτος) of essential nature (τί ἐστιν).[147]

As a prelude to his discussion of how the knowledge of an explanation is one with the knowledge of the thing explained, Aristotle gives a brief account of his doctrine of the four kinds of cause or explanation in Book *B* 11.[148] These kinds are: the essential cause, the material cause (understood in this context as "an antecedent which necessitates a consequent"), the efficient cause, and the final cause. Aristotle says that all of these are exhibited or revealed (δείκνυνται) through the middle term, and he goes on to illustrate how this is so.[149]

The importance of Book *B* 13 lies in its description of, and programme for, how we should hunt or search (θηρεύρειν) for those things which are predicated in (κατηγορούμενα) what a thing is (τὶ ἐστι).[150] This is the process of collecting the essential attributes of the kind in question that do not extend beyond the genus (for example, "oddness" belongs to the number 3, but it also belongs to other things grouped under the genus "number"). The essence of a thing will be found when the point described in the following quotation is reached:

> It is such attributes which we have to select, up to the exact point at which they are severally of wider extent than the subject but collectively coextensive with it; for this synthesis must be the

---

147   93[b]30; 93[b]38–39; 94 9[a]10. Tredennick, in dealing with the first kind of definition, translates λόγος by "explanation." This is liable to mislead, but it shows how palpable is the problem of conveying in English what λόγος means in its many occurrences in Greek philosophical texts.

148   94[a]20–23. For his extended, detailed account of this doctrine, see either *Phys.* 194[b]21 or *Met.* 1013[a]24–[b]28, which contain similar accounts.

149   94[a]24 *et seq.*

150   96[a]20 *et seq.* This should be read alongside Aristotle's account of such a search contained in *An. Pr. A* 25.

substance [οὐσία] of the thing [πράγματος].[151]

The method of division (διαίρεσις) can be used to help in the search for definitions by making sure that we select the essential attributes and organize them in the proper order, paying attention to the appropriate differentiae. It can also help to reassure us that the selection we have made has overlooked nothing relevant.[152] Some salutary advice on how to develop definitions is given in the latter part of Book *B* 13. Division is also portrayed as a useful way of organizing problems.[153]

From the foregoing account of Aristotle's procedure in the *Posterior Analytics* down to Book *B* 14, the following points emerge. These passages present his conception of how a science may be organized so that the truths won by researchers may be presented in an intelligible, and thus a teachable, form. Barnes has gathered the evidence from the text of the *Posterior Analytics* that tends to support his interesting thesis about how we ought to view the treatise as a whole.[154] He claims that Aristotle develops the method of demonstration in that treatise as part of a programme of how scientific teaching, and not scientific investigation, should proceed. This thesis is advanced in response to what Barnes labels the "Problem of Demonstration," namely, why does Aristotle's practice as a scientific researcher and recorder as shown in his scientific and philosophical works not reflect the theoretical method expounded in

---

[151]   96ᵃ32–35. The last phrase in the quotation should be considered carefully, since οὐσία is sometimes used by Aristotle to mean something other than what we have come to associate with his doctrine of "substance" in the context of his metaphysics. He may on occasion mean by οὐσία something like what τὶ ἐστι elsewhere means, i.e., essence, or by what Barnes translates as "reality."

[152]   97ᵃ23–26.

[153]   98ᵃ1–3.

[154]   Barnes, *supra* n. 31. For a critique of Barnes's treatment of this problem, and for a different interpretation of the context in which Aristotle formulated the theory set forth in *An. Post.*, see Michael Ferejohn, *The Origins of Aristotelian Science* (New Haven: Yale University Press, 1991), pp. 140–41. A response and reiteration is provided in Jonathan Barnes, "Aristotle's Philosophy of the Sciences" (1993) 11 Oxford Studies in Ancient Philosophy 225–41.

the *Posterior Analytics*? After reviewing some of the attempts to solve this problem by showing the purpose of the *Posterior Analytics* to be different from what has been traditionally thought, Barnes gives four arguments in favour of reorienting our expectations about what we can learn from that work. He argues from the etymology of the verb meaning "to demonstrate" (ἀποδείκνυναι); from key passages in the treatise, such as the opening proposition which has been discussed in detail above; from a claim that the theory of demonstration rests on the formalized dialectical exercise that would have been practised in the Academy; and finally, from a close relationship which Barnes tries to show between the method of induction and how teaching proceeds.[155] He compares the discernible connections between teaching and demonstration with the suggestions in the *Posterior Analytics* that could be construed as aligning demonstration with research itself rather than the presentation of the fruits of research. He concludes that, on balance, Aristotle means by demonstration a way of providing structure to the knowledge that one wishes to teach. It is not meant to tell natural scientists how to go about their experimentation and observation in the course of doing scientific exploration. This is not the appropriate place to weigh and comment on Barnes's thesis. One might note, however, that he neither discusses nor cites one significant passage in the *Prior Analytics* which, it is submitted, tends to confirm his result. In the context of discussing how the attributes of the terms should be sought, Aristotle writes:

> Consequently, if the attributes of the thing are apprehended, our business will then be to exhibit readily the demonstrations. For if none of the true attributes of things had been omitted in the historical survey, we should be able to discover the proof and demonstrate everything which admitted of proof, and to make that clear, whose nature does not admit of proof.[156]

---

155   Barnes, *supra* n. 31, pp. 138–43.

156   46ª22–27. Allan notices this passage and sees in it a foreshadowing of Aristotle's enterprise in the *An. Post.*: D. J. Allan, *The Philosophy of Aristotle*, 2nd ed. (Oxford: Oxford University Press paperback, 1970), p. 107. See also Ackrill, *supra* n. 106, p. 98.

This is uncannily like the procedure that Aristotle prescribes for teachers in the *Posterior Analytics*. They must take what has been discovered in the way of scientific knowledge and conduct students through a demonstration of the essential attributes that can be proved. For those things which have to be assumed, or apprehended immediately (that is, without the use of a middle term), the teacher will make due allowance and present these in such a fashion that the learner will understand the difference between a knowledge-claim and a hypothesis, for example. In any event, the teacher must also be aware throughout as to whether the learner's belief is in line with the material being demonstrated, for if it is not, the learner will be immune to the force of the conclusion and the demonstration will therefore fail. All this is to say that Aristotle's theory of demonstration provides a body of terminology, distinctions, and helpful advice on how scientific knowledge may be taught and learned. The programme he gives, it must be emphasized, is "theoretical,"which means he is not giving practical tips on how to plan a particular lesson. Instead, he is both describing and prescribing a general method about the necessary and sufficient conditions of learning. A student can be said to have learned D when he has grasped how D can be explained by the conjunction of propositions P_1 and P_2. It is not enough for learners to be able just to repeat D by rote, for instance, in order to claim they have learned D.[157]

The next general observation about Aristotle's description of how a science should be organized is that his account is heavily dependent on the notion of the necessary and essential (and its opposite, the contingent and accidental) connection between classes of P's and classes of S's; or between attributes and subjects in the language of the Oxford translator. This dependence is evident not only in the *Posterior Analytics*, but in other logical works as well. For example, in the *Categories*, the term ὑποκειμένον is the favoured term for naming what in some sense underlies and is the subject of the sorts of things that may be predicated.[158] This notion lies at the root

---

[157] Hence the emphasis on the αἰτία.

[158] See also the use of ὑποκειμένον at 71ᵃ24.

also of Aristotle's explication of the premisses of syllogism as all showing the same form. In every instance the πρότασις includes the notion of something belonging to (ὑπάρχειν) something else. This is the hinge upon which each meaningful demonstrative premiss swings. This relationship between two different kinds of things is not made any clearer by our resorting to Aristotle's explanation in the *Categories* about how things may be said. One term is either said to be contained in another, or it is said to be predicated of another.[159] Nor is the account of definition in the *Posterior Analytics* or elsewhere much more helpful on this score. We might have expected, had we been operating under the assumption that all of Aristotle's works form a coherent whole in which no major doctrines are inconsistent with each other, that his discussion of the relationship of definition to demonstration would reveal, possibly through the use of examples, how a demonstration may be achieved by taking from one of the sciences a definition of a substance (about which sort of thing is all that we can have knowledge *simpliciter*). Then, with this as a starting point, and by conjoining this with other terms to form a demonstrative premiss-pair, he might prove to us a necessary conclusion about the subject of our inquiry. Nowhere in the whole of the *Posterior Analytics* can such an example be found. The nearest that Aristotle comes to this is when he gives demonstrative explanations of thunder and of the lunar eclipse, but in each case, the subject is not a substance but rather what we would call a natural phenomenon or event. This omission of any examples detracts from the intelligibility of Aristotle's scheme.

In response to the above criticism, it might be maintained that Aristotle never shows any intention to present his theory of demonstration in the context of showing how the knowledge which had been achieved by his day could be fitted into his description. Instead, he offers in his *Posterior Analytics* an ideal model, so to speak, of how a complete, and not just a partial, science may be organized so as to be grasped by the learner. The problem with such

---

159   *Cat.* 1ᵃ20–23. As Ackrill points out, the ideas expressed in this distinction "play a leading role in nearly all Aristotle's writings." See J. L. Ackrill, *Aristotle's Categories and De Interpretatione* (Oxford: Clarendon Press, 1963), p. 74.

an interpretation is that Aristotle's generalizations about the identical structure for each separate science are drawn from and relate back to things which he feels are already known. It should be granted that he makes no claim that all scientific knowledge had been won in his time. Through his work in the *Posterior Analytics*, though, runs a visible thread that the possibility of making such a complete inventory of our world is very real and perhaps not far off. Furthermore, what is already known indicates how what we may subsequently discover can be demonstrated when it is fully grasped. There is no doubt that at least some things were already known in the strongest sense, for Aristotle's purposes, when he composed this theory of demonstration. For whatever reason, none of these things finds its way into the *Posterior Analytics*.

There also arises out of that portion of the work so far surveyed the assumption on Aristotle's part that the definitions attained in each science about the objects appropriate to that science are real, and not just nominal or verbal.[160] In addition, it is not for the scientist to have to sort things out into the order that will make demonstration possible. In some arcane sense for Aristotle things are already sorted out in nature and our definitions reflect these natural classifications.[161] This key part of Aristotle's scheme is aptly expressed by Grene in the following:

> For the establishment of scientific knowledge depends first and foremost on the possibility of stating *real definitions* of *limited kinds of things*. Substances fall naturally into classes in such a way that we can specify, in carefully chosen formulae, their essential natures. We can follow nature in keeping to *"the peculiar substance*

---

[160]   See Ackrill, *supra* n. 106, p. 94.

[161]   See the concise comment in Ackrill, *supra* n. 159, p. 75:

> He assumes each thing there is has a unique place in a fixed family tree. What is "said of" an individual, X, is what could be mentioned in answer to the question "What is X?", that is, the things in direct line above X in the family-tree, the species (e.g. man or generosity), the genus (man or virtue) and so on. Aristotle does not explicitly argue for the view that there are natural kinds or that a certain classificatory scheme is the one and only right one.

of each thing, and what it is to be that thing."[162]

It is such a set of unstated assumptions, about what makes language possible and explicable, about how what we say reflects the world and natural and necessary connections among kinds of things, and about the subsistence and knowability of such kinds, that gives impetus to both the researcher and the teacher. For if there were no essential concomitances in nature and we were dumb to indicate them by way of speech, then we should not be interested in explaining why things are the way they are and how they can change.

This restricted interest in relations between kinds of things—what may be determined as falling under category, genus, species and sub-species—means that scientific knowledge has no place for what may be peculiar about an individual thing. Demonstration is concerned only with knowledge in the strongest sense, and this requires that the premisses be universal propositions. This is pointed out by Aristotle in the following unmistakeable terms:

> It is also clear that if the premisses from which the syllogism proceeds are commensurately universal, the conclusion of such demonstration—demonstration, i.e., in the unqualified sense—must also be eternal. Therefore no attribute can be demonstrated nor known by strictly scientific knowledge to inhere in perishable things.[163]

There also looms throughout the *Posterior Analytics* the implication that demonstration is a distinctly armchair type of activity. There is no exhortation aimed at luring the investigator into the field. Instead, demonstration seems to be a matter of imparting knowledge, which scientific investigators have obtained, through lectures in which the student audience is quiescent and passive. Aristotle does, as we have seen, allow the possibility of a syllogistic or scientific question (ἐρώτεμα), in which a premiss is framed in the interrogative.[164]

---

162   Grene, *supra* n. 6, p. 81 (emphasis in the original).
163   75^{b}21–25.
164   77^{a}36–40.

Asking an inappropriate question, either because the person to whom the question is posed is not an expert in the science which might contain the answer to the question or because the question itself is framed so as to be inapplicable to that field in which the answerer has knowledge, is a form of ignorance that Aristotle discusses in Book *A* 12. The possibility of the syllogistic question would seem to indicate that the method of demonstration is not wholly guided by a pedagogic purpose. This is what Barnes thinks. He explains away what he perceives to be this flat contradiction by postulating that the passages cited above in respect of the syllogistic question are notes left over from an early course delivered by Aristotle. These notes have somehow been retained in the extant version of the *Posterior Analytics*.[165] This question will be examined again in Chapter Six, along with the cogency of Barnes's proposed explanation.

A final significant feature of Aristotle's account of demonstration worth emphasizing is the precondition for all scientific knowledge that the real explanation of the conclusion should be contained and exhibited in the premises. This requirement of showing why something is or why it occurs is readily seen as central to the things that a teacher ought to be doing. Aristotle even gives a relatively helpful example to illustrate the difference between deduction that shows the mere fact of an event and the "reasoned fact" (in Mure's translation) of it. In this case, the event is the twinkling of a star, discussed above.

The acquisition of first principles

The treatment of this topic is long delayed by Aristotle, until it occupies only the final chapter of the *Posterior Analytics*. The promise that this topic will be dealt with in due course has been hinted at several times throughout the preceding parts of that treatise, and there are oblique references to it as well in the *Prior Analytics*. Aristotle is interested in how the learner grasps or comes to know (γνῶσιν) the immediate (ἄμεσον) principles from which all

---

165   Barnes, *supra* n. 31, p. 142.

demonstration derives. He has been at pains to show that not all knowledge is demonstrative; it is through this proposition, *inter alia*, that he meets the challenge of the skeptic on the ground of an infinite regress in Book *A* 3. Aristotle is also interested in what state (ἕξις) can be developed in the human mind so as to achieve the learning of such things.

On the first question of how the first principles are acquired, he examines three alternative explanations. These are the following:

(1) they are grasped in the same way as the "mediate" premisses used in demonstration;

(2) the knowledge of the first principles is not scientific knowledge in the same sense that knowledge of demonstrative premisses is scientific; or

(3) whether the states (ἕξεις) are not present in us initially but only come about, or whether we possess them without recognizing it.[166]

Aristotle rejects the arguments that we have always possessed such states and that we have no capacity (δύναμις) to acquire them. Instead, he argues that there is a faculty developed in us that starts with what all animals have in common, namely, an innate (σύμφυτος) capacity (δύναμις) for discrimination (κριτική) that is called perception (αἴσθησιν).[167] For some animals the perception persists (ἐγγίγνεται), while for others it does not.[168] The sense impression that does persist is retained in the soul (ψυχή) of the percipient. The repetition of such perceptions gives rise to memory (μνήμη) and repeated memories give rise to experience (ἐμπειρία).[169] The memories are numerically many (πολλαὶ τῷ

---

[166] 99^{b}22–26.

[167] 99^{b}34–35.

[168] 99^{b}36–37.

[169] 100^{a}3–5. This capacity for perception plus memory is stated in the *Met.* to give rise to the capacity for being taught, not only to humankind, but other animals as well. See *Met. A* 980^{a}27–^{b}25.

ἀριθμῷ), but the experience is single (μία).[170] The experience is the universal (καθόλου) wholly established or stabilized (ἠρεμήσαντος) in the soul. It represents the starting point (ἀρχή) of all art (τέχνη) and science (ἐπιστήμη), the former having to do with things coming to be (περὶ γένεσιν), and the latter with things that are (περὶ ὂ ὄν).[171] The final summing up of this account is the *locus classicus* in Aristotle's writings of the relation of the particular to the universal as mediated by capacities specific to the human soul, as told in vivid imagery. In Book *B* 19 he writes:

> We conclude that these states of knowledge are neither innate in a determinate form, nor developed from other higher states of knowledge, but from sense-perception. It is like a rout in battle stopped by first one man making a stand and then another, until the original formation has been restored. The soul is so constituted to be capable of this process.[172]

Aristotle goes on to restate this account in theoretical language, trying thereby to show how the perception of the first particular of a kind (for example, Callias) is already a perception of the universal (human).[173] Subsequent perceptions lead to the establishment (or a "stand is made"—ἵσταται) in the soul of the "ultimate" (Tredennick) or "true" (Mure) universals, which are the categories, or genera that themselves cannot be divided into genus and differentia.[174] From the foregoing account Aristotle concludes that:

> ... it is clear that we must get to know [γνωρίζειν] the primary premisses [τὰ πρῶτα] by induction [ἐπαγωγή]; for the method by which even sense-perception implants [ἐμποιεῖ] the universal is inductive.[175]

---

[170] 100ᵃ5–6. What separates humans from other animals in this regard is their capacity for having connected (μετέχει) experience, and for developing arts (τέχναι) and reasonings (λογισμοί): see *Met. A* 980ᵇ25–28.

[171] 100ᵃ6–9.

[172] 100ᵃ10–14.

[173] 100ᵃ16–ᵇ1.

[174] 100ᵇ1–3.

[175] 100ᵇ3–5.

Aristotle next casts about to see if there is any intellectual state, except for intuition or comprehension (νοῦς) more accurate (ἀκριβέστερον) than scientific knowing.[176] He finds that opinion (δόξα) and calculation or reckoning (λογισμός) do not qualify for this description, as they both admit what is false. Since primary premisses are more knowable than intermediate premisses, and since all scientific knowledge involves discourse (λόγος), the primary premisses must be grasped by the superior form of knowledge, which he has argued by exclusion must be νοῦς.[177] It follows from this argument that there can be no scientific knowledge of the first principles; there is only intuition of them. Νοῦς itself is the source (ἀρχή) of scientific knowledge, since by means of it we are enabled to acquire the first principles (ἀρχαί).[178] One should note the play on the ambiguity in meaning of ἀρχή, which Aristotle uses here to establish yet more symmetry in his conclusions.

To summarize, then, Aristotle has answered his two questions raised at the start of Book *B* 19 in the following way. The method by which the first principles are acquired is induction. We might justifiably hesitate to say they have been learned by this means; instead, the notion of "acquisition" has been employed advisedly. Learning in its focal sense is intimately tied up with the possibility of demonstration, and these first principles which are at the foundation of demonstration cannot themselves be demonstrated (and hence learned). His second important conclusion is that the state or faculty (ἕξις) by virtue of which we are capable of grasping such principles is νοῦς.

This discussion of the role of νοῦς in a full explanation of how demonstration is possible brings us full circle in our reading of the *Posterior Analytics*. Demonstrative knowledge, or scientific knowledge, which is knowledge in the unqualified sense and the kind that is amenable to being taught and learned, itself depends on

---

[176] 100^{b}5–6.
[177] 100^{b}7.
[178] 100^{b}14–17.

previously existing knowledge.[179] This latter form of knowledge will be obtained by induction, and the distinctively human capacity for using this method and deriving what is universal out of the host of φαντασίας (appearances) and μνῆμαι (memories) is νοῦς. We are in a position to understand Aristotle's opening statement in the *Posterior Analytics* in all its ramifications only after we have understood the closing chapter of his treatise.

While being careful not to digress too far, we should question here whether induction is the only method for achieving an awareness of first principles. Certainly it appears so if we confine our vision to the *Posterior Analytics*; but in the *Prior Analytics A* 30, when considering how we should go about selecting premisses for our syllogisms, Aristotle concludes that chapter by saying that a detailed (ἀκριβής) discussion of this issue may be found in his treatise on dialectic, that is, the *Topics*.[180] This is generally taken as a cross-reference to the *Topics A* 14, and Ross's remark on the passage in the *Prior Analytics* just referred to is cautionary, namely:

> It is, of course, only the selection of premisses of *dialectical* reasoning that is discussed in the *Topics*; the nature of scientific reasoning is discussed in the *Posterior Analytics*.[181]

Indeed, if we restrict our glance to the *Topics A* 14 among all the chapters of that treatise, Ross's comment seems fair enough. If we examine other parts of the *Topics* though, we may be surprised to find how Aristotle views one role of dialectic in our coming to know the first principles of each compartmentalized science. In the *Topics A* 2, where the context of his discussion is the several different uses

---

[179]   Note Hamlyn's comment:
> That principle, incidentally, illustrates the extent to which Aristotle thinks of demonstration not just as a method for the justification of truth-claims *per se*, let alone the ascertainment of truth in an absolute sense, but as part of a learning context in which different people participate with different teaching/learning roles.

D. W. Hamlyn, "Aristotelian Epagoge" (1976) 19 Phronesis 167–84, p. 173.

[180]   *An. Pr.* 46ª28–30.

[181]   Ross, *supra* n. 16, p. 396.

of dialectic, Aristotle notes that:

> For the philosophic sciences it is useful, because, if we are able to raise difficulties on both sides, we shall more easily discern both truth and falsehood on every point. Further, it is useful in connection with the ultimate bases of each science [τὰ πρῶτα τῶν περὶ ἑκάστην ἐπιστήμην ἀρχῶν]; for it is impossible to discuss them at all on the basis of the principles peculiar to the science in question, since the principles are in relation to everything else, and it is necessary to deal with them through the generally accepted opinions [ἐνδόξα] on each point. This process belongs peculiarly, or most appropriately to dialect; for, being of the nature of an investigation [ἐξεταστική], it lies along the path [ὁδός] to the principles of all methods [μεθόδων] of inquiry.[182]

This point seems consistent with Aristotle's claim that the starting points of demonstrative knowledge cannot themselves be demonstrated. They must be acquired through some other means. How does the method of dialectic compare with the method of induction for this purpose?

In the first place, dialectic proceeds from plausible premises that may coincide with the views of the many, or to those counted wise among them. These premises do not of themselves command belief, as Aristotle expresses it in the *Topics* 100^{b}21-22. Therefore, it is possible to argue pro or contra on either side of the proposition. This is how a dialectical argument proceeds: by opponents debating with one party posing questions and the other answering by means of yes or no answers. As the passage above has been characterized by a modern commentator:

> So once again we find running through the whole passage 101^{a}34–^{b}4 the closely connected notions of debating both sides of the case, arguing from *endoxic* views, and being critical rather than didactic.[183]

---

[182] *Top.* 101^{a}34–^{b}4 (translation by E. S. Forster).

[183] J. D. G. Evans, *Aristotle's Concept of Dialectic* (Cambridge: Cambridge University Press, 1977), p. 32.

This method seems wholly at variance with becoming aware of first principles through a process beginning with sense perception and ending with the recognition of a universal. Does Aristotle have two alternative accounts to offer on the same subject that conflict with each other, or are they complementary? Evans, who was quoted above, tries to explain away any apparent discrepancy by pointing to the "difference of interest" between first, the terminal chapter of the *Posterior Analytics,* and second, the account given in the *Prior Analytics A* 30 and its extension, the passage referred to above in the *Topics.*[184] The first is concerned, on Evans's account, with:

> . . . the psychological question of how the cognitive apparatus which every individual possesses can be developed to the point at which the rare and privileged apprehension of the first principles can be obtained.[185]

We might well ask, incidentally, whether Evans is not guilty of some hyperbole in his use of the adjectives "rare and privileged" in reference to the grasp of the starting points of demonstration. Aristotle, unlike Plato, usually gives no grounds for our tagging him with the doctrine that the things at the root of all knowledge can be glimpsed by a select few. Quite the contrary, for the general tenor of Aristotle's epistemology is that all persons, in so far as they possess the usual complement of human faculties, are capable of knowing scientifically.

To continue with Evans's exegesis, he views the discussion outside the *Posterior Analytics* as an attempt to spell out the "sort of logical procedure which must be employed if we are to harness our covering first principles."[186] This dichotomy of interests, psychological and logical, is not altogether satisfactory as a description of what Aristotle is trying to show in either case, since it may be equally possible to characterize the account in the *Posterior Analytics B* 19 as a "logical" account, rather than one having to do with our cognitive faculties themselves. For example, Hamlyn

---

[184] *Ibid.,* p. 33.

[185] *Ibid.*

[186] *Ibid.*

borrows the expression "genetic epistemology" to describe Aristotle's discussion in respect of induction, and says that Aristotle therein tries to "make clear the general terms in which an account of the development of knowledge is to be given" and not to give such an account himself.[187]

I would argue that the key to reconciling Aristotle's contention in the *Topics* that the first principles can be reached by dialectic and that in the *Posterior Analytics* whereby those principles are reached by induction, does lie in a "difference of interest" in the two treatises, but not in the way Evans portrays. The whole thrust of the *Posterior Analytics* is that teaching and learning proceed by demonstration, and demonstration in turn requires pre-existing knowledge on the part of the learner, or on some occasions, theses or postulates in its place. Is the teacher's role confined to just mechanical demonstrations with no control over the starting points? No, Aristotle's theory is richer than that. It is for the teacher to lay out the definitions, assumptions, theses or postulates from which demonstration will proceed, and, in general, to impress upon the learner the coherence and completeness of the system of knowledge. Aristotle is concerned in the latter part of the *Posterior Analytics* with how the starting points may be understood by the learner and engage her assent, for without this the learner will not grant the force of the conclusion to be derived. There will not then be any learning of the kind Aristotle calls διανοητική. The *Posterior Analytics* is imbued with this problem of finding the appropriate starting points, for without them the enterprise of teaching would be a non-starter itself. It would be bound to fail just as would any apodeictic syllogism fail whose premisses we refused to admit were true or were necessary or were universal. The account by Aristotle in the *Topics* is not written with the same chief problems in view. Aristotle is not there asking how the learner may be presented with first principles in a way in which she will grasp what is to be assumed or what is necessary because it is universal to the genus and essential. This is the "didactic" aspect that Evans himself recognizes and contrasts with the "critical" role of dialectic. This critical use of

---

[187] Hamlyn, *supra* n. 179, p. 171.

dialectic may find its home in the discussions between investigators about first principles, between Aristotle and Theophrastus, say, on the shores of the island of Assos, where the two participants are knowledgeable already in a certain science. It is not designed for the classroom, where the whole process of teaching would be disrupted by a student's countering the teacher's utterance of a definition with an utterance of the negation of that definition. This distinction between the pedagogical context of the *Posterior Analytics* and the contentious *sic et non* atmosphere that prevails in the *Topics* is more helpful in interpreting the thrust of each of Aristotle's two accounts, than is the rather pallid distinction between "logical" and "psychological" as used by Evans.[188]

---

[188]   In further support of this interpretation of the difference between the accounts in question, see *S.E.* 172^{a}18–21 which reads:

> Dialectic, however, does proceed by interrogation, whereas, if it aimed at showing something, it would refrain from questions, if not about everything, at any rate about primary things and particular principle. (Aristotle, *On Sophistical Refutations*, trans. E. S. Forster, Loeb Classical Library [London: William Heinemann Ltd., 1955; Cambridge, Mass.: Harvard University Press, 1955]).

Teaching, as discussed throughout the *An. Post.*, is essentially concerned with "showing things," therefore the teacher must employ some method other than dialectic in showing what the first principles of a science are. There may be another, equally plausible way of putting into perspective the discussion of the use of dialectic in the *Top.* Owen assigns this work to Aristotle's early period, when he was still active in the Academy, and may conceivably have been as busy influencing Plato as being influenced by him, if the evidence in Plato's later dialogues may be fairly interpreted in this way. Owen writes with his customary lucidity:

> In any event Aristotle accepts dialectic on these terms and codifies its procedures in the Topics, not merely as a device for intellectual training or casual debate but as essential equipment in constructing the sciences. Yet, as he insists, the material of dialectic remains common convictions and common usage, not the self-evident truths which his admiration of mathematics persuades him are characteristic of science.

G. E. L. Owen, "The Platonism of Aristotle," 1965 Dawes Hicks Lecture on Philosophy to the British Academy, originally published in (1965) 56 *Proceedings of the British Academy* 125–50 at p. 144, and reprinted in *Articles on Aristotle: 1. Science*, Jonathan Barnes et al. (eds.) (London: Duckworth, 1975), pp. 1–34 at pp. 29–30)

Owen goes on to argue that Aristotle eventually rejected Plato's large

We may re-focus our attention now to the account of induction in the *Posterior Analytics,* and ask how coherent is this "magnificent account of the unbroken development from sense to reason."[189] As Hamlyn acutely observes, Aristotle's explanation of how sense impressions are retained as memories and how the universal is somehow built up out of memories through the process of mere repetition amounts to a very brief and cryptic account. Aristotle's attempt to illustrate how the first universal is grasped in a way similar to the man taking a stand in battle during a rout of his forces does not go very far towards answering the question about how induction somehow "implants" the universal in the soul, which process would be equivalent to the first soldier making a stand. Instead of a genetic account, we are given a metaphor.

In the past two decades several important articles have discussed how the account of induction is supposed to join up with, or relate to, the account of νοῦς. Articles by Kosman and by Lesher have been noteworthy in this respect and they may be briefly mentioned here, for they bear some implications for our overriding interpretation of the *Posterior Analytics* as an assay in describing the conditions necessary for teaching to succeed and learning to occur.

Most modern commentators on the last chapter of the *Posterior Analytics* agree that induction is related, in Aristotle's account, to νοῦς in the same way as a process is to a finished state (or a ἕξις, in Aristotle's lexicon).[190] The disposition, if that is properly what a ἕξις involves, to see the pattern of things in this world so that the first principles are clear to the learner is established by the learner's first practising the inductive procedure of starting with sense impressions of particulars exhibiting some attribute in common and concluding

---

claims for dialectic, for example, that it was a master-science, and by implication then, we may assume that Aristotle later deviated from the concept of dialectic as expressed in the *Top.* If this is so, then the account therein of the method of dialectic as a means by which to reach the first principles was later superseded by Aristotle's account of induction to achieve that purpose.

189   W.D. Ross, *Aristotle,* 6th ed. (London: Routledge, 1996), p. 53.

190   For example, see Kosman, "Understanding, Explanation and Insight in Aristotle's *Posterior Analytics,*" *supra* n. 2, pp. 385 and 390; and Hamlyn, *supra* n. 179, p. 175.

with an apprehension of the universal. Kosman goes further than this and sees induction as the very act of insight. On his interpretation, ἀπόδειξις (which he translates as "understanding" rather than "demonstration") is a reciprocally related activity. Ἐπαγωγή (induction) thus stands to ἀπόδειξις as teaching does to learning, or seeing to being seen.[191] They are actually different descriptions of the same thing; hence, when the learner proceeds towards the universal by the inductive process, the teacher moves in the opposite direction, figuratively speaking, and lays out principles and explanations appropriate to the particulars in question. Kosman's interpretation will be the subject of further scrutiny in Chapter Six.

Lesher attacks the orthodox opinion, identified with·Ross for example, that νοῦς is somehow a faculty of intuition and that it is restricted in its operation to the grasping of first principles.[192] Lesher claims that on this interpretation, νοῦς has no relation to Aristotle's empirical account of how we grasp a universal in the process of observing particulars. He contends that there is sufficient evidence in the *Posterior Analytics* to justify the interpretation that νοῦς has a broader scope than this, and that besides apprehending first principles the concept of νοῦς is also meant to explain how principles and insights may be grasped through induction at many different levels in Aristotle's epistemology. Lesher seeks to broaden our reading of what νοῦς is capable of, according to Aristotle. If Lesher's argument is sound, he is justified in claiming that the relation between Aristotle's theories of perception and demonstration is not that assumed by Barnes in constructing the thesis about the pedagogic purpose of the *Posterior Analytics*. Lesher's argument, too, will be examined in a subsequent chapter.

This chapter has spelled out a summary of Aristotle's arguments in the *Posterior Analytics* in favour of a strong thesis about how teaching and learning ought to be organized. He gives us a programme, based on philosophical principles, in which such organization is meant to reflect the logical system of the syllogism

---

[191]   Kosman, *supra* n. 2, p. 389.

[192]   Lesher, *supra* n. 17.

which he develops in the *Prior Analytics*. If he is correct in his assumptions and their implications for the human activity of teaching, we have gained by reading the *Posterior Analytics* a powerful tool with which we may organize a curriculum, plan the units of knowledge to be imparted in each science, and judge whether or not an attempt to teach has been successful. Aristotle's account has not gone unchallenged, as the several immediately preceding paragraphs attest. The programme in the *Posterior Analytics* was the subject of much obloquy during early modern times for what were perceived to be its absurd strictures on scientific investigation. Our next task, after two relatively short interludes for treating special problems arising out of the *Posterior Analytics*, will be to see what there is of lasting educational value in Aristotle's programme, and to see, if it goes wrong in some respects, what can be learned from that too.

CHAPTER FOUR

Aristotle's Criticism of Learning in the *Meno*

The *Meno*, traditionally placed among Plato's earlier or Socratic dialogues, has had a long and honourable connection with the study of the history and philosophy of education.[1] It is one of those canonical texts that continue to serve both as a prime elementary introduction to perennial problems in the theory of what teachers do or ought to do, and also as a source of recurring fascination to veteran practitioners of the philosophy of education.[2] Owing to its provocative, witty, and paradoxical contents, it has attracted a large body of scholarly literature. Our purposes in this chapter will be to examine the theory of learning put forth by Plato in that dialogue

---

[1]   See A. E. Taylor, *Plato: The Man and His Work*, 7th ed. (London: Methuen, 1960), pp. 25–26 for the traditional rationale behind this grouping. Ryle's chronological thesis places the *Meno* among the "eristic" dialogues, as Ryle calls them, which were composed and delivered to audiences before the trial of Plato, among others, in the late 370s on charges of defaming public figures, but published after such trial. Thus the participation of Antyus is a late insertion into the original text of the dialogue. See Gilbert Ryle, *Plato's Progress* (Cambridge: Cambridge University Press, 1966), pp. 152–53, 217, and 219.

[2]   For a modern example, see Brian Hendley, "The *Meno* and Modern Education" (1981–82) 12 Educational Studies 425–29.

and to examine also the criticism made by Aristotle of that theory. Both Plato and Aristotle try to avoid or rebut the same dilemma about how and whether learning is possible. The explication in this chapter of Plato's theory in the *Meno* is fairly long and detailed. This is so because to state his theory in a few words would almost always be to burlesque it. In addition, there is an aspect of his theory that has been generally overlooked. It receives attention here, for it curiously prefigures some of Aristotle's contentions in the *Posterior Analytics*. Out of our examination we may isolate certain dominant problems and ideas that have a great impact on the methods of teaching, particularly those which place emphasis on the importance of learners discovering something without the teacher telling them what it is. As often happens with our task of understanding Aristotle, this task is made easier by comparing his ideas with those of his forerunners, who often produce the knots that Aristotle tries to unravel.

First, something brief should be said about our understanding of the role of Socrates in the *Meno*. All of the named characters who appear in that dialogue (Meno, Socrates and Anytus) were historical personages, and extrinsic evidence allows us to fix the approximate dramatic date at around the final few years of the fifth century B.C.[3] We cannot be sure of the precise nature of Socrates's teachings and hence we must be careful about reading more into Plato's dramatic use of his old master than may be warranted by a comparison with other sources that have come down to us on the work of Socrates.[4] For this reason we ought to be wary about attempts to attribute such doctrines as that of ἀνάμνησις to Socrates, as if he were the inventor, and Plato the mere chronicler, of them. This caution is mentioned here because of some of the broad-brush portraits of this era of Greek educational philosophy that contain a portrait of the historical Socrates as if he were the creator of some advanced and programmatic philosophical doctrines. These portraits may

---

[3]   Taylor, *supra* n. 1, p. 129.

[4]   A review of the biographical sources, which often give conflicting evidence about the life and opinions of Socrates, is contained in A. R. Lacey, "Our Knowledge of Socrates" in Gregory Vlastos (ed.), *The Philosophy of Socrates: A Collection of Critical Essays* (Garden City, N.Y.: Anchor Books, 1971), pp. 22–49.

altogether omit mention of Plato.[5] A notable example of this tendency is to find a necessary connection between the so-called Socratic method of teaching and the theory of ἀνάμνησις. This connection is no more logically necessary or factually indissoluble than that between the Socratic method and the metaphysical theory of the Forms. For Plato, there might be said to be a way of meshing certain methods of teaching (perhaps exemplified by Socrates) and philosophic inquiry with his peculiar theory of learning. We must be careful not to saddle Socrates with the same conception, for there remain many gaps in our knowledge about has positive doctrines. In what follows, references to Socrates will be to the dramatic, not the historical, Socrates. With this caveat in mind we may proceed to spell out and consider some extremely curious notions propounded by Socrates in Plato's *Meno*, paying particular attention to the initial efforts to define ἀρετή and the subsequent attempt to give a lively illustration of the theory of ἀνάμνησις. For the most part, the translations of key terms from the *Meno* used in this chapter are drawn from Guthrie's translation.[6]

The theory of ἀνάμνησις in the *Meno* and dispensing with the need for teaching

Commentators never cease to remark on the abrupt beginning of the dialogue. Without salutation or prelude, Meno asks Socrates in which of the following ways ἀρετή (virtue or excellence) is acquired:

---

5   This tendency is marked in Harry S. Broudy and John R. Palmer, *Exemplars of Teaching Method* (Chicago: Rand McNally and Company, 1965). These authors write at p. 38:

   As to what causes the insight, Socrates has his theory of innate ideas and reminiscence, a theory that to many is not convincing. But is there a convincing theory?

   The authors do not, incidentally, answer that terminal question.

6   Plato, *Meno*, trans. W. K. C. Guthrie, in *The Collected Dialogues of Plato*, ed. Edith Hamilton and Huntington Cairns, Bollingen Series (Princeton: Princeton University Press, 1961). References hereafter in the text and notes simply to Stephanus line, column, and page will be to the *Meno*.

by teaching (διδακτόν), by practice (ἀσκητόν), or by nature (φύσει).[7] After some self-deprecating remarks about how an Athenian such as himself will be less inclined to answer such a query in a bold (ἀφόβως) and grand (μεγαλοπρεπῶς) manner than would a Thessalian (that is, someone such as Meno or Gorgias, of whom it is later hinted Meno is a protégé), Socrates at first evades the question.[8] He wonders instead whether a preliminary question should not first be answered. Once we have satisfied ourselves on the answer to it, we may then carry on with a consideration of Meno's question. The first order question Socrates has in mind is: What is ἀρετή itself (αὐτο)?[9] Once we know what the εἰδώς (common character or pattern) of ἀρετή is, or as Socrates also expresses it, the οὐσία (essential nature) of it, then we will be in a position to understand and articulate how it is acquired by men.[10] Questions of the order, "What is X?" and "Is X Y?", are common in Plato's early dialogues, and we can discern a fluctuation of interest in the *Meno* between two different primary questions, namely, "What is ἀρετή itself?" and "Is ἀρετή teachable?"[11] Socrates says that he himself has never met anybody who could answer the first of these two questions, although he grants that Gorgias may have answered it and Socrates simply has forgotten his answer.[12]

On the prodding of Socrates, Meno tries to answer the question "What is ἀρετή?" He gives different sorts of ἀρετή, according to

---

[7]   70ᵃ1–3. The importance of the concept of ἀρετή in fifth-century Greek philosophical speculation is thoroughly canvassed in Werner Jaeger, *Paideia: The Ideals of Greek Culture*, trans. Gilbert Highet, 3 vols. (Oxford: Oxford University Press, 1943–45). Jaeger sees changing notions of ἀρετή as so central a thread in Greek cultural beliefs that he might almost be said to have apotheosized the concept. See *ibid.*, 2: pp. 44 *et seq.* for a discussion of how Socrates effected a change in his contemporaries' conception of ἀρετή.

[8]   70ᵇ6–7.

[9]   71ᵃ3–6.

[10]   For Socrates's use of εἰδώς, see 72ᶜ5–ᵈ1; and for his request for the οὐσία, see 72ᵇ1.

[11]   Richard Robinson, "Socratic Definition" in Vlastos (ed.), *supra* n. 4, pp. 110–12, originally published as Chapter Five of Richard Robinson, *Plato's Earlier Dialectic*, 2nd ed. (Oxford: Clarendon Press, 1953).

[12]   71ᶜ2–3.

whether the person who possesses it is a man, woman or child.[13] This fails to satisfy Socrates, of course, who wishes to learn from Meno what is common to all these sorts of ἀρετή.

Meno's second attempt to define ἀρετή is to state that it is the capacity to govern men.[14] This answer is plausible only if ἀρετή is conceived of as an excellence peculiarly confined to statesmen or rulers of the πόλις. Socrates shows the inadequacy of this definition by pointing out that a slave or a child, both of whom are relatively powerless, may be said to possess ἀρετή.[15]

Undaunted, Meno, tries once more by giving a list of things that are ἀρεταί, such as justice, courage, temperance, and wisdom.[16] This, although different from a list of sorts of virtues, still gives us only a multiplicity of ἀρεταί and not the common nature of ἀρετή that runs through or permeates them all (διὰ πάντων τούτων ἐστίν).[17] To help Meno grasp the subject of their joint quest, Socrates produces the analogies of geometrical figure and colour.[18] Just as we may ask "What is figure?" (τί ἐστιν σχῆμα;), or "What is colour?," so may we ask "What is ἀρετή?"[19] This is a different mode of question from asking "What is *a* colour?" or "What is *a* figure?," to which we might reply "white" or "triangle," respectively. On this analogy, "courage" will be an appropriate answer to "What is an ἀρετή?" but not to "What is ἀρετή itself?" Socrates tries to help Meno further by going through some definitions of colour and shape.[20]

With this instruction behind him, Meno makes a further attempt to define ἀρετή. He says that it is the desire of beautiful or fine

---

13   71^{e}1–72^{a}4.

14   73^{c}7–^{d}1.

15   73^{d}2–8.

16   74^{a}3–4.

17   74^{a}5–7.

18   The adjective "joint" is used here advisedly because Socrates specifically distinguishes at 75^{c}8–^{d}1 the current discussion between himself and Meno by saying that he is not a clever (σοφῶν), disputatious (ἐριστικῶν), and quarrelsome (ἀγωνιστικῶν) questioner (ἐρόμενος).

19   74^{b}3 *et seq.*

20   75^{b}8–76^{d}5.

(καλῶν) things and the ability to acquire them.[21] Socrates undermines this definition through the proffering of one of the Socratic paradoxes; in this case, about the inability of any man ever truly to desire things that are bad (τὰ κάκα) and therefore harmful to him. Meno concedes Socrates's argument on this point. His frustration at failing to produce a definition of ἀρετή that will withstand Socrates's corrosive scrutiny leads Meno to complain about what, figuratively, Socrates is doing to him. It is as if Socrates were practising some kind of magic on him that reduces Meno to ἀπορία (perplexity or helplessness).[22] He also compares Socrates to that species of fish called the νάρκη, whose sting has a numbing effect on the senses of its victim. Socrates, with typical mock irony, admits the justice of the comparison only if it be recognized that he himself is somehow numbed in the process.[23]

The action in the dialogue next has Socrates take up Meno's query about how we can search for ἀρετή when we do not already know what it is.[24] The effect of Meno's point is that we cannot learn something unless we already know what it is, but if we know what it is, how can we reasonably be said to learn it? Socrates refers to this as an eristical or contentious argument (ἐριστικός λόγος) and he refuses to admit its validity.[25] He begins his refutation of it in a curiously indirect way. He states that he has learned, on the

---

21   77^b2–4.

22   80^a1–3.

23   80^c6–7.

24   80^d5–8.

25   80^e2. This same eristical trick is introduced in the *Euthydemus* at 276᛬5, and according to Socrates in that dialogue, the dilemma turns on an ambiguity in the word μανθάνειν, which can mean both "to learn" and "to understand." For both Plato and Aristotle, "eristic" is something different from "dialectic." In this connection we might note Ryle's summary at *supra* n. 1, pp. 105–106:

> In the Greek world in general elenchic duelling is normally called "eristic", but this word has acquired pejorative connotations for both Plato and Aristotle. They use this word and its variants for commercialized forms of the exercise practised by certain sophists who stoop to all sorts of tricks in order to make sure of winning.

By contrast, dialectic has an important place in the philosophical and heuristic method of both Plato and Aristotle and it is a valuable part of the better sort of education that each recommends.

authority of persons in touch with the divine (some priests and poets), that man's soul is immortal (ἀθάνατον) and, although subject to many births and deaths, is never finally extinguished.[26] From this information Socrates infers that each soul already has learned everything that can be learned. What in ordinary language (καλοῦσιν ἄνθρωποι) we call learning (μάθησιν) is nothing but the recalling (ἀναμνησθέντα) of certain knowledge already present in the soul.[27] Learning (μανθάνειν) simply is ἀνάμνησις, and this is the way of avoiding the eristical argument about the impossibility of learning.

Meno is not convinced by Socrates's mere statement of this doctrine. He wishes to have proof, and so asks Socrates to teach (διδάξαι) him that this is what learning is. Socrates says he cannot "teach" it to him (for if learning is mere ἀνάμνησις, then there is no teaching, properly speaking), but he can demonstrate (ἐπιδείξωμαι) it to Meno.[28] For this purpose he summons Meno's slave boy and engages him in a dialogue about certain geometrical figures.

This dialogue takes the form of Socrates asking questions meant to elicit affirmative or negative answers from the boy. Socrates hopes to show that, at most, the boy is only being reminded (ἀναμιμῃσκόμενος) of certain propositions rather than learning them.[29] The topic of the interrogation is the now celebrated proof of the dimensions of a square whose area is twice that of a two-foot square. The boy at first thinks that each side of the sought-after square must be four feet in length, but Socrates's questions reveal that the area of such a square would be sixteen square feet, not eight. After some floundering about, the boy admits to Socrates that he is in perplexity as Meno is about the nature of ἀρετή, and he not only does not know the answer, but also does not think that he knows.[30] Socrates views this discovery as a necessary juncture on the path (ὁδός) of ἀνάμνησις, for it will stimulate the boy into inquiry (Socrates even descends to the use of the verb to learn, μανθάνειν,

---

26   81ᵇ3–4.
27   81ᵈ2–5.
28   81ᵉ4–82ᵇ1.
29   82ᵇ5–6.
30   84ᵃ7–ᵇ1.

in this context).[31]

Notwithstanding the boy's perplexity, Socrates resumes his questioning and points out that he is not thereby teaching.[32] It is difficult not to find Socrates's repeated protestations on this point something like the assurances of sleight-of-hand artists that there is nothing up their sleeve. Nevertheless he claims just to be interrogating (ἀνερωτῶντα) the boy on his opinions (δόξαι). Socrates describes a figure composed of four equal squares. The diagonals of each of these squares may be seen as forming the four sides of a larger, diamond-shaped square. Each side of this larger square is the hypotenuse opposite the sides of the four original squares. The inscribed square, the boy is led to agree, has an area twice that of the area of each of the four original squares, because the diagonal bisects each of the latter squares. Therefore the length of each side of the inscribed square is equal to the length of the hypotenuse of the original two-foot square.[33] Socrates is again at pains to point out, and to have Meno concede, that the boy's realizing this is the result, not of any teaching, but of Socrates's inquiring into and bringing forth the boy's opinions.[34] Socrates expressly contends that his procedure has shown that those opinions are in some sense "in" the boy even when it was previously shown that he did not think he knew the length of each side of a square covering eight square feet.[35] This locative sense of "in" is important for those interpreters who see a formulation of a theory of innate ideas, in a Cartesian sense, in Socrates's demonstration. In the first stage of his being questioned, that is, the procedure to which he has just submitted, the boy merely has true opinions (ἀληθεῖς δόξαι) about the answer to the question, without knowing (μὴ εἰδῇ) what the answer was.[36] Socrates describes those opinions, being freshly aroused, as having a dreamlike quality about them.[37] Through repetition of the same

---

[31]   84ª3–4. For the use of μανθάνειν, see 84ᶜ4–5.

[32]   84ᵈ1 *et seq.*

[33]   84ᵈ4–85ª8.

[34]   85ᵇ7–ᶜ1.

[35]   85ᶜ2–4.

[36]   85ᶜ6–7.

[37]   85ᶜ9–ᵈ1; 86ª6–7.

questions, presumably in the same progression, the boy will recover (ἀναλαμβάνειν) the knowledge (ἐπιστήμη) for himself (ἐξ αὐτοῦ).[38] It will most emphatically not be attained by teaching (διδακτόν). Such recovery of knowledge Socrates calls ἀνάμνησις. This description will hold not only for knowledge of geometry, but also for knowledge of all sorts and subjects. The corollary of this argument is that the boy must have acquired such true opinions at some previous time. If so, contends Socrates, it was in some previous life.[39]

Moreover, Socrates claims that even if his account is wrong in some key respect, he still maintains that, contrary to the eristical argument, it is better for us together (κοινῇ) to look for (ζετεῖν) that which we do not know rather than to rest smugly in our ignorance because what we do not know we can never discover (εὑρεῖν).[40] On both grounds, then, the theory of ἀνάμνησις and the never-say-die attitude built on a preference for inquiry over skeptical sloth, Socrates thinks that he and Meno should continue their pursuit of the answer to the question about ἀρετή.

This concludes Socrates's demonstration to Meno of what ἀνάμνησις is by illustrating how the slave boy can think for himself and arrive at a correct conclusion without his interrogator telling him what it is.[41] The remainder of the dialogue may be summarized as

---

[38]   85ᵈ3–4.

[39]   85ᵈ9–86ᵃ6–7.

[40]   86ᵇ6–ᶜ5.

[41]   This emphasis on the boy thinking for himself about what is entailed by certain geometrical relations, and not just looking and seeing what the rough figures drawn by Socrates tell him, is central to Socrates's proof. The discovery by the boy is not "a purely empirical one" made "on the evidence of his eyesight," as Ross supposes, but involves the boy's reasoning powers. Vlastos gives some examples to show that ἀνάμνησις is more a matter of reasoning than of observing. Socrates's remarks later in the dialogue about being able to calculate the αἰτία as the mark that distinguishes knowledge from true belief lend further support to Vlastos's interpretation. See Gregory Vlastos, "Ἀνάμνησις in the *Meno*" (1965–66) 4 Dialogue 143–67, which includes the relevant passage from Ross. Note also Crombie's comment:

It is not true, as it is sometimes said, that Socrates' methods are empirical. He does not, for example, get out a foot rule.

I. M. Crombie, *An Examination of Plato's Doctrines*, 2 vols. (London: Routledge

follows. Socrates and Meno make a fresh beginning at 86^{d}3. Socrates again advises that the target of their inquiry should be shifted to the nature of ἀρετή itself, rather than to the question of how it may possibly be acquired. Presuming that the answer to the latter question cannot be known, Socrates proposes and elaborates two hypotheses, a method of using propositions that evidently is well known by this time to geometers but less familiar to philosophers. The first hypothesis is that virtue is that attribute of the soul called knowledge (this is an inelegant way of putting Socrates's assertion in English, but it is faithful to the original); the second hypothesis is that virtue is something good (τι ἢ ἀγαθὸν).[42] Socrates eventually rejects both of these hypotheses, primarily on the ground that attributes of the soul may be advantageous or harmful, depending on their use: for example, learning (μανθανόμενα) and discipline or training (καταρτυόμενα) may prove harmful (βλαβερά) without practical wisdom (φρόνησις).[43] Socrates never really addresses the third possible means of acquisition suggested at the outset by Meno, namely, practice (ἀσκητόν). We have to wait until the *Republic* before we learn what role practice has in the formation of the characters of citizens of the ideal state.

Socrates does go on to give further arguments why ἀρετή is not acquired through instruction.[44] Anytus enters upon the scene during these deliberations. He reveals himself as a doubter of the Sophists' pretensions about their ability to inculcate ἀρετή in their clients, though he confesses that he himself has never encountered a Sophist. Anytus exits from the scene of the dialogue after muttering sombre and portentous advice to Socrates about how his denigration of fellow Athenians will cause future problems for Socrates.[45] After briefly considering the question of teachability further, Socrates ventures a positive theory about how ἀρετή may be acquired. He reverts to his distinction between knowledge and true opinion (ἀληθὴς δόξα). He claims that the latter of this pair may be as good

---

and Kegan Paul, 1962–63), 2: 138.
[42]   87^{b}4–^{c}3; 87^{d}2–3.
[43]   87^{e}4–88^{c}3.
[44]   89^{d}3 *et seq.*
[45]   94^{e}3.

a guide (ἡγεμὸν) as the former for the purpose of conducting oneself rightly (ὀρθότητα πράξεως).[46] At this point he draws his famous comparison between true opinions and the statues of the mythical artificer, Daedalus.[47] These statues are reputed to run away unless they are secured. Just so will true opinions fly from the mind unless the explanation for them is formulated (δήσῃ αἰτίας λογισμῷ). The necessary process is ἀνάμνησις. It ties down (δεσῶσιν) these fugaceous opinions, which by virtue of the success of the process of ἀνάμνησις become knowledge (ἐπιστήμη) and become stable (μόνιμοι). This tie or fetter (δεσμός) distinguishes (διαφέρειν) knowledge from true opinion. Socrates grants that this metaphorical description is itself only a figure of speech (εἰκάζων) rather than a piece of knowledge (εἰδὼς) in its own right.[48] The source of such true opinions is not easily identified, but Socrates in the end claims that it is by divine dispensation (θείᾳ μοίρᾳ) that a man's soul originally receives them.[49] He concludes the dialogue by leaving open the possibility that there may be a kind of statesman (πολιτικός ἀνδρός) who can shape another like himself in terms of ἀρετή. Obviously, from Socrates's remarks, such a statesman was not to be found among such fifth century luminaries as Pericles, Themistocles and Thucydides, all of whose offspring turned out rather poorly.

A couple of points raised in Plato's dialogue deserve emphasis. It is frequently urged by Socrates that Meno observe how, in his dealing with the slave boy, Socrates deliberately refrains from teaching (διδακτόν) and concentrates instead on questioning. Through his questions, of course, Socrates is not engaged on some open-ended debate or brain storming session, which will lead to a destination that nether participant knows beforehand. He has in mind before he begins his interrogation, aimed at showing the boy that he does not know what he thinks he knows, what kind of responses the untutored slave will likely give. When Socrates begins the second set of questions, designed to lead the boy to the correct answer to the original question, he sets out questions in a

---

46   97ᵇ8–ᶜ3.
47   97ᵉ2–98ᵃ7.
48   98ᵇ1.
49   100ᵃ1–7.

progression that he has a good idea beforehand will result in the boy finally grasping what Socrates himself knew all along. This method of assisting the learner to hit upon the correct answer by the guidance of well-chosen leading questions is traditionally called Socrates's "maieutic" method, after his frequent references to himself as a midwife attending at the births of other people's ideas.[50] Prima facie, this conception of what a teacher can do contrasts strongly with what Aristotle has said about teaching in the *Posterior Analytics*. This difference will be followed up in the final part of this chapter.

Secondly, we have concentrated in our summary on the *Meno* and have left untouched the issue of how the theory of ἀνάμνησις is treated in other Platonic dialogues, such as the *Phaedo* and the *Phaedrus*. These are interesting in their own right, but it is not absolutely necessary to admit them to our discussion in order to gain some insight into Aristotle's criticism of the theory.

Thirdly, Plato's depiction of the relation between true opinion and knowledge is another topic of broad scope, but it here is given only a brief treatment for the light it throws upon the doctrine of ἀνάμνησις. A discussion of how that relation is spelled out in the *Theaetetus* would be out of place here. For our purposes, it is important to keep closely to the text of the *Meno* and to note well how Aristotle's idea of knowledge ἁπλῶς (or, as we have referred to it in Chapter Three, knowledge *simpliciter*) echoes the requirement in the latter part of the *Meno* that the knower must be aware of, and be able to state, the explanation or reason (αἰτία) for his opinions.[51] The necessity of repeating the process of ἀνάμνησις until the opinion is

---

50   This is an uncommon adjective. An early recorded instance of it in English is the following:

> Of Platonick Discourse there are two kinds, Hyphegetick and Exegetick (of which a sub-division is called Majeutick).

Thomas Stanley, *The History of Philosophy*, 1655, xv, 46, quoted in *The Compact Edition of the Oxford English Dictionary*, 2 vols. (Oxford: Oxford University Press, 1971), p. 1696 s.v. "maieutic." For Socrates's description in this vein, see the *Theaetetus* 149ª1 *et seq.*, where in typical self-mocking fashion he claims to be fit for midwifery because he himself has always been barren. He claims that part of his skill consists in bringing forth and distinguishing between offspring that are real and those which are mere phantoms.

51   See *supra* n. 47.

"tethered" also puts us in mind of the Aristotelian theory about repetition being necessary for the stabilizing of the universal in the soul, as presented in the *Posterior Analytics* B 19. This passage, which occurs late in the *Meno*, regarding the tethering of the learner's opinions is crucial for an understanding of what the slave boy episode is meant to show. Among modern commentators, only Vlastos has taken significant notice of it. He views ἀνάμνησις, where it is used by Socrates in the *Meno*, as meaning "any enlargement of our knowledge which results from the perception of logical relationships."[52] This interpretation goes far beyond the rather crude notion that Socrates thinks all souls are naturally omniscient and ἀνάμνησις is simply a matter of bringing to the forefront of the mind through another's "reminding" what is already present in the background. This crude interpretation has been perpetuated somewhat by the rendering of ἀνάμνησις into Latin as *reminiscientia* and into English as reminiscence. The very thing which Socrates does not want to have imputed to him is that he has reminded the boy of the correct answer, in the sense that to remind a person, X, that Y or of Y is to tell X that Y or of Y. Because of the use by Socrates of the notion of αἰτία, Vlastos claims:

> Thus to say that knowledge is true belief "bound" by the αἰτίας λογισμῷ is to imply that a statement becomes known when it is seen to follow logically from premises sufficient for the purpose: to "recollect" it, then, would be to see that these premises entail it.[53]

This suggests to Vlastos's mind that Plato has, as the underpinnings of everything he has to say about ἀνάμνησις in the *Meno*, a sophisticated view of knowledge as capable of being systematically axiomatized. On Vlastos's interpretation, then, learning will be:

> . . . not just a matter of increasing his stock of true beliefs, but of acquiring *knowledge*, that is to say, true beliefs logically

---

52   Vlastos, *supra* n. 41, pp. 156–57.
53   *Ibid.*, p. 155.

bound to the reasons for their truth.[54]

The method of teaching exemplified in Socrates's questioning of the slave boy will then be important for disclosing the grounds that underlie the conclusion as well as the conclusion itself. The circumstantial guarantee that the conclusion is a piece of knowledge and not just a true belief lies in the joint progress of the guide and the learner through the progression of questions leading up to the learner's culminating insight into the answer to the original question.

This is a very significant and worthwhile attempt to put the use of ἀνάμνησις into perspective by noting the calculation or reckoning of the αἰτία as a precondition of knowledge. It illuminates a fascinating aspect of the procedure Socrates follows with the slave boy, for it shows that the process must include certain elements if the correct answer is to be reached. The procedure cannot be, for example, one of trial and error: for the participants might hit upon the right answer without having formulated and stated the reasons why it is right. Vlastos has performed a valuable service in bringing this notion into prominence, though his interpretation has been little remarked upon by subsequent writers. His discussion shows neatly how ἀνάμνησις and the method of interrogation are meant to serve the same ultimate purpose. He goes possibly too far, however, in construing the notion of a rigorous and all-embracing deductive system, with primitive and derivative propositions, out of the suggestion of the requirement for an αἰτία. This accomplishment is left to Aristotle, for whose theory of demonstration the αἰτία is a cornerstone. Vlastos's interpretation, possibly out of enthusiasm for attracting attention to this neglected part of the *Meno*, begins to take on the appearance of an Aristotelian gloss on the text of the *Meno*. That text does not, unfortunately, give sufficient grounds for saying that the process of ἀνάμνησις leads to an "enlargement" of a learner's knowledge; the whole flavour of the doctrine is that in some sense the learner's knowledge is "recovered," and that the teacher may guide the learner in achieving this, not by adding to what she believes, but by pertinent questions about what she already believes,

---

[54]   *Ibid.*, p. 159. For the suggestion of atomization, see *ibid.*, p. 155n.24.

so as to separate his true and reasonable beliefs from false and groundless ones. In this way, and through its repetition, certain beliefs are "tied down."

Vlastos also interprets Plato's doctrine in the following way. He contends that to "recollect" is a notion developed by Plato in the *Meno* as a technical way of expressing the following:

> When these [relationships] are inter-propositional to "recollect" a previously unknown proposition is to come to know it by seeing that it is entailed by others already known.[55]

There are two problems with this interpretation. The first is that it seems to credit Plato with a theory of valid inference. There are very slim grounds for such an imputation. Vlastos is reading into the concept of αἰτία fairly sophisticated notions of entailment, criteria for an adequate definition, and the central role of explanation in the sciences that Plato is, at best, only dimly aware of in the *Meno*. Secondly, this interpretation tends to slight that aspect of the doctrine that gives it the title ἀνάμνησις. This is really to repeat what is said above about the importance of Plato's language wherein he elaborates a picturesque background in which souls are endowed with learning that is coextensive with what can be known; without this supposition the eristical argument triumphs over the attempt to save the appearance of learning. In addition, if the Platonic doctrine were as Vlastos portrays it, then Aristotle, far from criticizing it for being too simplistic as we shall see presently, presumably would have embraced it as a natural precursor to his own theory about how learning proceeds from what is already known. If we agree that there is this defect in Vlastos's interpretation, notwithstanding its salutary effect of bringing to light this interesting part of the *Meno*, the cause of the defect is not obscure. A major impetus for Vlastos's argument is his reaction against the interpretation, promulgated by Ross and Taylor in particular, that the *Meno* shows that all knowledge is somehow dependent on sense-experience. Vlastos vigorously tries to refute this, and to substitute his own construal by which all

---

[55]   *Ibid.*, p. 157.

knowledge recovered by ἀνάμνησις is, in a sense, deductive, even demonstrative knowledge in the fully-fledged Aristotelian sense. This vigour has carried Vlastos somewhat beyond the data of the theory in Plato's text.

We may summarize the foregoing in the following way. There appear to be two possible constructions of the point of the doctrine of ἀνάμνησις that can mislead us as to what Plato meant. The first is to look at the doctrine solely within the ambit of the slave boy episode, extending from 80^d to 86^c, and, on the basis of this section only, to impute to Plato the theory that teaching is simply a matter of reminding the learner of something, in the crudest sense of "remind." The second way of misinterpreting the point of ἀνάμνησις is at least much more interesting than the first. It involves detecting in the dialogue traces of a major theory of learning and then claiming that the whole theory itself has been worked out in Plato's mind. This is a doubtful inference but at least it provides a point of comparison with the later architect of that major theory, namely Aristotle. A relatively balanced interpretation, that sees in the αἰτίας λογισμώς a requirement that the learner must grasp more than just the true belief, but also the reason for that belief, and that Plato has in mind some deductive process (though this does not mean that he envisions an axiomatic system capable of encompassing and yielding all knowledge), can be found in Bluck.[56] In this connection it might also be noted that Moravcsik considers and rejects the interpretation that "recollection and the corresponding sense of 'learning' are to be understood as the intuitive grasp of simple concepts and the drawing of deductive inferences."[57]

One must also be aware that the doctrine of ἀνάμνησις is not always accorded the prized status of a theory that is, on its own merits, capable of explaining what we understand to be the facts of learning and teaching. It must be said, however that the sort of serious discussion surrounding the doctrine in the commentaries by Vlastos, Bluck and Crombie tends to counterbalance the view that

---

[56]   R. S. Bluck, *Plato's Meno* (Cambridge: Cambridge University Press, 1961), pp. 412–13.

[57]   Julius Moravscik, "Learning as Recollection" in Vlastos (ed.), *supra* n. 4, 1: pp. 60–61.

ἀνάμνησις is a mere myth or metaphor, not to be pressed too hard for its literal meaning.[58]

Aristotle's discussion of the doctrine of ἀνάμνησις

In several isolated passages in his work, Aristotle goes straight to the heart of Plato's theory of ἀνάμνησις and tries to show it is misguided. According to Bonitz, Aristotle mentions the *Meno* by name twice in his extant works, and he further alludes to that dialogue in the *Nicomachean Ethics*.[59] In the latter context he is discussing philosophical dogmas which he ascribes to Socrates. In addition, in his short treatise entitled *De Memoria*, part of that group called the *Parva Naturalia*, he devotes the second part of his discussion to the concept of ἀναμιμνήῄσκεθαι (recollecting) and finds it different from, though related to, memory.[60] This discussion will receive some slight comment hereafter, but the major part of this section will be taken up with two important passages in the *Analytics* that contain his criticism of Plato's doctrine.

The first passage is found in the *Prior Analytics A* 21. Aristotle there raises the concept of ἀνάμνησις in the course of discussing how it is possible that we can err in our conception or judgment (ὑπόληψιν) of terms (ὅρων) that we set out in syllogism.[61] There is, for example, the possibility of mistake in the extension of terms. Where P belongs to both S and T καθ' αὐτὰ (that is, essentially) and S and T both belong in turn to U, a learner may judge that P belongs only to S and hence to U.[62] She may fail to realize that P belongs to U through T as well. In such a case, according to Aristotle, the

---

58   On the notion of Plato's doctrine as a mere myth or metaphor, see B. Phillips, "The Significance of Meno's Paradox" in Alexander Sesonske and Noel Fleming (eds.), *Plato's Meno: Text and Criticism* (Belmont, Ca.: Wadsworth, 1965), pp. 80–81, originally published in (1948–49) 42 The Classical Weekly 87–91; and Moravscik, *supra* n. 57, p. 69.

59   H. Bonitz, *Index Aristotelicus*, 2nd ed. (Graz: Akademischer Druck—u. Verlagsanstalt Graz, 1955) s.v. *Menon*; and N.E. 1260ª23, 27.

60   *De Mem.* 451ª21 *et seq.*

61   *An. Pr.* 66ᵇ18.

62   *An. Pr.* 66ᵇ22 *et seq.*

learner may have knowledge and ignorance about the same thing (namely, P) in relation to the same thing (U).[63]

He illustrates this type of error by letting P stand for "two right angles" (though he seems to mean that this is elliptical for his standard example, "the sum of its interior angles is equal to the sum of two right angles"), M for "triangle," and S for "this particular diagram of a triangle" (αἰσθητὸν τρίγωνον). A person might perfectly well know that P a S, but fail to realize that S exists (μὴ εἶναι), in which case she has universal (καθόλου) knowledge but not particular (καθ' ἕκαστον) knowledge.[64] By her knowledge of the universal she knows that the sum of the interior angles of any particular triangle equals the sum of two right angles, but she does not grasp the particular knowledge having to the triangle placed before her.[65] Aristotle is careful to indicate that universal and particular knowledge do not constitute two contrary states of mind (οὐχ ἕξει τὰς ἐναντίας), for they may coexist within the same person at the same time, or one may be present and the other absent.[66] It is from this standpoint that he launches his criticism of the doctrine of the doctrine of ἀνάμνησις.

He contends that the doctrine can be criticized on the ground that it presupposes the contrariety of those two states of mind. Plato's attempted solution to the eristical argument posed by Meno, instead of asking in how many different senses we may be said to know something, rests upon Plato's theory (λόγος) that learning (ἡ μάθησις) is simply synonymous with ἀνάμνησις, and that which we learn we already know at some level of our understanding.[67] Ἀνάμνησις becomes the process by which this foreknowledge is dredged up.

We do not have to argue for this identification if we recognize, according to Aristotle, that we do not have previous knowledge of the particular. Instead, by the process of ἐπαγωγή we acquire (λαμβάνειν) knowledge of the particular just as though we could

---

63   *An. Pr.* 66[b]25–26.
64   *An. Pr.* 67[a]8–15.
65   *An. Pr.* 67[a]19–21.
66   *An. Pr.* 67[a]20–21.
67   *An. Pr.* 67[a]21–22.

remember (ἀναγνωρίιζοντας).[68] This similarity between coming to know by ἐπαγωγή and by the process of remembering must have been what confounded Plato and caused him to make the unwarranted generalization that learning was just remembering. As Aristotle shows, the possibility of error arises not because a learner's universal knowledge is contrary to their particular knowledge, but because she may be mistaken in her particular knowledge (for example, wrongly think that M is a triangle).[69] This might easily happen when learners have never considered the proposition disclosing the universal in conjunction with the proposition disclosing their knowledge of the particular.[70] Besides universal and particular knowledge (the latter is also called by him, knowledge proper to the object or τῇ οἰκείᾳ), there is actual (ἐνεργεῖν) knowledge.[71] It seems we have the latter when we are actually apprehending a particular object at the moment and, as it were, exercising our universal knowledge. These three sorts of knowledge relate to one another, in the words of Cherniss, in the following way:

> [There is] . . . a distinction of two senses of *eidenai*, the knowledge of the universal being potential knowledge of the particular case actualized when the particular is recognized as coming under the universal.[72]

---

68   *An. Pr.* 67ᵃ22–25. The verb γνωρίζειν was discussed above in Chapter Three, n. 36, where a justification of it as "to recognize" is suggested. This observation applies *a fortiori* to the verb used in this context, namely ἀναγνωρίζειν; for the prefix ανα- signifies a repetition of the action signified by the verb.

69   *An. Pr.* 67ᵃ27–30.

70   *An. Pr.* 67ᵇ7–10.

71   *An. Pr.* 67ᵇ4–5.

72   Harold Cherniss, *Aristotle's Criticism of Plato and the Academy*, 2 vols. (Baltimore: Johns Hopkins University Press, 1944), 2: 69. There is a dearth of literature on the subject of Aristotle's treatment of the theory of ἀνάμνησις. Besides Cherniss's comments, which are very brief, we might note the following discussion: John Catan, "Recollection and *Posterior Analytics* II, 19" (1970) 4 Apeiron 34–57. Catan makes some exegetical notes on the passage in *An. Pr. A* 21 which we have been discussing. Those notes are mystifying and inconsistent, as illustrated by the following excerpts from p. 46:
       Some confusion is generated by the rejection of Recollection at line 22

The second significant passage to be considered is the *Posterior Analytics A* 1. As part of his discussion of the necessity of previous knowledge for learning to occur, he mentions the *Meno* and the ἀπορήμα raised in that dialogue. He again discusses one of his favourite examples of universal knowledge, the one about the sum of the angles of a triangle. Then, in an account that parallels that just discussed in the *Prior Analytics,* he points out that the learner will recognize (γνωρίζειν) a particular geometrical figure (that is, *this* figure drawn for her) as a triangle as she is led (ἐπάγειν) to relate the particular to the universal.[73] This process gives rise to the possibility that the learner may be said to know, and yet in another sense not to know, the very same thing. Until the relation (ἐπαχθῆναι) or the deduction (συλλογισμός) is made, the learner may be both ignorant and knowledgeable about the same thing.[74] This does not create a paradox for Aristotle that he must resolve, for he has constructed an apparatus to handle the analysis of different sorts of knowledge claims.

----

which is based on Aristotle's denial that there is any prior "knowledge" of the singular. But the singular (*to kath' ekaston*) [sic] turns out to be as universal as interpreted by the example. Thus Aristotle is to be understood as rejecting any prior knowledge of the universal.

and pp. 46-47:

Therefore Aristotle denies the existence of learning as *Recollection* because there is no prior knowledge of the concrete sensible particular. Thus for him the origin of knowledge both scientific and non-scientific is sensation. *Recollection* denies that origin but let us note *Recollection* as presented in the text above is viewed as going from universal to universal i.e. in terms of the example, from "triangle" to "two right angles." This, of course, is not Plato's doctrine but the closest thing in Aristotle's doctrine of knowledge to it.

In both passages Catan indicates that "two right angles" is a phrase to be taken literally and not as an ellipsis for "the sum of its interior angles is equal to the sum of two right angles," which is Aristotle's standard example of the predicate that belongs to the universal "triangle." Catan's comments are, as a whole, extremely difficult to grapple with, and Aristotle's own text, supplemented by his arguments in the *An. Post.* are generally easier to follow.

[73]   *An. Post.* 71ª20–21.
[74]   *An. Post.* 71ª24–26.

The account in the *Posterior Analytics* is also valuable for the distinction there drawn by Aristotle between universal knowledge and knowledge *simpliciter*. The latter is defined at 71^b12 and includes the knower's cognizance of the αἰτία of the subject and the necessity by which P might be said to belong to S. Universal knowledge is still not the most accurate, comprehensive knowledge and should be distinguished from scientific knowledge, which is knowledge *simpliciter*. The latter is defined at 71^b9-12 and includes the knower's cognizance of the αἰτία of the subject and the necessity by which P may be said to belong to S. Universal knowledge is still not the most accurate, comprehensive knowledge and should be distinguished from scientific knowledge, which is knowledge *simpliciter*. At 71^b29 Aristotle indicates that the failure to acknowledge this distinction was Plato's downfall in trying to evade the eristical argument raised in the *Meno*. Aristotle's precise words are:

> If he did not in an unqualified sense of the term *know* the existence of this triangle, how could he *know* without qualification that its angles were equal to two right angles? No: clearly he *knows* not without qualification but only in the sense that he *knows* universally. If this distinction is not drawn, we are faced with the dilemma in the *Meno*: either a man will learn nothing or what he already knows.[75]

For Aristotle, the idea that a learner already knows in an unqualified sense everything that can be known and it is just a matter of finding the method by which to bring it, so to speak, to the surface, is philosophically repugnant. He tries to save the possibility of learning against the skeptic by saying that the limb of the dilemma which reads, the learner can learn only that which he already knows, can be spelled out in such a way that it will not offend our good sense. Having once attained to universal knowledge, the learner in

---

[75] *An. Post.* 71^a26–30. He goes on (71^a30–$^b4$) to repudiate the idea that universal propositions should be qualified by learners according to the breadth of their experience. Such qualified propositions obviously will not serve as appropriate starting points for demonstration. The process of ἐπαγωγή will result in a recognition of the universal, not just a generalization of experience which holds good for all enumerated instances.

a sense then learns in particular what she knows in general. This just makes actual what is already potential. Aristotle views his versatile distinction between ἐνέργεια and δύναμις as more sophisticated than anything in Plato's philosophic apparatus. Once again, he has used that distinction to avoid the snares set by his forerunners.

By comparison with Plato's apparent desire to turn all learning into a mode of ἀνάμνησις and to banish the activity of teaching in favour of the activity of interrogation, Aristotle's account of demonstration seems much less radical. Indeed, the Platonic depiction of learners in the charge of a maieutic guide, who helps them make discoveries for themselves, is at the opposite pole, conceptually, from the Aristotelian depiction of the teacher who proceeds by demonstration and lecture, and who assumes that the only existing knowledge with which her learners may be credited is what she or another teacher has arranged for them to have through prior demonstration, or what the learner may have gained from ἐπαγωγή.[76] Aristotle's conception of teaching and learning is shot

---

[76]   See Taylor's capsule comment on the "exact point" of the doctrine of ἀνάμνησις at *supra* n. 1, pp. 136–37:

> And the philosophical importance of the doctrine is not that it proves the immortality of the soul, but that it shows that the acquisition of knowledge is not a matter of passively receiving "instruction", but one of following up a personal effort of thinking once started by an arresting sense-experience . . . We see, then, why both Socrates and Plato hold that "knowledge" can only be won by personal participation in "research"; it cannot simply be handed from one man to another.

There are some serious prooblems with this interpretation. For a start, Taylor's emphasis on the need of "sense-experience" as initiating the process of learning depends on the notion of a prior empirical discovery that was argued for by Ross, but is rejected by Vlastos with some strong reasons: see *supra* n. 41. Secondly, the words set off in inverted commas, instruction, knowledge, and research, represent for Taylor some peculiar sense of the ordinary meaning of those words, but he fails to clarify what is the sense of each. Note also Taylor's liberal use of inverted commas in the following recapitulation of the point of the doctrine (*supra* n. 1, p. 139):

> . . . *all* "learning" is an active response of personal thought and efforts
> to the "hints" derived from a mare mature fellow-learner.

These qualified assertions and terms tend to compound the obscurity of Plato's original metaphor or analogy, rather than to elucidate it.

through with the didactic responsibility of the teacher, and the learner's state of mind is of concern to the teacher only in so far as the learner must in some degree assent to the premises of the demonstration in order for the conclusion to be telling. Plato, on the other hand, represents learning as occurring only where the teacher abdicates and gives up the lectern and turns instead to the cross-examination of the learner with the aim of bringing forth ideas already once grasped but afterwards become fuzzy until they are recalled through the agency of a teacher such as Socrates. This process harkens back once again to that dialectic exercise referred to in Chapters Two and Three above. It is a dialogical procedure that results in ἀνάμνησις, and in a sense "dialogical" is preferable as a description of the teacher's role illustrated in the *Meno*. If we applied the adjective "dialectical," there would be some danger of unintentionally suggesting some Platonic tenets that are conspicuous in his later writings. For the moment, the point is to liken what happens in the *Meno* with the dialectical exercise common in the Academy, whereby one party plays the interrogator and the other the defender of a proposition. The defender is restricted to making yes or no answers while he tries to stave off refutation.[77] That this type of procedure, or a refinement of it, may be engaged in profitably by a pair of seekers after the truth (or essential natures of things) is revealed in the *Meno* , where Socrates invites Meno to join him in the quest without fear that Socrates will try to win the debate at all costs.[78] Finally, as another way of comparing Aristotle's and Plato's notions of ἀνάμνησις, some attention should be paid to the *De Memoria*. In that little treatise Aristotle draws a sharp distinction between remembering (for which he uses the verbs, μεμνῆσθαι and μνημονεύεῖν) and recollecting (ἀναμιμνήκεσθαι). He claims that ἀνάμνησις is not the recovery of memories, for no memory must necessarily have preceded it in time (though memory may follow ἀνάμνησις).[79] It is possible to recover scientific knowledge

---

77 Plato's views on dialectic, which seem to evolve over the course of his philosophical career, are summarized and assessed in Ryle, *supra* n. 1, pp. 125–29.

78 See *supra* n. 18.

79 *De Mem.* 451^{a}21–22.

(ἐπιστήμη) or a perception (αἴσθησιν) in the sense of ἀνάμνησις.[80] The result of this is that, unlike Plato, Aristotle sees the role of ἀνάμνησις as, at most, the relearning of an object of ἐπιστήμη; but it has no bearing on its original learning. Aristotle does not expressly refer to Plato's use of ἀνάμνησις, but it is clear from the tenor of *De Memoria* that the original learning does not take place in a previous lifetime of the individual. Furthermore, the process of ἀνάμνησις, as set forth in that treatise, is something that the person does on his own; it does not require the interrogation of him by another.[81] The learner can recollect in tranquillity.[82]

The learner's dilemma and the educational use of the learner's perplexity

Both Plato and Aristotle feel compelled by Meno's eristical argument to give a solution to the problem of how learning is possible. The complex constructive dilemma, as a logician would call it, is formulated by Socrates in the *Meno* at 80ᵉ1. It may be stated in the following way:

(P$_1$)   If X knows what Y is, X does not have to seek or to learn Y, and, if X does not know what Y is, X will not recognize Y when he sees Y.

(P$_2$)   But either X knows what Y is or he does not.

(C)   Therefore, either X does not need to seek or to learn what Y is or he will not recognize Y when he sees Y.

If the major premiss, composed of two hypothetical propositions,

---

80   *De Mem.* 451^{b}2–5.
81   *De Mem.* 452^{a}4–6, 11.
82   A better sketch that that given here regarding points of difference between plato annd Aristotle about ἀνάμνησις is contained in Richard Sorabji, *Aristotle on Memory* (London: Duckworth, 1972), pp. 35–41. On several key issues Sorabji argues that Plato's account is superior to that of Aristotle.

is conceded, along with the minor premiss, which affirms alternately the antecedents of the major, then the conclusion follows and the search for both the known Y and the unknown Y appears futile. In addition to being problematic for the searcher and the researcher, it is a dilemma facing the would-be teacher and learner, for it appears to foreclose on the possibility of X learning anything he does not already know. The skeptic, of course, need not answer the question how X ever came to know anything in the first place. Let us just say that it is through some means other than seeking or learning.

This constellation of seeking, searching, and learning is not accidental. In the *Meno* the activities described by the verbs to seek or inquire (ζητεῖν), to learn (μανθάνειν), to discover (ἑυρίσκειν) and to rediscover (ἀνευρίσκειν) are all used associatively, and Socrates takes seriously the claim that all such enterprises involving those activities are equally susceptible to the skeptic's attack.[83] All of these verbs seem to be entwined with what the slave boy is doing, even though to seek or search connotes a process, while to learn or discover are success verbs.

Plato's attempt to escape the dilemma takes the following form. In the *Meno* Socrates is somewhat equivocal about whether there is any learning left at all for men to achieve. On the one hand, he states that what is ordinarily called learning is really nothing but ἀνάμνησις, and since X may be said to have already learned Y at some previous time, the fact that he cannot, according to the skeptic, learn it again has no ruinous consequences for Socrates's theory of teaching. On the other hand, Socrates persists on occasion to use the

---

[83]   The best example of where these occur together in the *Meno* is at 84^c3–^d1 where Socrates and Meno have the following exchange:

SOCRATES: Do you suppose then that he would have attempted to look for [ζητεῖν], or learn [μανθάνειν] what he thought he knew, though he did not, before he was thrown into perplexity, became aware of his ignorance, and felt a desire to know?
MENO: No.
SOCRATES: Then the numbing process was good for him.
MENO: I agree.
SOCRATES: Now notice what, starting from this state of perplexity, he will discover [ἀνευρίσκειν] by seeking [ζητεῖν] the truth in company with me.

language of seeking, learning and discovering in the context of describing what he and Meno are doing with respect to ἀρετή and what he and the slave boy are doing with respect to arriving at a certain geometrical theorem. In the result, Plato does not need to deny the truth of the implication in either proposition in the major premiss, because his theory of teaching is not designed to help the learner grasp something he never knew before; instead, the teacher is cast as an aide or guide to whom the learner resorts in order to understand better or more clearly, metaphorically to bring to the surface, something that at first is grasped only weakly and darkly. From this solution, it may be seen that the force of the dilemma is not denied. Plato simply slides around both pincers of the dilemma by denying that the learner must learn anything in the sense of "originally" learning anything. Rather, the distinct emphasis in the *Meno* is on inducing the learner to set forth what he thinks and open it up to examination.

The last sentence in the immediately preceding paragraph provides a transition to a second way of seeing Plato's account; it calls into play a different aspect of ἀνάμνησις. Again, it is not an instance of Plato escaping the dilemma by grasping its horns or jumping through those horns or any other standard route of escape. On this second account, Socrates may be seen as denying that the learner has any knowledge beforehand that will serve to denude the learner's search for such knowledge of any purpose. This way of interpreting the *Meno* is far different from the standard account of Plato's theory, but there is textual evidence to support it. As repeatedly emphasized in the slave boy episode, the learner may be presumed to possess opinions. These may be true or false. If true, they can, through the process of ἀνάμνησις, be secured and thereby change their epistemic status and become knowledge. This will not happen on the first occasion that the learner grasps something, but it will be the natural result of the process being repeated by a competent guide.[84] This second account differs from the first in

---

[84]　One might wonder whether learners could ask themselves the same series of questions and thus confirm their answers and render themselves knowledgeable. Socrates's procedure implies that the process of repetition must also be done by the learner in concert with the guide.

respect of what the learner may be said to have previously learned. On the first account, we would credit him with knowledge, that is capable of being "aroused," in Plato's lexicon, by ἀνάμνησις; on the second account, the learner's previous learning is only in the domain of opinion and ἀνάμνησις is the process by which such learning is transmuted into knowledge.

In either case, what is the knowledge of? For Plato, as for Aristotle, the concern is with the learner possessing or coming to possess knowledge than can be stated in true propositions. Such knowledge will be about subjects that can appropriately be fitted into the queries, "What is X?" and "Is X Y?" Finally, as we have seen from examining Socrates's demands of *Meno* near the beginning of the dialogue, the answer to these questions will be in the form of providing the εἰδὼς or οὐσία of the subject of discourse. This is a harbinger of Aristotle's own preoccupation with definition and the paramount importance of being able to state essential attributes of things and the differentiae that mark one kind off from another. This ability is what allows the teacher to construct demonstrative syllogisms, which is teaching *par excellence*.

An evident step in the teacher's enterprise, according to Plato's vivid little drama in the *Meno*, is the drawing of the student into ἀπορίαι.[85] Socrates first reduces Meno himself to perplexity by the sharp questioning of Meno's rather facile attempts to answer the question of "what is ἀρετή." This is not a comfortable position to be in, as Meno's retorts about Socrates being a sorcerer and a νάρκη illustrate. Yet it seems for Socrates to be an essential stage that must be passed through on the path of ἀνάμνησις. The slave boy must first be shown that his initial opinions about the dimensions of the square were wrong and shown thereby that he does not think he knows the answer. The next step beyond this, in Socrates's method, is to have the learner start again on his search and, humbled by what he does not know, eventually reach a satisfactory resolution. Ἀνάμνησις is cast throughout as a succession of steps. Placing

---

[85]   The concept of ἀπορία does not seem to have passed directly into English intellectual discourse, carrying with it some of its ancient Greek philosophical resonance, but instead has been transmitted through the French *aporie*, with connotations of the "impassable point" which it meant for Plato and Aristotle.

ἀπορίαι along the path of the learner might be said to be a necessary part of the teacher's task, not only for the purpose of deflating intellectual pride, but for showing how reaching an *impasse* in our thinking is a precondition of discovering something for ourselves.

Aristotle, though his works do not in general show the same esteem for the teacher's purposeful driving of the learner into an ἀπορία, recognizes in the *Nicomachean Ethics* that the unravelling (λύσις) of an ἀπορία is discovery (εὑρῆσις).[86] In his view, the philosopher must marshal, at the beginning of his inquiry, the difficulties with which his topic is beset. This has several purposes, each of which he discusses in the *Metaphysics B*. The passage is worth reproducing at length:

> For those who wish to get clear of difficulties it is advantageous to discuss the difficulties well; for the subsequent free play of thought implies the solution of the previous difficulties, and it is not possible to untie a knot of which one does not know. But the difficulty of our thinking points to a "knot" in the object; for in so far as our thought is in difficulties, it is in like case with those who are bound; for in either case it is impossible to go forward. Hence one should have surveyed all the difficulties beforehand, both for the purposes we have stated and because people who inquire without first stating the difficulties are like those who do not know where they have to go; besides, a man does not otherwise know even whether he has at any given time found what he is looking for or not; for the end is not clear to such a man, while to him who has first discussed the difficulties it is clear. Further, he who has heard all the contending arguments, as if they were the parties to the case, must be in a better position for judging.[87]

This passage shows Aristotle himself employing a variation on the theme of the eristical argument in the *Meno*. The survey of the ἀπορίαι will be one way to ensure recognition of the solution. This

---

86   *N.E.* 1146ᵇ6.

87   *Met. B* 995ᵃ26–ᵇ3. Translation from the *Metaphysics*, trans. W. D. Ross (Oxford: Oxford University Press, 1924).

passage is a commendation as to how philosophical thinking should proceed; it is not necessarily related to how the learner must grasp what has already been discovered. In the *Posterior Analytics* there is no mention of the pedagogical virtues in luring a class of students down a blind alley and thereafter leading them back onto the correct path. The teacher is demonstrating from the beginning. The method of conducting our philosophic inquiries will be different from teaching the sciences.

It is further interesting to note that in neither Plato's nor Aristotle's mind will ἀπορίαι tend to smother the learner's or inquirer's intellectual curiosity. In the *Meno* at 84ᶜ4 to 6, Plato appears to take it for granted that the slave boy's perplexity will naturally be succeeded by a desire to know. He will not simply and willingly continue in his ignorance. Aristotle for his part opens his *Metaphysics* with the claim that "All men by nature desire to know," and he goes on to indicate how we know this.[88]

On the matter of solving Meno's dilemma (which Aristotle calls an ἀπορήμα), Aristotle's solution may be characterized in either of two ways. First, he may be taken to be challenging the material truth of the first hypothetical in the major premiss, that is, if X knows what Y is, he does not need to seek or to learn what Y is. He distinguishes among several different senses of "know," to the effect that X might know what Y is universally, by the knowledge proper to it, and actually. If X has actual knowledge of a particular Y, and thus knows that Y falls under the universal, then indeed X cannot learn it again in any meaningful sense of "learn." It might be possible for X to "relearn" what Y is, in the sense of ἀνάμνησις spelled out by Aristotle in *De Memoria*, but this is not what Plato meant by ἀνάμνησις. On the other hand, if X knows the universal and potentially therefore the particular Y, he can still be said to be able to go on and learn. Thus the consequent in the major premiss of the dilemma does not follow from the antecedent. How did X learn what the universal is? This is not, for Aristotle, properly an instance of learning, but rather is achieved through the process of ἐπαγωγή. This

---

[88] *Met. A* 980ᵃ1: Πάντες ἄνθρωποι τοῦ εἰδέναι ὀρέγονται φύσει (translation by Ross).

latter process differs from Plato's account in that ἐπαγωγή does not occur in some previous incarnation of the soul, but is what all persons endowed with the proper human quantum of perception and memory can achieve early in and throughout their lifetime.

The second way of describing Aristotle's rebuttal of the dilemma is as a challenge to the material truth of the minor premiss, that is, that either X knows what Y is or she does not. The use of "knows" here again is ambiguous as between Aristotle's several senses; and these different senses are not contraries, in the sense that X cannot logically be said to know in the different senses at the same time and about the same object of knowledge. Therefore the alternatives contained in the minor premiss are not exhaustive. As a result Aristotle escapes through the horns of the dilemma.

To Aristotle's way of thinking, Plato's answer to the eristical argument is not telling. The theory of ἀνάμνησις, if interpreted literally, would require that X have all sorts of knowledge about the universal and the particular Ys falling under it. This move is illicit, because it oversimplies what it means to know and conflates the different sorts of states by the possession of which a person is said to know. Is Aristotle's criticism fair? In so far as Plato's doctrine of ἀνάμνησις is understood in the sense of the first account given above, where the learner may be said to know in the strongest and complete sense to possess ἐπιστήμη, as Aristotle uses that term in the *Posterior Analytics,* then Aristotle's judgment seems right on the mark. Plato has failed to deal with the dilemma raised in the *Meno,* and resorts to declaring that both teaching and learning are otiose concepts, because the learner already possesses within himself that which can be learned as learned already. The teacher becomes, on this account, an intellectual obstetrician (and, if we add in Socrates's irony, teachers are qualified for this role because of their own lack of original ideas). The learner need not be shown anything. If, however, ἀνάμνησις is seen in the light of Plato's account of how learners possess opinions only and the process of ἀνάμνησις has as its goal the securing of those opinions by the learner's coming to grasp the αἰτία, then Aristotle's criticism is rather wide of the target. He would not be alone in this, for the received interpretation of the *Meno* concentrates on the first account of ἀνάμνησις and tends to ignore the second. Vlastos's article and to a lesser extent Crombie's commentary are the exceptions to this.

Whichever construction is placed on Plato's doctrine, the implications for teaching will differ widely from what Aristotle theorizes in the *Posterior Analytics*, both about the conditions of knowledge and the means by which a teacher transmits such knowledge. For Plato (and this generalization is based on what is said in the *Meno*, and not in the other parts of his corpus), teaching is conducted with a view to what the learner in some sense already knows or opines. For Aristotle, teaching will be demonstration, with the learner busy primarily in absorbing information from the teacher. Although the learner may be presumed to have previous knowledge, the explanation of how this arises by ἐπαγωγή and through the faculty of νοῦς has nothing to do with the divine allotment of those opinions among the souls of humans, nor with the eliciting of the learner's opinions and the confirming or confounding of them through cross-examination.

CHAPTER FIVE

The Syllogism and
the *Petitio Principii*

One argument about the function and value of the syllogism, with which all modern students of traditional logic are familiar, is that syllogistic reasoning embodies a fallacy.[1] Such reasoning has a universal proposition as its major premiss and that premiss, in some sense, without going further, already contains the conclusion purportedly derived from the conjunction of it and the minor premiss. Thus, the syllogism is inherently guilty of the fallacy of *petitio principii*. There is some irony in this, for we owe the earliest systematic description of this type of fallacy to Aristotle himself.[2]

This argument is of ancient lineage, though most often we come across it in one of its modern revivals during controversies among

---

[1]   This charge is usually brought against syllogisms consisting of categorical propositions, such as Aristotle recognized. The so-called hypothetical and disjunctive syllogisms, developed and formalized by Aristotle's successors, the Peripatetics as they were known to ancient commentators, were also condemned for fallaciousness, but this will not be touched on in the discussion which follows.

[2]   See *Top.* 162^{b}34; *An. Pr.* 64^{b}50; and his comments on circular demonstration in *An. Post.* 72^{b}33–73^{a}5. In general, see Jonathan Lear, *Aristotle and Logical Theory* (Cambridge: Cambridge University Press, 1980), pp. 76–90 and John Woods and Douglas Walton, "The Petitio: Aristotle's Five Ways" (1982) 12 Canadian Journal of Philosophy 77–100.

British logicians in the nineteenth century. Sextus Empiricus, who flourished at the beginning of the third century A.D., in the course of dealing with what he calls certain inconclusive (ἀσύνακτος) arguments put forth by the Stoics and Peripatetics, points out a vicious circle in the following argument pattern: "Every man is an animal; Socrates is a man; therefore, Socrates is an animal."[3] The major premiss in the foregoing argument is, according to Sextus, established (βεβαιέται) by induction (ἐπαγωγή) from particular instances (κατὰ μέρος). If those instances include Socrates, then the conclusion has already been noted and used in establishing the major. The attempt thereafter to prove the conclusion by deduction is therefore redundant.[4] If the particulars surveyed did not include Socrates, then the induction, being incomplete, might still be overturned should it happen that Socrates, for instance, proves not to be an animal. The first possibility, wherein Socrates is among the instances grounding the induction, gives rise to the claim that using the syllogism is a trivial form of reasoning, for it has no probative value. This is because to syllogize is invariably to commit the fallacy described in standard textbooks in similar form to the following:

> If one assumes as a premiss for an argument the very conclusion one intends to prove, the fallacy committed is that of *petitio principii*, or begging the question.[5]

Sextus's charge was repeated from time to time, and again was raised to prominence in the writings of certain British logicians

---

3   Sextus Empiricus, *Outlines of Pyrrhonism*, trans. R. G. Bury, Loeb Classical Library (London: William Heinemann, 1933; Cambridge, Mass.: Harvard University Press, 1933; reprinted 1967), 2: 195–96. This work is hereafter referred to as Sextus, *Pyrrh.*

4   Sextus, *Pyrrh.*, 2: 65.

5   Irving M. Copi, *Introduction to Logic*, 6th ed. (New York: Macmillan, 1982), p. 107. As stated in a later edition of this text, a *"petitio principii* is always valid— but always worthless, too." See Irving M. Copi and Carl Cohen, *Introduction to Logic*, 8th ed. (New York: Macmillan, 1990), p. 102.

preceding Mill.[6] Whately, for one, thought he had provided a defence to the charge. It is Mill who formulates the issue afresh and attempts to settle it once and for all by showing how the territory of deductive logic, which he argues is coterminous with syllogism, fits into the general landscape of human reasoning.

This chapter combines three tasks. First, I shall review the allegation of *petitio principii* as it is understood and represented by Mill. Then I shall examine his views on what role the syllogism, and deductive procedures in general, play. On his account, they turn out to have fruitful applications not only in science, but in such fields as theology and jurisprudence as well. In the third and concluding part of this chapter I shall compare Mill's views with what Aristotle himself wrote about the purpose of demonstration through the construction and use of syllogisms.

I can state a preview of what that comparison yields. At the end of this chapter several arguments are advanced which depend for their substantiation on the earlier, expository parts of this chapter and on what has already been observed about Aristotle's formal and material logic in previous chapters. The attempt to impugn the syllogism as being, by its very nature, fallacious, only makes sense if it is supposed that the syllogism is fundamentally a method of inquiry or investigation, the success of which is to be judged by its ability to yield new discoveries. From our reading of the *Analytics* and the other parts of Aristotle's logical corpus, we may very well doubt whether the uniform purpose of the syllogism, in Aristotle's system, is to make possible the finding of wholly new knowledge embodied in the conclusion on the basis of what is already known (contained in the premises). The flaw in Mill's argument is that Aristotle sees in syllogistic reasoning a host of different purposes, not all of which are related to Mill's ideas of, and hopes for, scientific

---

6   Mill draws up his conclusions in opposition to the opinions of Richard Whately, whose *Elements of Logic* first appeared in 1826. Whately, in turn, was answering the charges of George Campbell, an eighteenth-century associate of Thomas Reid's Common Sense school: see W. R. Sorley, *A History of British Philosophy to 1900* (Cambridge: Cambridge University Press, 1920, reprinted in paperback, 1965), p. 203, and also John Passmore, *A Hundred Years of Philosophy*, 2nd ed. (Harmondsworth: Penguin Books, 1968), p. 21.

methods. The charge of *petitio*, in Mill's formulation, also ignores the context in which the formal description of the syllogism was first developed. Aristotle does not find his data by introspectively examining the contents of his own mental processes.

Secondly, the allegation of *petitio* rests on an assumption that the syllogism may reasonably be exemplified in the form stated by Sextus, and taken over by Mill, so that the criticisms made about it will apply in equal measure to all types and forms of syllogisms. In Sextus's historical treatise, we will recall, the minor premiss and the conclusion of the sample syllogism are each singular propositions, in which the subject is a substance (according to Aristotle's doctrine of categories). It will be questioned at the end of this chapter whether the adoption of this example does not further the critics' cause at the expense of distorting the strictures laid down by the father of the original system.

Mill's statement of the problem and his suggested resolution

It is particularly interesting to examine Mill's restatement of the traditional charge levelled against the syllogism, because it receives its classic though sometimes misread elaboration in the temperate and generally lucid *System of Logic*.[7] We know that Mill's own

---

7   John Stuart Mill, *A System of Logic, Ratiocinative and Inductive; Being a Connected View of the Principles of Evidence and the Methods of Scientific Investigation*, 8th ed. (London: Longmans, Green and Co., 1906, reprinted 1967), hereafter referred to as simply *Logic*. The first edition was published in 1843. The adjective "temperate" is applied because of such treatments of the issue of the value of syllogism as that of F. H. Bradley in *The Principles of Logic*, 2nd ed., 2 vols. (Oxford: Oxford University Press, 1922, reprinted 1928), 1: II, I, §§1–8, where Bradley acerbically commented that: "the syllogism itself, like the major premise is a mere superstition"; "the syllogism is a chimaera"; and "[w]e can not for ever with eyes fast closed swallow down the mass of orthodox rubbish in which that truth has wrapped itself up." These paragraphs are reprinted in Irving M. Copi and James A. Gould (eds.), *Readings on Logic*, 2nd ed. (New York: Macmillan, 1972), pp. 112–15. Mill's discussion of the traditional critique of syllogistic reasoning has not always been construed in the even-handed way he approached it: see Passmore, *supra* n. 6, p. 21, where it is noted:

Mill's attitude to syllogism is often misunderstood; he is read as being,

precocious education included the Organon as a staple. He attributes great value to his early training in it and has a high opinion of how it can discipline the thought of every normal mind.[8] In the *Logic* he puts the proper use of deductive reasoning, as he conceives it, into perspective alongside the scientific methods of inductive reasoning. As is well known Mill reaches the conclusion that induction is the sole form of real inference, while deduction, including syllogistic reasoning, is only apparent inference. Though he does not think it possible to exonerate syllogism from the charge of *petitio*, Mill finds a useful place for it among the instruments of the scientist's labours and in the intellectual endeavours of other types of reasoners. Before going into that topic we ought to trace his statement of the traditional criticism.

His discussion of deductive reasoning (or "ratiocination," in his vocabulary) follows immediately after the presentation of what we

---

like Locke, an unsparing critic of the traditional logic. This is not at all the case; indeed, he is always ready to defend formal logic against those empiricists who condemn it out of hand as a "medieval rigmarole."

[8]   See John Stuart Mill, *Autobiography* (New York: New American Library, 1964), pp. 35–36:

From about the age of twelve, I entered into another and more advanced stage in my course of instruction, in which the main object was no longer the aids and appliances of thought, but the thoughts themselves. This commenced with logic, in which I began with the *Organon*, and read it to the *Analytics* inclusive, but profited little by the *Posterior Analytics*, which belong to a branch of speculation I was not yet ripe for . . . It was his [James Mill's] invariable practice, whatever studies he exacted from me, to make me as far as possible understand and feel the utility of them; and this he deemed peculiarly fitting in the case of the syllogistic logic, the usefulness of which had been impugned by so many writers of authority . . . My own consciousness and experience ultimately led me to appreciate quite as highly as he did the value of an early practical familiarity with the school logic. I know of nothing, in my education, to which I think myself more indebted for whhatever capacity of thinking I have attained . . . I am persuaded that nothing, in modern education, tends so much, when properly used, to form exact thinkers, who attach a precise meaning to words and propositions, and are not imposed on by vague, loose, or ambigous terms.

would call his theory of language and meaning. He deals first of all in the *Logic* with the question of how words have meaning, in both their referential and descriptive uses.[9] He then goes on to explain how "names," which is his nearly all-embracing category for meaningful words, are arranged in sentences to form different types of propositions that also mean something.[10] This is all done to prepare the reader for grasping the nature of valid reasoning, which is accomplished through chains or series of propositions.[11] With such a background, in which language has been subjected to an atomistic analysis, with sentences the molecules, do we arrive at Mill's discussion of the syllogism, and of logic in general, which he defines as:

> . . . the science of the operations of the understanding which are subservient to the estimation of evidence: both the process itself of advancing from known truths to unknown, and all other intellectual operations in so far as auxiliary to this.[12]

He gives an account of the elements of a syllogism, and of the logical maxim, of medieval origin, which had traditionally been supposed to underlie the syllogistic system, namely the *dictum de*

---

[9]   *Logic*, I, ii, and iii. I shall not here recount his important and influential discussion of the denotative and connotative meanings of names.

[10]   *Logic*, I, iv–vi.

[11]   This progression from simple words to complex sentences is scrutinized in Gilbert Ryle, "The Theory of Meaning" in C. A. Mace (ed.), *British Philosophy in the Mid-Century*, 2nd ed. (London: George Allen and Unwin, 1966), pp. 239–64. Ryle notes at p. 249 that:

> Word-meanings do not stand to sentence-meanings as atoms to molecules or as letters of the alphabet to the spellings of words, but more nearly as the tennis-racket to the strokes which are or may be made with it.

and at p. 241:

> In particular, Mill's theory of meaning set the questions, and in large measure, determined their answers for thinkers as different as Brentano, in Austria; Meinong and Husserl, who were pupils of Brentano; Bradley, Jevons, Venn, Frege, Peirce, Moore and Russell.

[12]   *Logic*, "Introduction," pp. 6–7.

omni et nullo.[13] Mill disputes the applicability of this maxim, on the ground that it relies for its force upon an outmoded metaphysical theory (and, we might add for Mill, an outmoded theory of language, since he has a broad conception of the scope of metaphysics).[14] In its place, he coins and substitutes a different Latin maxim, *nota notae est nota rei ipsius.*[15] He argues that this is a superior principle by which to explain the validity of that which follows from universal proposition.[16] He addresses next the much agitated question of the

---

[13]   That is, whatever may be affirmed of a whole may be affirmed of every part of the whole. The derivation of this maxim and the one favoured by Mill are discussed in William Kneale and Martha Kneale, *The Development of Logic* (Oxford: Clarendon Press, 1962), pp. 79 and 376.

[14]   *Logic*, II, ii, §2, pp. 114–15. The theory which has been discarded (according to Mill) is the realist position on the issue of universals, whereby genera and species and other classificatory names were each thought to denote a kind of entity.

[15]   *Logic*, II, ii, §4, pp. 118–19. That is, whatever has any mark, has that mark of which it is a mark, or as expressed in Kneale and Kneale, *supra* n. 13, p. 79: "what qualifies an attribute qualifies a thing possessing it."

[16]   Mill's final position on the relative value of these two competing maxims is shown in a footnote in the *Logic* (which means, as usual, he is thereby answering a query of Alexander Bain's), which reads:

> I conclude, therefore, that both forms have their value, and their place in Logic. The *dictum de omni* should be retained as the fundamental axiom of the logic of mere consistency, often called Formal Logic; . . . But the other is the proper axiom for the logic of the pursuit of truth by way of Deduction; and the recognition of it can alone show how it is possible that deductive reasoning can be the road to truth.

From the *Logic*, II, ii, 4, p. 119. This is a good example of Mill's predilection for conserving traditional concepts and distinctions, and seeing some utility in them even though he wishes to replace or improve them by his own account. No attempt will be made here to deal with the distinction between two rival views of the proposition, each of which, according to Anschutz, Mill embraces at different points in the *Logic*. On Anschutz's account, the class view of predication would be favoured by those who condemn the syllogism, while the attributive view would be favoured by those who defend the syllogism. Mill's maxim, *nota notae*, would be compatible with the attributive view, but his description of the function and value of the syllogism is couched in terms of the class view. Anschutz's explanation for this is: ". . . as on many other occasions, Mill wants to have it both ways." See R. P. Anschutz, "The Logic of J. S. Mill," (1949) 58 Mind 217–305, reprinted in *Mill: A Collection of Critical*

function of the syllogism.

He begins by canvassing those opinions that he has inherited from his predecessors. Mill has a deep-seated respect for traditional theories in logic. From his vantage point the opinions about the nature of the fallacy of *petitio*, if not in its application to the syllogism, are uncontroverted:

> We have now to inquire whether the syllogistic process, that of reasoning from generals to particulars, is, or is not, a process of inference; a process from the known to the unknown; a means of coming to a knowledge of something which we did not know before.
>
> Logicians have been remarkably unanimous in their mode of answering this question. It is universally allowed that a syllogism is vicious if there be anything more in the conclusion than was assumed in the premises.[17]

Mill confesses that he thinks there is a *petitio* inherently involved in every syllogism, viewed as an argument meant to prove the truth of the conclusion. He largely follows Sextus's explanation of how the fallacy is committed, though he does not invoke his name. For Mill, this doctrine is "irrefragable."[18]

Mill expressly rejects, however, the consequences of the *petitio* that is assumed by some critics, namely that of the "uselessness and frivolity" of syllogistic theory itself.[19] Mill claims to discern a serious function of the syllogism that has been overlooked by both the friends and the critics of the syllogism. This useful function is described below, after a discussion of why syllogism is only apparent inference.

For his target Mill uses the same form of argument used by

Essays, ed. J. B. Schneewind (Garden City, N.Y.: Anchor Books, 1968), pp. 46–83, p. 76. In the discussion below, we shall focus on Mill's treatment of the syllogism as if he adhered consistently throughout to the class view, as Anschutz expresses it. My topic will not be Mill's consistency on this point, but rather some assumptions he employs.

[17]   *Logic*, II, iii, §1, p. 120.

[18]   *Ibid.*

[19]   *Ibid.*

Sextus, and as used by numerous writers since Mill. In it, the minor premiss is the singular proposition, "Socrates is a man."[20] On this point Mill has made a significant departure from Aristotle's system as outlined in the *Analytics*. All syllogisms, for Aristotle, are composed of a universal proposition as the major, and either a universal or a particular proposition as the minor and the conclusion. All demonstrative syllogisms are, of course, made up of universal propositions only. In no case will the singular proposition be an element of a syllogism. This is stated expressly, and not just implied by Aristotle. The reason for this goes to the root of what syllogistic reasoning is supposed to accomplish, from Aristotle's point of view. We will return to this point in the third part of this chapter. Suffice it to say, Mill was not oblivious to the fact that his chosen example, the one by which he claims to show the empty pretensions of syllogism in the search for truth, was omitted from the class of valid forms of reasoning. Mill skirts the issue by writing that:

> . . . no place is assigned to *singular* propositions; not, of course, because such propositions are not used in ratiocination, but because, their predicate being affirmed or denied of the whole of the subject, they are ranked, for the purposes of the syllogism, with universal propositions.[21]

---

[20] To repeat what was previously summarized in greater detail in Chapter Two, Aristotle draws a distinction among the following types of propositions, according to what subsequent commentators have called the "quantity" of the proposition:
  Mortal belongs to every man—universal
  Rational belongs to some animals—particular
  White belongs to Socrates—singular.
  Mill also uses a syllogism involving the Duke of Wellington, for the sake of contemporaneity. The Duke did not die until the *Logic* had passed into its third edition.

[21] *Logic*, II, ii, §1, p. 109. This view is evidently not just a whim of Mill's: see P. F. Strawson, *Introduction to Logical Theory* (London: Methuen, 1952, reprinted as a University Paperback, 1971), p. 180:
  . . . when presented with a singular categorical statement such as one made with the words "Caesar is dead", which would now be classified as a singular predicative or class-membership statement, traditional logicians assigned it to the A form.

This is a rather bizarre justification, for it is difficult to see how "man" is applicable to every part of Socrates in the same way that predicate applies to every man who ever lived or will live. Perhaps the predicate "mortal" makes more sense in this regard; but we should certainly say that neither Socrates's arm nor leg nor any other part of him is itself a man. Nevertheless, it is important to Mill that such singular propositions should be allowed, for it facilitates the argument about *petitio*. He does not admit this, of course, nor has any commentator detected such a covert purpose in his choice of example. It does strain our credulity, after following Aristotle's careful dissection of the forms of argument, to hear that the syllogism cited by Sextus is, for Mill, a syllogism in Barbara.

Mill follows Sextus in another way. He claims that the universal proposition, "All men are mortal," is drawn on the basis of particular observations. This process of repeatedly observing different instances of the mortality of individual men and thereupon framing the generalization that every man who ever lived or who will live in the future is mortal is, for Mill, the process of induction. To it belongs the honour of being called real inference. The statement of such an inference in a universal proposition is characterized by him as follows:

> We then, by that valuable contrivance of language which enables us to speak of many as if they were one, record all that we have observed, together with all that we infer from our observations, in one concise expression; and have thus only one proposition instead of an endless number, to remember or to communicate.[22]

Induction is then the "inferring" part of the "process of philosophising," and the construction of general propositions is the "recording" or "registering" part of that same process.[23]

It is not necessary for the process of inferring that the observations

---

[22]   *Logic*, II, iii, §3, p. 122.

[23]   *Ibid.* The activity of philosophy is here referred to by Mill in its archaic sense as comprehending a broad range of different sciences and arts. See Ryle, *supra* n. 11, pp. 257–59.

of particulars be collected and expressed in a general proposition, for Mill also allows that reasoning can proceed "from particulars to particulars without passing through generals."[24] Children and brute animals, claims Mill, reason this way; on further reflection, he contends that some very competent adults do this in their ordinary lives as well. The formation and expression of sound judgment and what is called common sense depend on a person's relative skill in doing this.[25] This skill so impresses Mill that, after adducing numerous examples, he goes on to say that "all inference is from particulars to particulars."[26] This is apparently inconsistent with his earlier claim in the *Logic* that all real inference is induction, understood as the passage of the mind from particulars to generals. Notwithstanding this discrepancy, the universal propositions employed as major premises in syllogisms perform two distinct functions, one related to what has already been experienced and the other related to future experience. They are the registers of inferences already made (and in this way are an aid to memory), and secondly, they are "short formulae" for making further inferences. The conclusion reached by virtue of syllogistic reasoning is:

> . . . not an inference drawn *from* the formula, but an inference drawn *according* to the formula; the real logical antecedent or

---

[24] *Logic*, II, iii, §3, p. 123.

[25] *Ibid.*, pp. 124–25. This facility might be compared with Aristotle's description of quickness of wit (ἀγχίνοια), which is discussed in *An. Post.* A 34. Aristotle says it is the flair for hitting upon the correct middle term, and hence the explanation, with no apparent hesitation. He uses the example of inferring that the moon's brightness on one side is explained by that side's facing the sun, the source of the reflected light. The quick-witted person passes from the major term, "bright side facing the sun," and the minor term, "moon," to a recognition of why the moon's bright side is always turned towards the sun, without having to trace laboriously through the middle term in this syllogism. This process differs from that described by Mill, who focuses his remarks on the dispensability of the process of inferring particulars from generals; from the fact that A happened once, to the realization that A will recur, all other circumstances being the same. Mill and Aristotle are in agreement that different degrees of human reasoning abilities will allow the standard process of inference, as each views it, to be abridged by some exceptional minds.

[26] *Logic*, II, iii, §4, p. 126.

premise being the particular facts from which the general proposition was collected by induction.[27]

The rules of valid inference that were described by Aristotle and his school and that are embodied in the valid figures and moods of the syllogism become, on this view, a "set of precautions" to ensure that we read correctly the record of our past inductions.[28] As Mill elsewhere expresses this same point, these rules form the "indispensable collateral security" of the correctness of our generalizations. They are also the "system of securities for the correctness of the application" of formulae.[29]

The starting points of deductive reasoning are not always, despite Mill's empirical bent, framed from direct experience. Mill considers also, when discussing forms of deduction, the case where the premisses of a syllogism are grounded not on observation, but on authority. The rules of syllogism, in this context, become the

---

[27]   *Ibid.*

[28]   *Ibid.*, p. 127. The language used by Mill, namely that a collection of facts and the framing of a general proposition "warrant" a "given inference," has been likened to the relatively modern conception of formal logic as a system of "inference licences" or "inference tickets." See Gilbert Ryle, *The Concept of Mind* (Harmondsworth: Penguin Books, 1963), p. 288: ". . . we should have thought of the rules of logic rather as licences to make inferences than as licences to concur in them."

[29]   *Logic*, II, iii, §5, pp. 129, 131. No commentator appears to have remarked on the striking fact of Mill's use of legal terminology in describing the use of the rules of traditional logic. For example, the phrase "collateral security" is common coin in credit transactions. It is created by an agreement or assurance made by the debtor that is independent of and subordinate to the principal security. Thus a person may borrow money against the mortgage of her land and provide collateral security in, for instance, the form of a pledge of shares of company stock. Mill sprinkles different metaphors and analogies throughout the *Logic*, II, iii, §§4–6, and it is sometimes difficult to ascertain whether or not they are just intended to be elegant variations on the same theme. The idea that one's own deductive inferences are warranted by general propositions discovered by induction and supported by evidence is certainly different from the suggestion that the rules of logic are a secondary form of assurance because certain rights may be enforced by one person against another. Mill's language in this regard may be picturesque, but it hardly bears analysis.

guarantee of the correctness of the interpretation derived from the given starting points. In fact, he generalizes and says that "interpretation" may be the best omnibus term for describing the various functions of syllogism.[30] Whether the data to be dealt with are observations or authoritative pronouncements, syllogistic reasoning affords the advantage that, by using it, we are not likely to stray from the record of inferences made in the past, or from the received authority, in making our current or future inferences. In this sense, the syllogism is a mode of verifying an argument that begins with the unknown and terminates in a conclusion about the unknown.[31]

To be sure, there are some disadvantages and drawbacks attendant upon the use of syllogistic reasoning. It is not infallible. First in importance among these is that, if the inference is based on an insufficient sampling, the resulting generalization will obscure the true nature of the evidence grounding the inference and it will tend to promote and perpetuate wrong attributions. But this possibility of error, Mill thinks, is a "small set-off against the immense benefits of general language."[32]

The account above conveys the gist of Mill's argument that in some sense the major premiss contains already that which is purported to be proved in the conclusion, so that syllogistic reasoning cannot be a legitimate tool for discovery when used by the scientific inquirer. On the other hand, Mill, who is so averse to throwing out inherited intellectual baggage, salvages the syllogism for another purpose. He sees it as useful, not for inferring new things and making discoveries, but for providing assurance to the reasoner that he is making proper deductions from what is already known and on the table, so to speak. It "secures" the process of real inference. Syllogism is an ancilla to inference, but is no substitute for it.

---

[30] *Logic*, II, iii, §4, p. 127.
[31] *Logic*, II, iii, §5, p. 130.
[32] *Ibid.*, p. 131.

Applicability of Mill's arguments to Aristotle's syllogistic system

In the final section of this chapter, we shall examine the cogency of Mill's account, in particular with a view to determining whether it does justice to Aristotle's original theory. We shall see that Mill differs fundamentally from Aristotle on several key matters, including the following: the placement of the boundaries of the province of logic (to use one of Mill's favourite figures of speech), the original purpose and form of syllogistic reasoning, and the role of induction. The conclusion reached is that, in general, Mill presents an oversimplified version of the theory of syllogism and predicates his destructive criticism upon assumptions that do not reflect what Aristotle goes on about in the *Analytics*. These assumptions are not peculiar to Mill, but are shared by other critics who see a *petitio* in the syllogism.

A passage from the *Prior Analytics A* 4 adorns the beginning of Book II of the *Logic* as an epigraph.[33] The opening paragraphs to Book II imply that, just as syllogism is broader than and comprehends demonstration, so may the topic of deduction be subsumed under his account of inference. At the bottom of this account is his theory of the meaning of propositions; and in this regard his theory bears some resemblances to Aristotle's writings on the same matter. In his discussion of the denotation and connotation of words Mill differs from the Aristotelian tradition, though he adopts some familiar principles from it.[34] Real propositions, which are about the attributes of things, and verbal propositions, which give, *inter alia*, the definition of a word, compose the entire set of meaningful propositions. Mill's theory of the import of propositions recognizes the distinction between subject and attribute, and accounts for all assertions by representing them as either the

---

[33]   *An. Pr.* 25^{b}26–31.

[34]   For example, Mill adheres to such views as that: the standard form of proposition comprises a subject and a predicate (though he adds the copula as an essential element as well), the meaning of a word or expression ("many-worded name") is to be sought in what it names, and the meaning of a proposition will be the composite of the individual meanings of its elements.

ascription of an attribute to a subJect, or of one attribute to another.[35] None of Mill's theorizing forms a radical shift away from hundreds of years of philosophizing that is largely rooted in some doctrines regarding language and logical analysis spelled out first by Plato and Aristotle.

The situation is different with Mill's description of the uses of reasoning and, in particular, the prescribed ends of a deductive system of logic.[36] What is both remarkable for its narrowness and the cause of some fundamental misconstructions is how Mill, and how other logicians before and after him, interpret the purpose of the syllogism in Aristotle's account.[37] The syllogism is useless, claim the critics, for the job of discovering new knowledge because the conclusion is always contained in the major premiss. What is purportedly proved is already assumed, tacitly at least, by the general form of the major.

On Mill's account the real inference takes place in the drawing of the universal proposition (or the particular conclusion, depending on which part of the *Logic* we emphasize) out of the observed particulars. Having agreed with the critics thus far, and held that a *petitio* is inherent in the very form of the syllogism, Mill is reduced to finding some compensatory advantages in the use of syllogism, that save it from ridicule as a frivolous mental exercise that is without probative value and therefore logically uninteresting.

It should be noted that the argument in favour of the *petitio* rests on the assumption that the syllogism lays serious claim to being a means of scientific investigation. Mill concentrates his energy on showing the only department of the general activity of reasoning

---

[35]   And hence his taking issue with the *dictum de omni*, which supposes that predication is a matter of class inclusion rather than attribution: see *supra* n. 16.

[36]   The word "prescribed" as used here may not be entirely accurate, since it is at least arguable that Mill is only documenting what actually takes place. Any dispute over this would have to take up the issue of how much of Mill's representation of psychological experience in the *Logic* describes armchair theorizing.

[37]   For example, see Bradley, *The Principles of Logic*, as excerpted in Copi and Gould (eds.), *supra* n. 7, p. 113: "It sins against the third characteristic of inference, for it does not really give us any new information."

which can execute such an office is induction. Only induction leads to discoveries. Hence only it is inference. He devotes the preponderance of his discussion in the *Logic* to the canons which will guide such inference. By contrast, he resurrects ratiocination, or syllogism, as a body of rules for regulating the use of inductions already made and memorialized.

The problem with Mill's outlook is that he omits from his characterization of the function of syllogism some very significant features. These are not buried in Aristotle's work, but rather are prominently displayed therein. They are not incidental features, but are crucial for understanding what syllogism, and particularly demonstration, can be used for.

If we were to read Mill or some of his predecessors without first having looked at Aristotle's Organon, we would probably glean the impression that there was only one type of syllogism in Aristotle's logic, and its form could be adequately exemplified by the pattern evident in the piece of reasoning invoked and commented on by both Sextus and Mill, namely the deduction about the individual Socrates. Both of these impressions would be wrong. By relying on them we would have very little idea of the power and subtlety of Aristotle's actual account. He is very perceptive about the varieties of purposes and settings in human conversation, especially intellectual controversy and discourse (for it is in this area of human communication that he wants to systematize what can be said, what verbal moves can be made, and what consequences flow therefrom). The arguments employed in each type of intellectual exchange are not uniform, for they depend for their starting points and structure on the aims of the participants (that is, what goal they are striving for) and the types of things they are talking about and whether these can be known more or less certainly. The critics of syllogistic theory, who come down in favour of the fallacy of *petitio*, tend not to recognize in their assessments the multifarious types of discourse that may be cast in a syllogistic mould, as detailed by Aristotle. Instead they go on as if all syllogistic reasoning involves one type of discourse only. The single function imputed by such writers to syllogism is that of scientific inquiry as carried on by the researcher striving for originality. The single type of discourse is, on Mill's account at least, a sort of internal monologue conducted by the researcher as he works at the frontiers of established knowledge. There are no distinctions drawn between, for example, a dialectical and a demonstrative syllogism. By tailoring their arguments around one specimen syllogism, which itself has no standing in Aristotle's account, those critics seek to topple the whole theory. They fail to realize that they have destroyed a target fabricated out of whole cloth, in so far as they ignore the fine distinctions made by Aristotle in the *Analytics* and related by him to the everyday varieties of human discourse. Aristotle does not include among the types of syllogism a heuristic kind (if we call by that factitious term a syllogism structured so as to allow the reasoner to pass from what is known by him to what was hitherto known by nobody). The demonstrative syllogism seems closest in spirit to such a putative kind. Yet it is not designed for proof in the sense of revealing new discoveries, but proof and revelation in a didactic sense, whereby the learner grasps something he did not grasp before. This misapprehension of Aristotle's purpose is caused, in part, by the ambiguity in such key logical terms as "proof," "disclosure," and "discovery." This ambiguity and its meaning for both logic and the logic of teaching will form a topic for discussion in Chapter Six.

Demonstration by means of the apodeictic syllogism is discussed, as we have seen, in the context of how some things are taught and learned. Aristotle is preoccupied in the *Posterior Analytics* with the necessary and sufficient conditions which entitle us to say that a learner has come to acquire scientific knowledge. This process is not portrayed at the level of examining the individual learner's capacity for sense impressions, and then finding another capacity for building some mental construct out of impressions that bear a similarity. Aristotle's account rests on what he takes to be the commonplace process of a teacher leading a class from what they already grasp to an understanding of the reasons why things are the way they are, according to the knowledge already achieved in the appropriate science. This model of teaching, with the teacher's resources including axioms, hypotheses, definitions and a knowledge of the explanations that will serve as appropriate middle terms in the process of demonstration, holds together the various parts of the *Posterior Analytics* and clarifies what would otherwise be fairly obscure parts of that treatise.

There is a significant difference between this pedagogical use of the syllogistic form and the method, long sought by experimenters, for guaranteeing that advances will be made in the discovery of new knowledge. It is the latter topic that dominates Mill's organization of the methods of induction. In his *Logic* he gives instructions to researchers, in what we would call the natural and social sciences, about how to arrive at sound scientific generalizations. In the *Posterior Analytics*, on the other hand, it is assumed as an essential background that such generalizations have already been found and now are available for inclusion in the course of studies in the pertinent science. There is no longer any need for a "collateral security" or "set of precautions" in respect of the learner's inferences. The task that devolves upon the teacher is distinct from that fulfilled by the working scientist. The demonstrative syllogism is an apparatus for the former, not the latter; its home is the school, not the research laboratory. Because of his views on induction, Mill is forced to reassign syllogism to a new role in the scheme of human reasoning; but this is only because he and his predecessors in the *petitio* controversy attributed a function to the traditional logic that has little in common with what Aristotle himself claims.[38] Possibly Mill and the others were misled by some of the accessions to Aristotle's system made in the Hellenistic and medieval periods. That would be important to know; but it is not properly a topic of this chapter.

---

[38]   Among Mill's commentators, the seed of this idea seems to have been noted by F. E. Sparshott, "Introduction" to *Collected Works of John Stuart Mill*, ed. J. M. Robson, 12 vols. (Toronto: University of Toronto Press, 1978), XI: *Essays on Philosophy and the Classics*, where Sparshott writes at p. xi:

> But he [Mill] shows no sign of having noted what Aristotle has to say about syllogisms in investigation. To turn from Whately to the *Posterior Analytics* is to enter a different and saner world, in which the conclusion of a scientific syllogism is not a proposition like "The Duke of Wellington is mortal" but one like "The moon suffers eclipse," and the inquiry which it concludes does not take the form of discovering classes to which its subject belongs but that of discovering causal relations in which it is involved.

Sparshott's account is acute but not impeccable: the notions of investigation and causality in the *An. Post.* must be handled cautiously and without the conditioning of subsequent philosophical discourse.

Furthermore, Aristotle's work in the *Analytics* is based on his conception of formal logic as the description of what he has distilled out of how arguments (whether contentious, conversational or rhetorical) and, the in the case of teaching, demonstrations, proceed with at least two participants, one of whom takes the lead in attacking or sustaining a set proposition. This is completely alien to the conception of logic espoused by Mill, who states:

> For to this ultimate end, naming, classification, definition, and all other operations over which logic has ever claimed jurisdiction, are essentially subsidiary. They may all be regarded as contrivances for enabling a person to know the truths which are needful to him, and to know them at the precise moment at which they are needful. Other purposes, indeed, are also served by these operations; for instance, that of imparting our knowledge to others. But, viewed with regard to this purpose, they have never been considered as within the province of the logician. The sole object of Logic is the guidance of one's own thoughts; the communication of those thoughts to others falls under the consideration of Rhetoric, in the large sense in which that art was conceived by the ancients; of the still more extensive art of Education. Logic takes cognizance of our intellectual operations, only as they conduce to our own knowledge, and to our command over that knowledge for our own uses. If there were but one rational being in the universe, that being might be a perfect logician; and the science and art of logic would be the same for that one person as for the whole human race.[39]

This passage has been quoted at length because in it Mill throws logic into relation with education. The latter remains a broadly conceived art, to Mill's mind, for it concerns at least the study and teaching of all communication. Logic in both its inductive and deductive aspects has been completely severed from the realm of teaching and learning. Logicians have no standing to judge what teachers do in tutoring students, even though such teaching involves the use of definitions, classifications, and so forth. Any discourse

---

[39]   *Logic,* "Introduction," p. 3.

presupposed by logic is the internal, mental chain of thoughts. It is for the logician to help the original thinker by developing rules that validate this process and reassure him on his progress to discovery.

Aristotle recognizes, as we have witnessed from the passages surveyed or reproduced in Chapters Two and Three, that syllogism has uses that stretch beyond the task of teaching. In addition to the apodeictic syllogism, there are the dialectical and rhetorical syllogisms. Each type is distinguishable according to the modal designation and truth value of its constituent propositions and the speaker's objective in confuting or defending a conclusion. The different effects that can be achieved by syllogism, such as establishing scientific knowledge in the learner, or being persuaded or moved by a probable conclusion, may indeed take place, on Aristotle's account, in the individual soul. But the process of syllogizing finds its original home at the level of one speaker participating in a conversation with another, with certain well understood goals in mind that determine how the process will begin, will conclude and will be judged successful.[40] The "guidance of one's

---

[40]   See *supra*, Chapter Two, pp. 42 *et seq.* One of the foremost Mill scholars grasps in outline the genesis of a syllogistic system, though he does not carry an insight he credits to Francis Bacon as far as we have pressed it here. See the following:

> Like some contemporary scholars, Bacon thought of the syllogistic logic as a development of Aristotle's attempt to regularize the sort of disputations that are recorded in Plato's dialogues. In this context, moreover, he considered that the syllogism had an intelligible function as a way of settling a difference of opinion about some propositions by discovering other propositions to which both parties could agree and from which the disputed proposition or its contradictory could be inferred. If, however, logic is regarded as a means, not of seeking agreement among disputants, but of discovering the truth about things, then it is not at all easy, he points out, to see what purpose can be served by the syllogism.

R. P. Anschutz, *The Philosophy of J. S. Mill* (Oxford: Clarendon Press, 1953), p. 125. Anschutz also records in another passage a curious observation:

> The assumption here is that it is the dialectical syllogism which is fundamental in Aristotle's logic and that the scientific syllogism was added as an afterthought. This is an assumption which was made be most seventeenth-century philosophers and it has been revived by some recent commentators on Aristotle's logic.

own thoughts" by following syllogistic patterns as if they themselves could be discovered by introspection; the prototypical argument as a discourse with oneself and not with others; and the communication of thoughts being a mere byproduct of this ability to reason to oneself; all of these foregoing assumptions lie at the foundation of Mill's view of logic. Each one represents a radical departure from Aristotle's theory and programme. For Aristotle, the possibility of logic depends on there being more than just one rational, solitary thinker in the universe.

Contrary to Mill's demarcation between what is and is not beyond the pale of the logician, Aristotle sees logic as extremely useful in the "imparting of our knowledge to others." He sees this activity as capable of being encompassed in a system, namely his recommended method of demonstration. By the time Mill wrote his *Logic* there is no longer this connection between such activities. The principality of education has seceded, or been banished, from the province of logic. There is, then, a large discrepancy between the purposes for which Aristotle organized this branch of philosophy and the purposes attributed to it by some later writers who claim to detect a fundamental flaw that vitiates what they argue the syllogism is designed for.

Those writers further cloud the issue by adopting as their specimen of syllogistic reasoning an argument that has no place in Aristotle's account in the *Analytics*. In fact he specifically rejects the argument pattern that has a singular proposition as the minor premiss. In the *Prior Analytics* he gives us the following argument: "Being eternal belongs to Aristomenes as an object of thought [διανητός]; Aristomenes as an object of thought belongs to

---

R. P. Anschutz, *supra* n. 16, p. 67n. 22. Anschutz then refers to Kapp's small text, presumably as evidence of other authorities sharing this assumption. This characterization of the theory of demonstration as an "afterthought" is an unfortunate choice of wording. Kapp, for one, argues that the *Topics* on dialectical argument was completed before the *Analytics*, but it appears not just to be chronological order that Anschutz is alluding to. What is fundamental is not the dialectical syllogism but the practice of teaching in the Academy and the exercises in disputation that were encouraged therein. This, Kapp and Ryle agree, forms the material out of which Aristotle shapes his doctrines.

Aristomenes; therefore, being eternal belongs to Aristomenes."[41] It is difficult to see the point of such an example, as it is expressed in English. The important feature that example exhibits is the singular proposition that makes up the minor. This argument pattern is not, according to Aristotle, a syllogism, though it might at first appear to be one. The confusion is caused by failing to distinguish between saying "This belongs to that" (τόδε τῷδε ὑπάρχειν) and "This belongs to all of that" (τόδε τῷδε παντὶ ὑπάρχειν). The engine powering Aristotle's interest in syllogism is how classes of things that exist in nature relate to one another and how classificatory statements about those things disclose the reasons why of phenomena. The utterance of an essential predication is always a classificatory act. The syllogism depends for its force as an implement for achieving either conviction or scientific knowledge upon what may be said about Socrates *qua* Greek, or *qua* philosopher, or *qua* man and not *qua* an individual man. What Aristotle calls substances have no place in the propositions arranged into valid figures and moods, because they cannot be predicated of anything. He is interested in the different kinds of things that can, with increasing generality and extension, be predicated of classes of substances and those predications in turn. In the *Logic*, as we have noticed above, Mill recognizes that his standard example does not fit into any of the valid figures in the traditional system. He nevertheless ignores the lesson drawn by Aristotle that syllogism is based on what can be said of all of the things of a given sort, and demonstration is based on what can be said of them essentially.

Why is this point important to Mill? Why is he not content to use as his example one drawn from the traditional scheme? Its importance lies in the argument that a universal proposition is a mere composite of elements, and that it can be analyzed into a string of singular propositions. This is a cardinal feature of the *petitio* argument. Therefore Mill must introduce as his target a syllogism containing a singular proposition in the conclusion. Let us take a different specimen, say the following syllogism in Darii in the first figure:

---

41   *An. Pr.* 47[b]20 *et seq.*

All Greeks are mortal
Some kings are Greeks
Some kings are mortal.

On Mill's account, the major premiss represents an inference from the collocation of such propositions as Socrates is mortal, Plato is mortal, Speusippus is mortal, and so on indefinitely. Such a survey would be conducted solely on the basis of whether the individual in question is a Greek or not, however that nationality might be defined (for example, maybe exclusively, as "non-barbarian"). Some rulers, past or present, such as Philip or Lycurgus, might be included; but if so, it would be because they are Greeks, and not because they are kings. The universal proposition "All Greeks are mortal" is not formed with the criterion of political status or what we would call occupation in mind. It is not framed as a convenient way of noting and remembering (by a "contrivance of language") that all cobblers are mortal, all helots are mortal, all kings are mortal, and so forth, in so far as those cobblers, helots and kings are Greek. It is a composite of statements about individuals and not classes of individuals.[42] Therefore, the general proposition, not being formulated as an induction of classes of things, cannot be broken down into such classes. At least, it cannot be so broken down and still lend support to the *petitio* argument. That argument maintains that the truth of the conclusion has already been used to establish the truth (or, in Mill's system, the inference) of the major premiss. Yet the universal proposition and the particular proposition, in so far as they must be used as the minor premiss in a syllogism, bear a conspicuously different relationship to the major than does the singular proposition used in the role of the minor. Mill's argument about the inherent

---

[42] See, in support of this interpretation, Alan Ryan, *J. S. Mill* (London: Routledge and Kegan Paul, 1974), p. 72:

   . . . one needs to make clear an epistemological assumption which remains covert in Mill's own account. Mill thought that the world consisted of particular facts, particular states of affairs only. He was, like Locke, an atomist; everything that exists is particular . . . Hence the *facts* to which the general statement has to correspond are singular facts.

viciousness of the syllogism is much more plausible when the singular proposition is permitted; when it is not permitted into the system, it loses force. If we confine the permissible premiss-pairs to a combination of universal-particular or universal-universal, Mill's analytical and inductive account goes drastically awry. The conclusion is no longer somehow packed into the major premiss, so that in uttering the conclusion the reasoner is not merely repeating himself. The form of syllogism used by both Mill and Sextus becomes a stalking horse for their strategic purposes, but it is, unfortunately, in the nature of a chimera.

It is enlightening to try out Mill's argument about *petitio* using other syllogisms from the traditional canon instead of the one about Socrates, which belongs to a tradition of its own. They confirm how inapplicable are some of the *petitio* arguments about induction and the reverse analysis into atomistic propositions. For example, let us try: Mortal belongs to no man; every king belongs to man; not mortal belongs to some kings (a syllogism in Felapton in the third figure). Note that we have reverted to Aristotle's more or less standard form of proposition. Is it immediately obvious that the conclusion is one of the propositions used in establishing, by induction from individual men, the inference noted in general language in the major? This is hardly so. We can still be surprised, as learners, to see what interesting consequences follow from a general proposition, especially the first time we encounter a given argument pattern. When first going through Aristotle's fourteen valid syllogistic forms, as they might be expressed in an example each, we may be very likely to wonder how an argument that seems to lead to an intuitively surprising conclusion can be validated by the rules of immediate inference. Our surprise will wear off, of course, as we trace through it again and possibly depict the class relations by Venn diagrams or other such aids to understanding. Pretty soon we have mastered the argument and we are no longer surprised at all about the results we can obtain.

We cannot pass over without comment the issue of how Aristotle's few examples of demonstrative syllogisms fit or fail to fit within Mill's critical account. As noted in Chapter Three above, Aristotle is not forthcoming with more than a few examples. He gives us in the *Posterior Analytics A* 13 the syllogism about planets that he thinks illustrates the αἰτία or explanation that can be revealed by demonstration.[43] As we will recall, the proper scientific order of the propositions is:

> Being near belongs to planets
> Not twinkling belongs to being near
> Not twinkling belongs to planets.

It hardly needs saying that the conclusion of this syllogism is not a singular proposition which is, in some logical sense, contained in the major. The argument is not about Mars or Jupiter in particular, and it does not prove anything about planets that could not have been known at the outset. Its virtue lies in how the order and composition of the premisses disclose the reason for the proposition serving as the conclusion. Mill does not address this type of syllogism in the *Logic*.

There are some instances in the *Posterior Analytics* where it appears that Aristotle deals with syllogisms constituted of a universal and a singular premiss. When we reviewed in a previous chapter his response to the problem posed in the *Meno* we came across an example of just such a pattern.[44] It might be shown as:

> The sum of its interior angles being equal to two right angles belongs to triangle
> Triangle belongs to this particular diagram of a triangle
> The sum of its interior angles being equal to two right angles belongs to this particular diagram of a triangle.

This syllogism seems more of a piece with what Mill is constantly talking about. It looks here as if the induction leading to the framing of the proposition that serves as the major would be composed of such statements as that which serves as the conclusion. Two answers may be made in response to the allegation that this shows, by one of Aristotle's own examples, that syllogism is susceptible to the *petitio*

---

[43] See *An. Post.* 78ª31 *et seq.* and p. 75 above.
[44] See *An. Post.* 71ª20–26.

argument. The first is that the above argument does not exhibit a structure that entitles it to be included in Aristotle's formal system as outlined in the *Prior Analytics*. So it is not a syllogism. Secondly, Aristotle uses the above example in the *Posterior Analytics* in the context of discussing various kinds of knowledge which a learner may be said to have. If she knows the major, she has universal knowledge, and if she knows the minor, she has particular knowledge. But neither universal nor particular knowledge is, without more, scientific knowledge.[45] Such a piece of syllogistic-like reasoning cannot serve the end of demonstration; hence it is scientifically uninteresting. The purposes of syllogistic reasoning dictate that such an argument pattern involving a singular proposition has no use in Aristotle's system. Yet it is this outlaw form of argument that Mill represents as the standard type of syllogistic reasoning that bears all the virtues and all the defects of syllogism in general.

Lest one should think that Mill's use of the singular proposition in examining the function of the syllogism is an anomaly that can no longer be taken seriously, we should note that the syllogism about Socrates is a durable item that crops up repeatedly in modern discussions. For example, Toulmin uses the following sample pattern:

> Socrates is a man
> All men are mortal
> So Socrates is mortal.[46]

Toulmin is not examining the syllogism to see if a *petitio* is inevitably committed in such reasoning, but it is worthwhile to note for our purposes his following comment:

> Aristotle, himself was, of course, much concerned with syllogisms
> in which both the premisses were universal, since to his mind
> many of the arguments within scientific theory must be expected

---

45   See *supra* pp. 89 and 123.

46   Stephen Toulmin, *The Uses of Argument* (Cambridge: Cambridge University Press, 1969), p. 108.

to be of this sort. But we are interested primarily in arguments by which general propositions are applied to justify particular conclusions about individuals; so this initial limitation will be convenient. Many of the conclusions will, in any case, have an obvious application—*mutatis mutandis*—to syllogisms of other types.[47]

We shall not be concerned with whether the final sentence in this quotation from Toulmin is true within the context of his analysis. That final sentence does aptly serve, however, to summarize and disclose a fundamentally wrong assumption made by Mill and the proponents of the *petitio* claim against the syllogism. These writers are, of course, not the only commentators who have turned the triad of propositions showing Socrates's mortality into the apparent canonical form.[48]

It was remarked above that the impugning of the syllogism, because it cannot be the vehicle for making fresh discoveries, tends to obscure the pedagogical points raised by Aristotle in the *Posterior Analytics*. The aspect of logic focused on by Mill is that concerned with inquiry into the unknown rather than demonstration of the known. With demonstration, the order of our procedure is in the direction opposite to that followed by researchers who might begin, for example, with the working hypothesis of a general law as their major premiss.[49] Learners, on Aristotle's model, ought to begin with what is better known to them, and not with what is better known by nature. From this point they should be guided towards an understanding of the explanations of natural events. Such explanations are revealed to the learner by his seeing the major premiss and the conclusion related through the opportune introduction of the appropriate middle term. The process of learning, on Aristotle's account, is just as much a matter of progress from a conclusion to the explanation, as from a major premiss forward to a conclusion. Learners may be presumed to have already grasped that

---

47   *Ibid.*

48   See *supra*, Chapter Two, pp. 22–23.

49   This is only an illustration. It is not meant to be an accurate description of how a scientist would invariably proceed.

the planets, unlike the stars, do not twinkle in the night sky. Their learning will consist in grasping why this is so from premises that are scientifically respectable, that is, they are necessary and prior in nature (in the several ways that Aristotle uses that notion of priority). This is the sense of learning and adding to existing knowledge that forms Aristotle's topic in the *Posterior Analytics*. Very little of its subtlety or comprehensiveness as a theory of how science may be organized for the rational transmission of its achievements to learners initially unfamiliar with that science is suggested by Mill's account. The critics who allege that the syllogism is invariably guilty of a *petitio principii* have, ironically, assumed at the outset as their target a sterile and unrepresentative specimen of syllogism, in order to prove the barrenness of all syllogistic reasoning.

CHAPTER SIX

Critique of Aristotle's Programme for Teaching and Learning the Sciences

The preceding chapters have spelled out those features of Aristotle's logic that bear on the question of how to use demonstration to impart the knowledge gained by working scientists. As we have seen, Aristotle expounds a remarkably technical and comprehensive programme for the transmission and acquisition of such knowledge. It is a logical method, in the multiple senses of that phrase, including the Deweyan sense that will be discussed later. This chapter will be primarily critical in its orientation towards that programme. I shall test the verisimilitude of Aristotle's portrait of teaching by comparing it with what teachers typically do, with how textbook writers present what science has accomplished, and with what curriculum planners aim at in organizing and choosing the materials and activities for study in a science. This will not be an empirical comparison; indeed, it could hardly be so, given the scarcity of examples and lack of content in Aristotle's presentation of his progrmme. Rather, I am interested in examining the basic presuppositions of teaching in general, as laid out by Aristotle, and in reflecting philosophically on the validity of these by applying our concepts of such key items of educational discourse as teaching, learning, explaining and demonstrating.

We shall discover that a fundamental part of Aristotle's thinking is formulated in response to the same problem from which stems Plato's theory of ἀνάμνησις. The extended discussion of how Aristotle, like Plato, is deeply intrigued by that problem and how he attempts to solve it was provided in Chapter Four above. The position I develop in the second part of this chapter is that Aristotle's theory of learning is disfigured by his proposed solution, and this disfigurement is to such a degree that his theory cannot coherently explain how learning is possible. The trouble remains that, even on Aristotle's account, the learner must still already know what she is seeking to learn. A more reasonable solution, which is suggested by, and analogized from, how discovery is possible in non-teaching contexts, is supplied in this part of the chapter. I sketch out a notion of "previous knowledge" that both is in harmony with what happens in the classroom and stands up under philosophic scrutiny.

The third part of this chapter is devoted to explicating the relationship of ἐπαγωγή, as Aristotle understands it, and teaching. There have been some pointed remarks in the secondary literature on this topic. I argue that these generally miss the mark, because the process of ἐπαγωγή is to be contrasted with what the teacher does, according to Aristotle, and it is neither identical with nor analogous to teaching. What it is and how it allows for a second person to help it happen remain mysteries for the most part in Aristotle's brief description. This is a second weakness of Aristotle's theorizing about the type of knowledge that is a precondition to learning.

I shall then turn to a discussion of the role of the αἰτία or explanation in the acquisition of knowledge. I contrast the way in which Aristotle thinks the appropriate explanations can be discovered and imparted to learners with how scientific explanations play a key role in a concept of science and of scientific progress that is modern and distinctly non-Aristotelian. The contrast is between, on the one hand, the uncritical presentation to students of ready-made explanations and, on the other hand, the presentation of explanations of varying degrees of acceptability to students, who are encouraged to test such explanations and who, as one of the goals of science education, are put in the position of being able to try to formulate their own explanations in conformity with certain criteria.

In the last part of this chapter I consider the merits of Aristotle's claim that there is only one method by which teaching proceeds and ougt to proceed. The factual part of Aristotle's claim fails because teachers use many techniques and engage in many activities that are not at all demonstrative. In addition, the prescriptive part of his claim is plausible only in view of his hope or expectation that a science can be perfected, in the sense that no further principles or explanations are discoverable or need to be discovered. I shall argue that such a thesis is not sustainable on the evidence of the course of scientific progress down through history, nor is it foreseeable on the basis of such evidence that it will prove true in the future. Aristotle's conception of the possible completeness of the theoretical sciences influences his conception of science teaching, and the fate of his view on the first possibility will necessarily be shared by his view that demonstration is teaching *par excellence*. In this part of the chapter, I also contrast demonstration with the use of dialogue by the teacher in the classroom and the use of dialogue in classroom texts. The exposure of learners to participation in, or observation of, debates and discussions is not a mark of the immaturity of a science, but rather is a necessary ingredient of any science education.

It should be made clear before embarking on this chapter that Aristotle's theory, interpreted as a method of scientific inquiry, was long ago rejected by natural philosophers as they were then called and ignored by educational theorists, both groups of whom, like Locke's putative infant, wished to start intellectual life with "white paper, void of all characters, without any ideas."[1] From the high eminence among the leading texts that brought European culture out of the so-called dark ages, Aristotle's logical texts, particularly the *Posterior Analytics*, were demoted by early modern thinkers. They have since been little noticed by philosophers, either of science or of education.[2] The few paragraphs that follow illustrate how thorough

[1]   John Locke, *An Essay Concerning Human Understanding*, ed. A. D. Woozley (London: Collins, 1964), II, ch. i, 2, p. 89.
[2]   Typical of the modern reception of Aristotle's ideal model of scientific organization is Stephen Toulmin, *The Philosophy of Science* (London: Hutchinson University Library, 1967), p. 31:
      Certainly none of the substantial inferences that one comes across in the physical sciences is of a syllogistic type. This is because, in the physical sciences, we are not seriously interested in enumerating the

the rejection was and how it continues still. These remarks and quotations are placed here as a prelude to our critical evaluation, so that they may be an object lesson (not in the Herbartian sense) about how philosophy of education tends to reinvent itself continually. Aristotle's system has never been built upon.

As was pointed up in the introductory chapter, Aristotle's contributions to questions arising about the concept of education have, to modern eyes, been visible only in so far as they were explicitly rejected in the course of the rise of modern scientific thought and have not been accorded much concentrated attention since. This is just one example of how theorists who aim to deal with the topic of human knowledge and hence, human learning, feel disposed, again and again, wilfully to rid themselves of any conceptions influencing their predecessors. We might recall in this regard Bacon, Descartes, and Dewey. With respect to the first of these, it has been concisely summarized that:

> Bacon firmly believed that progress in knowledge was possible only when the ground had been completely cleared and a new foundation laid. Men must begin, he says, from the very foundations and effect a total reconstruction of all sciences. Especially must the mind be freed from every opinion or theory, and proceed straight to nature . . . Reason, or logic, says Bacon, has for so long been divorced from facts that it has fixed errors rather than discovered truth, and, therefore, the important step is to return to a purely sensuous knowledge of natural things, and from that foundation to work slowly upward, constantly guiding and controlling the mind by observations and experiments.[3]

---

common properties of sets of objects, but are concerned with relations of other kinds.

[3]   Richard Foster Jones, *Ancients and Moderns: A Study of the Rise of the Scientific Movement in Seventeenth-Century England*, 2nd ed. (St. Louis: Washington University Press, 1961), pp. 49–50. See also ch. 6 of Jones's book, which records, during a pamphleteering age, some very tart language used by magicians, astrologers and alchemists who, according to Jones (*ibid.*, p. 123), "formed a tatterdemalion army under the aegis of Bacon . . . They maintained a constant barrage and sulphurous smoke-screen on the entrenched positions of the ancients."

Dewey was keen on having us go beyond both Baconian philosophy and the antiquated method of scientific inquiry it supplanted. For him, "[e]ssential philosophic reconstruction represents an attempt to state these causes and results in a way freed from incompatible inherited factors."[4] This strong desire to clear the ground and to rebuild on the basis of answers to the root problems, realigning antitheses, and assigning new meaning to concepts if need be, is common in the philosophy of education.[5] Such a tendency has led to the following acute remark: "To an extraordinary degree, the history of educational theory is a history of repeated fresh starts rather than of continuous progress."[6] The trouble with such an attitude is that theorists are obliged to reinvent some quite useful early ideas which had fallen by the wayside of a path we fail to look back on. Aristotle deserves to be reconsidered, not because a demolition of his ideas is a necessary prerequisite to a true beginning, but because getting straight about his work is a worthwhile beginning itself. The attempt to appreciate and criticize is instructive because we realize the depth of Aristotle's programme. There is little that is educationally trite about it.

Previous knowledge and demonstration

Three facets of Aristotle's work in the *Posterior Analytics* illustrate how important it is to show that previous knowledge is necessary for all teaching to take place. First, this express idea is the overture, so to speak, to that treatise, brought out resonantly in the opening sentence. Secondly, the achievement of that kind of knowledge

---

4   John Dewey, *Reconstruction in Philosophy*, rev. ed. (Boston: Beacon Press, 1948), p. 51.

5   For example, note the emancipation declared by Comenius. As retold by Jones, *supra* 3, p. 131, there was:

> ... a treatise of Comenius entitled *Naturall Philosophie Reformed by Divine Light*, 1651, which declares that Aristotle's authority should not be tolerated in Christian schools as an absolute authority, but that men should be free to philosophize. "Why do we not, I say, turn over the living book of the world instead of dead papers."

6   John Passmore, *The Philosophy of Teaching* (London: Duckworth, 1980), p. 81.

deservingly called scientific or knowledge *simpliciter* depends on there being premises previous or prior to the conclusion in the order of deduction (if not in the order of actual learning by the student). Thus Aristotle avoids being entangled in the same problem that is encountered in the *Meno*. Thirdly, Aristotle constructs a theory of ἐπαγωγή, embracing both a process and a faculty, to answer the question about how first principles are acquired, if not by teaching. The notion that the learner must first know something before she can be taught anything else is fundamental to Aristotle's work in the *Posterior Analytics*. To a large extent, this theme is what makes the treatise cohere. It also shows how Aristotle shared certain problems with Plato. In the discussion below, the criticism will be made that for Aristotle and Plato both, the previous knowledge of X necessary to support learning Y is in some sense already the knowledge of Y. This is a mistake, because such accounts preserve the concept of learning against the skeptic's attack only at the cost of distorting how learning usually takes place. The knowledge of Y is not in some abstruse way already contained in the knowledge of X. What precedes Y in learners' understanding might be a knowledge of many sorts of things, from which they may, for example, be entitled to infer that Y.

It devolves upon us to re-examine this question of the necessity of previous knowledge. This is best done by trying to isolate some paradigm cases of a researcher discovering Y on the basis of what she already knows. Thereafter we may proceed to the situation of a student learning Y from a teacher, without the student's knowing Y in any sense beforehand. We must keep in mind that the knowledge is not of just any sort, but the potential learner must possess knowledge that she can state in the form of the answer to the question, "What is Y?" This is the kind of answer that Plato, in his early dialogues, has Socrates continually circle back to as basic to any further knowledge claim. The answer to it becomes the standard against which other claims to knowledge can be measured. For Aristotle, and for his theory of demonstration, the type of knowledge that is conveyed by teaching is knowledge about something as revealed by what can be essentially predicated of that thing. This is not stated in the conclusion to the demonstrative syllogism, but rather in the premises, and it is what also helps to show the explanation of that thing.

In response to both Aristotle's and Plato's presuppositions about how previous knowledge in the relevant educational sense is acquired, we might ask whether, and if so, in what sense, a learner must know what Y is before she can properly be said to learn Y. We can refer back to our discussion in Chapter Four for a description of how Aristotle and Plato give contrasting accounts of what this prior knowledge consists in and of what "learning" means as a result. Let us take an apparently simple case of an investigator, working at the frontiers of his science, learning something new. It is not new just to the investigator, but it is something that nobody before her has known.

The justification for proceeding in this way is that certain epistemologically relevant terms and expressions are ambiguous between what we may call, in verbal shorthand, a research context and a teaching context. For example, both research physicists and students who are only novices in physics may be said to learn important truths, though we recognize that there are two senses of the same verb being applied here. The same point is relevant with respect to such activities as discovering, researching, and inquiring. The interplay between the two contexts has had some influence on teaching methods; for instance, in the argument that teaching ought to be less a matter of instruction and more of a means for allowing the learner to re-discover knowledge that is already included in the inventory of a science, and that such re-discovery should proceed in the same way in which the original discovery was made.[7] This, and the related though distinct theory that scientific subjects should be learned by an inquiry method, have been frequently invoked in

---

[7] For criticism of this theory, see P. H. Hirst and R. S. Peters, *The Logic of Education* (London: Routledge and Kegan Paul, 1970), pp. 78–79; and David P. Ausubel, "Some Psychological and Educational Limitations of Learning by Discovery," in *Readings in Science Education for the Secondary School*, ed. Hans O. Andersen (New York: Macmillan, 1969), pp. 97–114. There is also a good, common-sensical discussion in R. F. Dearden, "Instruction and Learning by Discovery," in R. S. Peters (ed.), *The Concept of Education* (London: Routledge and Kegan Paul, 1967), pp. 135–55.

discussions about how science teaching should be organized.[8] They show how strong is the attraction to assimilate what students should do with what scientists are perceived as doing. For us, this constellation of concepts is important because Plato presents the learner's dilemma as also affecting the possibility of research and original discovery. Ανάμνησις is a way of accounting both for the elementary grasp of geometry and for the progress of Socrates and Meno in their quest into uncharted philosophical territory. If the one activity is possible, then so is the other. Our strategy in the following discussion will be to accept this parallel and to try to show how previous knowledge is related to original discovery, and what this implies for the extent of knowledge necessary to the student's learning.

There have been several occasions in the history of astronomy during the past three centuries when investigators have discovered a new planet in the solar system. For instance, Herschel discovered Uranus in the eighteenth century, Neptune was discovered around sixty years later, and then Pluto was finally observed in the 1930s.[9]

---

8   For a detailed discussion of the method of learning by inquiry, see Joseph J. Schwab, "The Teaching of Science as Enquiry," The Inglis Lecture, 1961, in *The Teaching of Science* (Cambridge, Mass.: Harvard University Press, 1966), pp. 1–104. Schwab relates the two contexts we have been discussing, as his prosposal for a secondary school science curriculum makes clear (*ibid.*, p. 71):

> It is important to recall, now, that we are discussing only one version of the enquiring curriculum—the most complete one, one which combines to the highest degree both aspects of the matter: *science* as enquiry and *learning-teaching* as enquiry . . . Of the two components— science as enquiry and the activity of enquiring—it is the former which should be given first priority as the objective of science teaching in the secondary school.

The important point is to see how this relationship between what scientists do and what students ought to learn by doing is somehow felt to be logical, or at least made logical. See also Michael Martin, *Concepts of Science Education* (Glenview, Ill.: Scott, Foresman and Company, 1972), pp. 7–9.

9   The following discussion about the interesting circumstances of Sir William Herschel's discovery of Uranus is chosen because it is well-documented by the discoverer himself in papers communicated to the Royal Society and in his letters to scientific acquaintances. The information summarized about his procedure and results is drawn from Constance A. Lubbock, *The Herschel Chronicle* (Cambridge: Cambridge University Press, 1933), as well as Michael

In Herschel's case, the discovery he made depended on his several systematic surveys of the heavens, in which he used the telescope he painstakingly constructed for himself.[10] He spotted what at first he took to be a comet among the stars in the constellation of Taurus. He surmised that it was a comet because repeated observations showed that it moved from Taurus into other constellations. In fact, Herschel's initial report to the Royal Society was entitled "Account of a Comet."[11] After more detailed observations and after calculations of its angular motion, direction of travel and so forth, it was finally determined by other astronomers of Herschel's day that the seventh planet had been discovered. Its elliptical orbit and perihelion were calculated. Herschel went on to discover, by further examination through his telescope, the first two of Uranus's five known satellites. Though there had been some speculation since Kepler's time that a new planet might be awaiting discovery, it was generally thought that such a planet would most likely be found at an orbit interposed between those of Mars and Jupiter, and not in the trans-Saturnian region. It seems that Uranus had been on many occasions recorded as a star before Herschel recognized in what ways it did not share starlike aspects, in particular because of its relative change in position and because it appeared more as a disc than as a point of light.

Herschel's discovery is presented as an example of an investigator learning about Y without first knowing what Y is. He learned, through his observations and by virtue of the confirmatory calculations done by other scientists more professional than he, that Uranus was not a star and not even a comet, though the latter was Herschel's initial description. The sighting of Uranus, which was not

---

A. Hoskin, *William Herschel and the Construction of the Heavens* (New York: W. W. Norton , 1963).

[10] Note Herschel's own account of the background of his observation on the evening of March 13, 1781 (from Lubbock, *supra* n. 9, pp. 78–79) :

It has generally been supposed that it was a lucky accident that brought this star to my view; this is an evident mistake. In the regular manner I examined every star of the heavens, not only of that magnitude but many far inferior, it was that night *its turn* to be discovered.

[11] *Ibid.*, p. 81.

even suspected to exist before Herschel spied it, differs somewhat from the later sightings of Neptune and Pluto. In the latter cases the existence of each planet was to some extent predicted by astronomical tables, calculations and pre-discovery observations.[12]

What previous knowledge was available to Herschel about Uranus? He might have consulted the then existing star charts, though he need not have. Although an amateur astronomer (his occupation at the time was teaching music), he was aware of the different aspects of stars, of comets, and of planets. He had such knowledge that, when presented with an anomalous light in the sky, that showed an unusual position and outline, he could make some basic calculations about it, such as speed, direction of motion, and relative size of the light source. He could even, after his initial discovery, use his powers of observation to descry that the orbit of Uranus's satellites is retrograde (and he had no precedent to suggest this, since this was the first observation of such retrogressive motion in the solar system).[13]

The point of enumerating these types of prior knowledge is to test Herschel's discovery against the skeptical claim that what Y is cannot be learned without Y being already known to the learner. We might say that Herschel knew, comparatively speaking, a great deal about astronomy and nothing about Uranus prior to discovering it. He knew about the constituents of the heavens and their motions and appearances. But what sense does it make to say that Herschel must have already known that Uranus was the seventh planet before he sighted it and recorded his observation in his astronomical journal?

---

[12]   See William Graves Hoyt, *Planets X and Pluto* (Tucson: University of Arizona Press, 1980), ch. 2 and *passim*.

[13]   His powers of observation were trained and practised, in the sense conveyed by the following excerpt from one of Herschel's letters, written in 1782 (from Lubbock, *supra* n. 9, p. 101.:

> . . . I do not suppose that there are many persons who could even find a star with my power of 6540, much less keep it, if they had found it. Seeing is in some respect an art, which must be learnt. To make a person see with such a power is nearly the same as if I were asked to make him play one of Handel's fugues upon the organ. Many a night have I been practising to see, and it would be strange if one did not acquire a certain dexterity by such constant practise.

One of the points to be observed about Herschel's actual procedure and his first attempt to categorize his observation is that he got the category wrong. He saw something which he took to be a comet and which was subsequently confirmed to be a planet. The fact that he was the first to see that speck of light as emanating from something other than a star is what apparently gained him credit in his own day as the discoverer of Uranus.[14] This entitled him, for example, to suggest a name for the newly discovered planet, though his suggestion did not catch on and the choice of another namesmith prevailed. A skeptic might take refuge in the claim that Herschel did as might be predicted on the skeptical account: because he did not already know what Uranus was he failed to recognize it when he saw it. The skeptical position would be, of course, that Herschel could never have recognized it unless he first knew that it was a planet. That there is something wrong with the skeptic's position is shown by how Herschel proceeded and how his observation was taken up by other astronomers. The processes of seeing something, such as Y, and of determining what Y is, are logically distinct. We may have evidence, based on observation or even calculation, of Y and yet this is no less knowledge just because we cannot as yet say what Y is. We may even be wrong and, on a misconstruction of the evidence, say that Y is an F when it turns out to be a G. Such error in no way diminishes the fact that the other, evidential knowledge remains something we grasp. As in Herschel's case, the observer who puts us on the right path may rightfully be called the discoverer, even though some of his observations and his categorization of his own discovery may be quite wrong. This line of argument is meant to show how odd it would be, given our experiences of scientific discovery, to think that we have to know what something is before we can be said to discover it.

Aristotle's account could arguably handle the case of the discovery of Uranus described above. A committed Aristotelian might point out that we, or Herschel in the above circumstances, had in mind the essential attributes of planets or at least, comets as contradistinguished from those of stars. This would be our universal

---

[14] Herschel was awarded the Copley medal and elected to the Royal Society before it was ascertained that Uranus was a planet and not a comet.

knowledge, as Aristotle calls it. Then, when we came across a new planet, we gained through perception particular knowledge by realizing that the body subsequently called Uranus falls under the universal. So there is some apparent sense in saying that Aristotle's account is consistent so far with our common experience in scientific discovery. But his account is not wholly vindicated by such experience. How would it handle, for instance, the discovery of pulsars in outer space? In this case the discovery is not in the form of the observation of a particular type of star, which is capable of being completely described in classificatory language. From the evidence of recorded radio signals and perhaps of flashes of visible light synchronized with such signals, a theoretical account of pulsars has been developed. This account depends at bottom on the atomic theory of matter and on the relationship between mass and binding energy. To some extent what we may discover about pulsars, or in a more recent example, about black holes, may conflict with what we had previously thought was essential to stars as a genus. We might, for example, in our scientific definitions have assumed that all stars produce light as a result of physio-chemical reactions and that they would be luminous to some degree. Prior to the discovery of black holes, or at least the advent of the theory postulating them, what sense would it have made to say that one type of star does not allow light to escape its gravitational pull? Hence, there is a great deal more to the discovery of such phenomena and their scientific explanation than Aristotle's distinction between universal and particular knowledge would account for. The scientist who, upon observing the Crab nebula let us suppose, discovers such a phenomenon as a pulsar, far from fitting it into the known categories of stars, might find that she has to remake, to some extent, those existing categories in order to accommodate the observed phenomenon.[15]

It is just this process that is so often the most stimulating side to

---

[15]   The discovery of pulsars emanating from souces located in supernovae led to a link between the death of massive stars in a supernova explosions and their current remnants, dense neutron stars revolving at a frequency measurable only in microseconds. See Simon Mitton, *The Crab Nebula* (London: Faber and Faber, 1979), pp. 89–97.

a new discovery; discovering a new type of thing can be more exciting than discovering a new instance of an established type. The long-standing controversy between proponents of the corpuscular theory of light and those who supported the wave theory turned on just this issue of how to give an explanation by means of one universal (particle) rather than the other (wave). The true advance is made, on occasion, not by verifying which category is appropriate, but by developing an alternative theory in which both competing theories are superseded and so, too, are the categories associated with each. For example, we have witnessed in this century the rise of a theory of quantum electrodynamics and the concept of the photon which together explain more events than did either the corpuscular or wave theories alone. The question of which of two ultimate categories better explains the behaviour of light is less relevant than before.

Scientific inquiry is not unduly hampered by the objection that scientific researchers can at best only gain new knowledge in particular of what they already know in general. Although previous knowledge in the form of evidence, observations, confirmed inferences, and probabilities is used by scientists in the course of their investigations, it is a slippery philosophic move to look at the procedures of discovery retrospectively and to claim that what was finally arrived at was already present in some form in what the discoverer knew when he started.

There seems, then, to be some intelligibility to the notion that a researcher may say that he knows X and is seeking to discover what Y is, without him being taken to mean that the knowledge of what Y is, either potentially or in universal form, is among the things he already knows.

Let us look next at a paradigm case of investigation or inquiry outside of the physical sciences. The following example would be drawn from the practice of forensic investigations. Suppose a police officer is attempting to discover what implement was used to open a window of a house and thereby permitted a burglar entry. She will obviously be interested in gathering any relevant evidence or clues at the scene. For example, she will examine the marks left on the window frame and the paint thereon. She will apply her knowledge of similar housebreakings encountered in the past and the knowledge gained in her training. From the evidence she collects she may be able to formulate a conclusion (in a Sherlock Holmesian kind of deduction) that the implement was made of iron or steel, had a beak-like end 4 centimetres in width, and on that end had a V-shaped nick one-half centimeter from one corner. She may also surmise that it could be handled by one burglar alone (as shown by the footprints on the ground outside the window) and that it afforded sufficient mechanical advantage to allow a person of relatively small stature to pry up the window and to snap the window lock. The officer's observations and inferences at this juncture go so far as to allow her to know something about an implement, even though she does not yet know what that implement is. It might conceivably be a crowbar or a wide chisel with a pipe applied to its handle for extra leverage. It may turn out that, later on, her investigation leads to a local suspect, the tread and size of whose shoes match those imprints found outside the window of the burglarized home. Also in the suspect's possession are what have come to be known in the thieves' trade and defined under the criminal law as housebreaking tools. Found among these is a crowbar, one end of which matches perfectly the impressions left on the window frame of the house. The assembled evidence would then go towards establishing that the implement used to jimmy the window was this particular crowbar. We should note that the process of discovery here does not pass from knowledge of the universal crowbar to the suspect's particular crowbar. The previous knowledge relied upon by the investigating officer is not that of crowbars in general, but of the unique circumstances surrounding the commission of the particular break and entry. In this case it is clear how learning what the instrument is, in the sense of coming to identify it, is posterior, both logically and chronologically, to gaining knowledge about the instrument as yet unknown. A similar process would be exemplified by the forensic pathologist giving her opinion about the cause of death where no weapon was found, the garage mechanic diagnosing why a tire went flat, or an allergist narrowing down the range of possible causes and finally isolating the single cause of her patient's reaction. In none of these cases would we say that the investigator already knows precisely what the cause is before she begins to look for it in the ways appropriate to her art or technology. She may have a general idea or a hunch, based on her experience and training, but this would not exclude the possibility that the cause in a particular case will be unprecedented or unique, yet withal discoverable.[16]

We have now held up to scrutiny cases of discovery in astronomical science and in another, more mundane type of investigation. Aristotle's work in the *Posterior Analytics*, we have argued, is not primarily concerned with a method of how scientific discoveries may be made, but instead is focused on how sciences are and should be taught. It is knowledge, both as previous knowledge and as learned scientific knowledge, in this sphere that most concerns him. He wants to say that here, too, the student is said to learn in the sense that she comes to grasp in actuality something that she already knows potentially. Not all knowledge, we will recall from the summary in Chapter Three, is learned. One type of knowledge (viz., in the form of first principles) is achieved through another process. We shall explore this process of ἐπαγωγή in the third and succeeding part of this chapter. We ought to keep in mind that Aristotle argues for the necessity of the knowledge of first principles in order to avoid the problem of an infinite regress in his account of the premises necessary for effecting a demonstrative syllogism. In the discussion above of discovery and the role of previous knowledge for the practitioners of different fields of investigation, we extracted the lesson that where a discovery is made, what was known previously may have a direct connection with the discovery; but this falls far short of saying that the previous knowledge already includes, in some latent or general form, precisely the discovery subsequently made. A criticism based on a parallel distinction may be made against Aristotle's general account of learning, where what is being learned is being taught.

An example from a classroom setting helps illustrate this discussion. Aristotle is fond of using an example from geometry, but his theory of demonstration purportedly embraces all branches of theoretical science and in that category would be theoretical but not

---

16   For illustrations of such detective work, see William R. Maples and Michael Browning, *Dead Men Do Tell Tales: The Strange and Fascinating Cases of a Forensic Anthropologist* (New York: Doubleday, 1994).

applied physics, as we know them. Suppose a student is brought to understand a general principle of physics such as Newton's second law of motion as it can be expressed in the symbolic equation, $f = ma$. This states that the amount of force of an object equals the product of the mass of that object and its acceleration. This is often included as one of the basic principles introduced at the beginning of a secondary school physics course and used thereafter in explicating theories about the behaviour of objects that range in size from subatomic particles to celestial bodies. With such a broad principle in mind, it is tempting to say that students are taught by applying this principle to particular situations, and are led to discover things by virtue of it. For example, if the student is given or has herself obtained data in respect of two of the three variables shown in the equation, she can discover the amount of the third by using a pocket calculator. There is apparently no limit to the number of situations to which this principle can be applied. Such broad principles as Newton's laws, in their force if not their form, seem to resemble the sort of thing that Aristotle envisions as lying at the base of each particular science. Teaching will be tantamount to setting before learners the relevant basic principles (which are undemonstrable) and then taking learners through the deductions that may be made from them in conjunction with the minor premiss that exhibits an explanation. This example from physics is cited because it seems to be amenable to Aristotle's account; for what is previously known by the student in this instance exhibits some of the hallmarks of scientific premisses (that is, necessity, universality, priority). The student works from such premisses and by following a deductive pattern arrives at a conclusion that is also necessary and universal. The deductive procedure guarantees that the knowledge achieved is scientific. There is only one method of teaching and this is what it involves. And the student will not be able to claim she knows Y scientifically unless she can give the proper reasons for Y in the pattern which shows the demonstrative premisses leading up to Y in the conclusion. This is something like the mathematics teacher's insistence that the bare numerical answer to a problem is insufficient by itself to show that the learner grasps what he has been taught, but that the relevant formula and its manipulation must also be shown on the face of the answer. Or, if it is a geometry problem, the relevant hypotheses, inferences and justification for each step must be shown in the proof of the theorem. It is very enticing to think that all teaching and learning could proceed along these lines and that all knowledge gained from teaching would *ipso facto* be scientific. This method would be infallible.[17]

One flaw in this view is that, as Aristotle himself admits, learners can be said to learn the conclusion in actuality only if they can be said already to know it potentially. This is part of Aristotle's rebuttal of Meno's dilemma. It introduces a ghostlike sense of knowledge that stands behind every successful act of learning. The remarks made above about the connection drawn between trying to discover Y and already knowing what Y is are analogous here. It is certainly intelligible to claim that a learner can grasp something of which she has no prior notion or suspicion, let alone knowledge; for example, that Mars's period of revolution around the sun is 687 days. For Aristotle however, such a proposition would not count as a piece of scientific knowledge or be demonstrable. The only propositions that can be demonstrated, and thus taught and learned, in the strong sense of those terms, would be about planets in general, either some or all of them. We therefore are left with a very attenuated concept of learning. What is previously known about a kind of object will yield, through deduction, propositions (the demonstranda) that at first are better known to the learner. Looking back on the process, Aristotle's analysis is that the learner knew potentially the premisses all along. The trouble with such an analysis is that it robs the concept of learning of much of its force. Instead of being the passage from a state of ignorance about Y to a state of knowledge about Y, or from knowing X to knowing both X and Y, where knowing X is not equivalent to knowing Y, learning is construed on Aristotle's account

---

[17] This notion of infallibility is important throughout the history of philosophy of education, where the philosopher in question has tried to say something about method. As a theorist he wishes to develop a method which will work not just most of the tine with normal learners, but all of the time with all learners in every possible subject. Comenius's counsel that teachers should imitate the sun, which inevitably and laboriously performs its daily functions, antedates Hume's doubt about the sun as a paragon of causal necessity. See John Amos Comenius, *The Great Didactic*, in *John Amos Conenius on Education*, ed. Jean Piaget (New York: Teachers College Press, 1967), pp. 70–71.

as the passage from one form of knowledge of Y to another form of knowledge of Y.[18]

I have examined above and tried to spell out the significant features of a case of an investigator making suitable preparations before venturing on an hypothesis. There is an analogous sense of preparation on the part of the learner that is largely ignored by Aristotle's theory. A scientific researcher will read up on the current state of knowledge and available data that relates to the problem before her, and then perhaps ruminate over it. With various degrees of quickness (in a flash, an instant, or only after agonizing and laborious thinking and speculation) she might come up with a possible explanation. Such descriptive modifiers apply equally to a student's acquisition of understanding. This is not to say that a learner invariably resembles an investigator in this regard (the

---

[18]   We may note in this connection a modern attempt to resolve the dilemma stated by Meno. In Michael Polanyi, *The Tacit Dimension* (Garden City, N.Y.: Doubleday, 1966), pp. 22–24, Polanyi claims to have reached a solution, which he describes in the following terms:

> The solution which Plato offered for this paradox was that all discovery is a remembering of past lives. This explanation has hardly ever been accepted, but neither has any other solution been offered for avoiding the contradiction. So we are faced with the fact that, for two thousand years and more, humanity has progressed through the efforts of people solving difficult problems, while all the time it could be shown that to do this was either meaningless or impossible . . . The kind of tacit knowledge that solves the paradox of the *Meno* consists in the intimation of something hidden, which we may yet discover ... This kind of knowing solves the paradox of the *Meno* by making it possible for us to know something so indeterminate as a problem or a hunch, but when the use of this faculty turns out to be an indispensable element of all knowing, we are forced to conclude that all knowledge is of the same kind as the knowledge of a problem.

We might notice, without discussing the point at length, that the unravelling of the Menonian paradox, in so far as it is created by the question of how learning is possible, is not really helped by Polanyi's account. For we may still ask, as we do of Aristotle, how is the foreknowledge necessary to discovery or learning itself discovered or learned. The argument from a regress has not been dealt with. In both cases, we see that the defect lies in trying to characterize the previous knowledge necessary as already including what is to be learned.

assimilation of such different activities has sparked some lively debate in recent educational discussions), but the comparison does indicate what sense there is in saying that learning Y is doing something more than just trying to bring foreknowledge of Y to the surface.[19]

An alternative way of handling the problem of previous knowledge is exemplified in a solution proposed by D. W. Hamlyn, in the following terms:

> The point that I was making was meant to be a conceptual point —it is simply that someone could not come to knowledge of X, if this is to be learning, without other knowledge. But this other knowledge does not need to have been acquired previously in time. The priority that is necessary is a logical priority only. Someone who has come to see that q is implied by p may be said to have learned that q, but it is not necessary for this that he should have come see the truth of p before coming to see that of q; he may come to see both together. A slogan which would make my point would be that all learning is, in one way or another, connecting things, and it is in this way that experience develops. But the connecting may take many different patterns.[20]

Hamlyn's solution is directed towards the friction between so-called rationalist and empiricist theories of learning, though he acknowledges in the paragraph immediately preceding the one from which the above quotation is drawn that his solution has implications for the Menonian dilemma. We may leave aside Hamlyn's point about learning as connecting, and focus on his narrower conceptual point. His notion of logical priority as an explication of what previous knowledge means is suggestive, for by means of it a crucial portion of Aristotle's theory might be defended against the criticism we have been levelling. I would argue, however, that Hamlyn's distinction is not a life preserver for that theory, but rather throws us back into the quagmire stirred up by Aristotle. For

---

[19] See Martin, *supra* n. 8, pp. 9 and 11–14, for an interesting model of hypothesis generation and how this may prove suggestive for science teaching.

[20] D. W. Hamlyn, "Human Learning" in R. S. Peters (ed.), *The Philosophy of Education* (Oxford: Oxford University Press, 1973) pp. 178–94, p. 187.

how are we to acquire knowledge of *p* without knowing something else beforehand? All of our concepts cannot be so connected together that knowledge of one will give us knowledge of them all (though a Bradleian idealist might argue in favour of such a proposition). Learning and understanding take place over time and involve a succession of achievements. Often our learning is graduated, from elementary bits of knowledge to more sophisticated concepts. But these different things learned are not always (and not even usually) connected by a relationship of material implication. We learn a great deal piecemeal. What is needed to escape Meno's dilemma is not just some possibility of learning an analytic truth (if this is the sort of thing Hamlyn means by his relating *p* and *q* above), which remains an easy target for the sceptical claim that what we thereby call learning is something less than we had at first thought. What is needed instead is an account that shows how we can learn synthetic truths (to continue in the Kantian jargon).

We ought now to return to Aristotle's programme. The type of learning he envisions as resulting from teaching is in no way concerned with such information as Mars's period of revolution or that Canada is composed of ten provinces and two territories or that Socrates took a wife named Xanthippe. None of these types of information is about a kind of object, as opposed to an individual object, nor is the proposition expressing each type of information necessary or universal. Each is, therefore, indemonstrable and is incapable of being taught in the sense in which Aristotle wishes to use that verb.

The consequence of Aristotle's description of, and programme for, teaching and learning that is acquired by means of teaching, is that much of what we might ordinarily think can be taught is not eligible for such transmission under Aristotle's scheme. The student will never be presumed to be ignorant of the most basic principles of a science but will be presumed to have acquired them before teaching begins. A student cannot learn anything scientific about individual objects, such as Socrates, this country, this chair, or that planet; but only about humans or Greeks or philosophers, about nations, about wooden artifacts, or about planets as a genus. That is, learners' knowledge will be only about kinds of things, their essential natures, and their explanations or αἰτίαι, all of which can be comprehended and disclosed in syllogism. Ignorance is accounted for, not as the absence of knowledge of any sort, but as the failure to grasp the relations between kinds. This amounts to a very restricted view of what learning consists in. Even a cursory glance through a modern textbook in the physical sciences confirms that a great deal of information presented there would not qualify as scientific knowledge for Aristotle.

What could be Aristotle's purpose in so restricting the sphere of teachable knowledge that learning becomes only a small fraction of what would ordinarily count as accessible to learning and to transmission in the classroom? The answer lies in Aristotle's attempt to escape the learner's dilemma posed in the *Meno*.[21] Although Aristotle takes a tack different from that of Plato, the result of his maneuvering still runs him aground on the same shoals that caught Plato's doctrine of ἀνάμνησις. There remains for both of them the intractable problem that it is still necessary to know Y in some sense before what Y is is learned in another sense of the verb "to know."

---

[21]   The importance of this dilemma for the development of what Aristotle's logic was meant to accomplish has been recognized before, to varying degrees, by Dewey and Popper, for example. Note the following from John Dewey, *Essays in Experimental Logic* (New York: Dover, n.d., reprint ed. of the work originally published by the University of Chicago Press, 1916), p. 227:

> Ancient logic never got beyond the conception of an object whose logical *place*, whose subsumptive position as a particular with reference to some universal, was doubtful. It never got to the point where it could search for particulars which in themselves as particulars are doubtful. Hence it was a logic of proof, of deduction, not of inquiry, of discovery, and of induction. It was hard up against its own dilemma: How can a man inquire? For either he knows that for which he seeks, and hence does not seek: or he does not know, in which case he can not seek, nor could he tell if he found. The individualistic movement of modern life detached, as it were, the individual, and allowed personal (i.e., intra-organic) events to have, transitively and temporarily, a worth of their own.

and from Karl Popper, *Conjectures and Refutations* (London: Routledge and Kegan Paul, 1969), p. 12:

> Yet what interests us here is Plato's optimistic epistemology, the theory of *anamnesis* in the *Meno*. It contains, I believe, not only the germs of Descartes' intellectualism, but also the germs of Aristotle's and of Bacon's theories of induction.

The root philosophical difficulty is created by Aristotle's use of one criterion of knowledge as the model of how all learning takes place. We would say that, among other ways, we can see if A knows the concept of Y by seeing if he knows what counts as a Y, if there is one, when A comes across it. This is a criterion, a way of judging. Out of it Aristotle manufactures two sorts of knowledge and calls learning (sc. scientific learning) the passage from one to the other. In this way he avoids the imputation of an infinite regress; in the process he leaves us wondering why a person's moving from a state of pure ignorance about first principles to a knowledge of them sufficient to support demonstration cannot be learning, in the sense that such a knowledge cannot be acquired by teaching. For in some sense the acquisition of such "previous" knowledge is more educationally interesting than the conclusions derived by deduction. Yet Aristotle has declared that process out of bounds to the teacher, and has accounted for it in a brief and blurry description.

The relation of ἐπαγωγή to teaching

I have used above the example of Newton's second law of motion to illustrate a principle of broad application in the practice and study of physics. Granted, this is not exactly the sort of principle that Aristotle has in mind; but it will help to advance my argument. Aristotle's point in relation to it would be that it can be set before a learner as a basic starting point that itself is not learned, but is the foundation for all learning. That this sounds odd may be pointed up by the following. What does it mean to say that such a principle is not learned? Aristotle contrasts learning (by which he means learning as qualified by the adjective διανοητική, to the meaning of which we devoted some space in Chapter Three) with a process of ἐπαγωγή. This latter Greek term is commonly rendered as induction, though we must keep in mind that Aristotle is not bothered by Humean doubts about the validity of induction. The repetition of the process, and the operation of memory and experience result in the development of a state of νοῦς, or intuition. The trouble with thinking of this state as something like intuition is that it is hard to see how the relationship expressed by the equation, $f = ma$, could be grasped without the learner being able to state how she came to know it. This is because, being known intuitively, it has come to be known without an explanation or an intermediate term. This latter way of putting it is in a more or less Aristotelian spirit. In our classrooms, however, would the physics instructor be on firm ground in asserting that he could count on the learner's intuition for an understanding of Newton's second law? Hardly. He is more likely in fact to spend considerable time with the learner preparing the groundwork for coming to an understanding of the law and then having the student, through repeated exercises, gain a mastery of what he has learned about Newton's theory. The teacher needs to ensure that a learner first grasps the concept of force and the other concepts that underlie the law. This may require analyzing these concepts one step further back; for example, by undertaking to explain how acceleration is not just a change in the rate of speed of an object, but may also involve a change in the direction of that object's motion. There is also the advisability of first going over the conventions used to express the measure of each variable in the equation, for instance, force being expressed in newtons and acceleration in meters per second squared. The previous knowledge needed to grasp such concepts as measurement takes us back further still in the learning history of each learner. Where a teacher begins his presentation of a relatively sophisticated concept or principle, in a word, how he pitches it, is a question that will require his thinking through just what he can take for granted on the part of his students and what should be reviewed and refreshed before the new concept or principle is introduced.

These considerations are in considerable contrast to the process of ἐπαγωγή that Aristotle describes, in which the learner first grasps, without the teacher's planning or guidance or cooperation, out of a welter of perceptions of particulars, the universal that will be comprised in the ἀρχαί of science. In planning the lesson, the unit or the year's course of study, the teacher will take this achievement for granted and, if it is not true in the case of a student, the teacher, *qua* teacher, can do nothing about it. The notion of a universal, such as force, is limited to a knowledge by intuition only, with no possibility, logical or otherwise, of its being taught. This illustration shows how dubious a foundation the Aristotelian first principles of each science are for all science teaching.

The virtue of Aristotle's account of ἐπαγωγή and of νοῦς seems to lie in its emphasis on something that must take place before learning can occur. This "something" is previous knowledge. We have argued in the preceding part of this chapter that it is not necessary that such previous knowledge already contain in any sense what is to be learned. Indeed, to adhere strictly to such a position makes the process of learning virtually an empty concept. Yet it does make sense, practically and philosophically, to speak of learning as being dependent on what is previously known. This same point is applicable as well to the process of discovery. As noted in the examples of Herschel discovering Uranus and of a sleuth discovering the instrument used to pry open a window, both Herschel and the sleuth had sufficient previous knowledge to be able eventually to identify what it was they were looking for. This holds similarly in the case of the learner; and for her, as for those earlier seekers, she need not know what Y is before she attempts to learn what it is. It is sufficient, though not necessary, that she have some knowledge beforehand. This is the rationale for the idea that a teacher builds upon what the learner already grasps. If the teacher inadvertently or negligently proceeds to a principle without the proper preparation of the learner, without, that is, providing the bridge between what was previously grasped and what is now to be learned, the teaching is liable to fail. But that is the teacher's fault as much as the learner's.

Moreover, Aristotle's programme stimulates the question whether the knowledge built upon is always of the sort that could be expressed by the student in the form of general propositions about kinds of things. This may indeed sometimes happen in a class where the teacher is trying to guide the class from a principle of broad import to the derivation of a theorem or a corollary of a theorem already established. Yet a teacher may also do something quite unlike this, and begin her teaching at a level far less general. When she teaches about the causes of civil revolutions in history, she need not begin with general principles about the economic determinants of class attitudes. This may be incomprehensible as a starting point, from the viewpoint of many students in junior high school, for instance. Instead, the teacher may begin her unit with a particular example, such as U.S. Civil War or the establishment of the Paris Commune in 1871. This would be the sort of knowledge necessary for the teacher's more general point to be understood when she comes to it. It illustrates one context in which previous knowledge must be presumed for teaching to be successful and thus for it to be a precondition of learning. In another instance, a concept may have to be grasped by the learner before a principle has any meaning for her. The concept of acceleration must be learned before Newton's laws of motion can be understood and put to use in the school laboratory. This concept may in turn depend on the learner having previous knowledge of what velocity means in relation to the motion of an object. In yet a different area of textbook knowledge, the teacher may purposefully avoid the so-called principles of a subject in teaching the lower reaches of the knowledge appropriate to it. Often young students revel in learning historical data, such as dates, customs, or about important personages, for their own sake, and not as exemplifications of some general principle of historical change. To give another example from a different field, the mathematics teacher must first ensure that the learner is capable of multiplying integers before trying to teach her algebra and exponential functions. What use or chance of success would there be in trying to teach trigonometry before the learner has been given a grounding in geometry?

This is not to say that the textbook or classroom presentation of a science or other subject invariably postpones the mention of general principles until late in the unit or in the text's order of contents. Indeed, when setting forth the achievements in physics, for example, Newton's laws or Boyle's law (the latter represents the relationship between the pressure applied to a gas and its volume at a constant temperature) may be introduced early on and then used as a useful tool in particular applications. As at least one historian of science, Thomas Kuhn, has argued, this order of presentation may be used so often that it has given rise to a pervasive misunderstanding about how scientific discovery proceeds. For example, see Kuhn's following remark:

> . . . the manner in which science pedagogy entangles discussion
> of a theory with remarks on its exemplary applications has helped
> to reinforce a confirmation-theory drawn predominantly from
> other sources. Given the slightest reason for doing so, the man

who reads a science text can easily take the applications to be the evidence for the theory, the reasons why it ought to be believed. But science students accept theories on the authority of teacher and text, not because of evidence. What alternatives have they, or what competence? The applications given in texts are not there as evidence but because learning them is part of learning the paradigm at the base of current practice.[22]

This distinction between how scientific investigation proceeds and how the results of such investigation should be conveyed to students learning the relevant science is, I have argued, basic to our understanding of what Aristotle is theorizing about in the *Posterior Analytics*. The failure to recognize the fundamental nature of this distinction has led some commentaries far off track in attempting to explain how ἐπαγωγή is related to teaching.

The final remark in the preceding paragraph is especially pertinent to Kosman's argument, summarized briefly above in Chapter Three.[23] He argues that ἀπόδειξις is the activity (ἐνέργεια) of the state or disposition (ἕξις) of scientific knowledge (ἐπιστήμη). Because of Aristotle's emphasis on the revelation, through the use of the appropriate middle term, of the explanation (αἰτία), Kosman is led to characterize ἀπόδειξις as the understanding of "phenomena" (in the sense of being able to explain them), while ἐπαγωγή is the act of insight into the principles necessary for the explanation. All of this may be unobjectionable as an interpretation of what Aristotle means by these key terms, even though Kosman goes so far as to say that ἀπόδειξις and ἐπαγωγή are really the same activity, seen from different angles. Where Kosman's commentary is positively startling is his construal of ἐπαγωγή as teaching and of ἀπόδειξις as learning, and his claim that the two are correlated in such a manner. The first principles are not recognized, according to Kosman, until explanations are seen to follow from them. Thus ἀπόδειξις and

---

22   Thomas S. Kuhn, *The Structure of Scientific Revolutions*, 2nd rev. ed. (Chicago: University of Chicago Press, 1970), p. 80.

23   See *supra*, pp. 101–102, and L. A. Kosman, "Understanding, Explanation, and Insight in Aristotle's Posterior Analytics" in E. N. Lee et al. (eds.), *Exegesis and Argument: Studies in Greek Philosophy Presented to Gregory Vlastos* (Assen: Van Gorcum, 1973), pp. 374–92.

ἐπαγωγή go hand in hand and are not "radically independent" activities.

Kosman's interpretation is unfortunately an *ignotum per ignotius*, for it introduces and relies upon the notion that the ἀρχαί cannot be known and understood until the demonstration from them has been effected and grasped by the learner. Aristotle makes it abundantly clear that the grasp of first principles is logically prior to any process of demonstration. The principles are previously known, not just tentatively entertained and waiting for confirmation. He has in mind two distinct processes of coming to know, one of which leads to ἐπιστήμη and the other to immediate knowledge. There are slim grounds in the text of the *Posterior Analytics*, especially in Book *B*, chapter 19, for conflating these two processes until it is indistinct how ἐπαγωγή differs from ἀπόδειξις, save for the vantage point of the viewer.

One of the chief ways of distinguishing the two, on Aristotle's account, is that the latter is accomplished by the teacher and it leads to ἐπιστήμη that is διανοητική, while the former is not something the teacher can facilitate and it leads to a different type of learning from that with which most of the *Posterior Analytics* is concerned. Kosman nowhere mentions that one of the primary stimuli for Aristotle's development of an account of mediated versus unmediated knowledge in the *Posterior Analytics* is his attempt to avoid the eristical argument in the *Meno*.

Realizing this, however, puts the notion of ἐπαγωγή into a perspective that will prevent us from characterizing ἀπόδειξις as learning and ἐπαγωγή as teaching. If there is one thing that the idea of ἐπαγωγή should be kept entirely separate from, it is the claim that it is teaching. Hamlyn's discussion on the nature of ἐπαγωγή is for this reason more illuminating and helpful. He notes, for example, that:

> It must be remembered that Aristotle's original question was "How do the first principles become known and what is the knowing state?" . . . I think that as with the question about demonstration that he raises at the beginning of the *Posterior Analytics*, he means to ask how scientific truths and first

principles respectively become known by a learner.[24]

To claim, with Kosman, that the above question is answered by saying that the student learns first principles by ἀπόδειξις is highly misrepresentative of the thrust of Aristotle's account. Hamlyn also asks, in considering the question in the *Posterior Analytics B* 19 about whether first principles are innate or acquired:

> Why does he raise this issue? It seems to me that the question must have some reference to the issues raised in the *Meno*, just as the explicit reference at *Pr. An.* 67a22 to which I referred earlier. Aristotle obviously wants us to become clear about what learning consists in. More than this, there is some connection between what Aristotle says, even if that connection is oblique, and the dilemma put forward by *Meno* that led to Socrates's thesis about recollection.[25]

This brings us to the important issue of what is the relationship of ἐπαγωγή to teaching, if it is not the one conjectured by Kosman. The tenor of the *Posterior Analytics* is that teaching is associated strictly with demonstration and results in ἐπιστήμη, while ἐπαγωγή is a separate process and results in knowledge of the first principles. These must be known before the demonstration can be effected, and they must bear the characteristics of universality, necessity, and priority (in the several senses required). The teacher does not come on the scene, in Aristotle's account, until the learner has first grasped the primitive propositions from which demonstrations may be derived like theorems. This interpretation is not without controversy. It conflicts, for example, with one branch of Barnes's argument about the essentially pedagogic purpose of Aristotle's theory in the *Posterior Analytics*. He subscribes to the interpretation of ἐπαγωγή summarized in the following statement from Ross:

> . . . [ἐπαγωγή] comes to be used habitually of leading another person on by the contemplation of instances to see a general

---

[24]　D. W. Hamlyn, "Aristotelian Epagoge" (1976) 19 Phronesis 167–84, p. 181.
[25]　*Ibid.*, p. 173.

truth.[26]

Barnes adduces some textual evidence that, he claims, shows how demonstration and ἐπαγωγή are often yoked together as both being species of instruction.[27] These passages are few in number and hardly countervail the general thrust of the treatise, which is that demonstrative knowledge is peculiar to what is taught and learned, while knowledge of the ἀρχαί is acquired in some other way. This alternative way is not demonstration, and so *a fortiori*, it cannot be teaching and intellectual learning. The defect in Barnes's interpretation is that the "leading on," which Ross suggests is at the root of Aristotle's use of ἐπαγωγή, is not by itself a form of teaching for Aristotle.[28] If it were, then his bifurcation of things known into those grasped immediately (that is, by demonstration) and those grasped immediately (that is, by νοῦς) would no longer have any *raison d'être*. If both these types of knowledge are subsumed under the heading of what can be taught, in the restricted sense that Aristotle understands teaching, then Aristotle's programme, in so far as it is designed to surmount the problem of an infinite regress in what we can know and learn, is in danger of collapse. The logic of teaching, according to Aristotle's analysis, dictates that teaching begins with what is already known but that teaching itself is incapable of demonstrating first principles. An *obiter dictum* in Lesher's article, mentioned in Chapter Three above, indicates his criticism of Barnes's attempt to make a close connection between ἐπαγωγή and teaching.[29] Lesher, because his interest in νοῦς extends further than just its role as a faculty of intuition for grasping first

---

[26] W. D. Ross, *Aristotle's Prior and Posterior Analytics* (Oxford: Clarendon Press, 1949), p. 47.

[27] Jonathan Barnes, "Aristotle's Theory of Demonstration" (1969) 14 Phronesis 123–52, pp. 142–43.

[28] The attempt to extract a notion of teaching out of "leading on" is the counterpart of the equally questionable attempt to illuminate the concept of education by saying that it is a cognate of the Latin infinitives *educare* or *educere*, as if the etymology could give us the one criterion for picking out instances of when teaching was occurring.

[29] James H. Lesher, "The Meaning of *Nous* in the Posterior Analytics" (1973) 18 Phronesis 44–69, p. 57n.31.

principles, attempts to show how νοῦς has a central role in scientific investigation, as well as the teaching of science. Lesher's interest is not the same as ours, nor is his criticism of Barnes the same. Even if Barnes were wrong in arguing that ἐπαγωγή is just as much a didactic activity as is demonstration, his overall thesis that the *Posterior Analytics* is a treatise on the method of teaching a science is not thereby impaired. His support for that thesis is merely weakened by the loss of one prop. The argument here is that such a prop must be removed, or else Aristotle's account of the acquisition of the knowledge of first principles becomes more confused than it already is. Nor does Barnes's possible misconstruction of ἐπαγωγή assist the contradictory of his thesis, that the *Posterior Analytics* is not motivated by a pedagogic purpose.

The account in the *Posterior Analytics* B 19 as to how the universal is implanted in the soul is a prime example of obfuscation. Aristotle narrows down the process of acquisition by finding a form of knowledge superior to ἐπιστήμη that involves νοῦς rather than λόγος (discourse). We will recall from Chapter Three the passage in which the grasp of the universal is likened to the stand by the first soldier during a rout in battle; it is suggestive, but hardly deserves the approbation of "finely" describing the process of coming to know universals out of perceptions of particulars.[30] In psychological terms, the passage is from sense impressions, through memory and experience, to stabilization in the soul. This account, as Hamlyn suggests, leaves gaps at every stage that make us wonder why the next stage necessarily follows.[31] The important aspect, from Aristotle's point of view as revealed in the context surrounding the passage in question, is that the first principles are not innate in the soul, but have to be derived in some way from sense perception. There is an innate δύναμις (capacity) by means of which universals can be grasped. This capacity, when it is actualized, becomes a ἕξις (state) known as νοῦς. The teacher (*pace* Barnes) is not, *qua* teacher, the person who can conduct this process of ἐπαγωγή for the person

---

30   See *supra*, p. 100. For the commendatory language in relation to Aristotle's account, see George Howie (ed.), *Aristotle on Education* (London: Collier-Macmillan, 1968), p. 138.

31   See Hamlyn, *supra* n. 24, pp. 178–79.

seeking to acquire the first principles of a science. This stands in contrast to other contexts in Aristotle's work where he specifically discusses the formation of a ἕξις out of a δύναμις. We might note in this regard the following observation by Hamlyn, which again counts against the claim that ἐπαγωγή is one species of instruction:

> Moreover there is no reference in the genetic account of the development of knowledge to teaching or the part played by other people in upbringing, whereas at the beginning of E.N. II Aristotle does at least say that the intellectual virtues arise from and are increased by teaching.[32]

If our understanding of how Aristotle tries to counter the *Meno* dilemma is sound, then he would be opening himself up to a serious charge of inconsistency by allowing in the *Posterior Analytics B* 19 for teaching to take place before the requisite previous knowledge was acquired. Thus he has to be reticent on the matter. The person who leads on, or the "inducer" (as Barnes calls him), is mentioned on occasion elsewhere in that treatise, but not in the context where Aristotle discusses ἐπαγωγή directly and in detail and in relation to νοῦς.[33]

---

[32]   *Ibid.*, p. 180. For the sake of pointing out a significant symmetry, we should note that in Book *B* of the *N. E.*, Aristotle distinguishes between intellectual virtues (διανοητικαὶ ἀρεταί) and ethical virtues (ἠθικαὶ ἀρεταί) in correspondence to the subdivisions of the rational element of the soul: see *N.E.* 1103ª4–10. He contends that each type of virtue is acquired in a different way. Intellectual virtues are acquired by teaching and learning, whereas ethical virtues are acquired through ἔθος (which has often been translated into English as habit, though training, custom, and discipline are permissible variations, depending on the context: see *N.E.* 1103ª15–18). The repetition of an ἔθος, according to Aristotle, leads to the creation of a ἕξις (disposition or state) to be virtuous: *N.E.* 1103ᵇ21–22. Here again, the process of acquisition of a ἕξις is in distinct contrast to the process of learning something or, at least, learning as a result of being taught. The parallels between acquisition by ἔθος and by ἐπαγωγή, both of which are acquired by dint of repetition and by non-didactic means, serves to confirm that ἐπαγωγή should be kept separate and apart from Aristotle's general thesis that teaching is accomplished by demonstration. There is a deep rift between these two processes at each turn in Aristotle's work.

[33]   Barnes's article, *supra* n. 27, contains the list of such references.

Explanation, scientific knowledge, and the perfection of science

As we have seen, one of the prominent themes in the *Posterior Analytics* is that demonstration will reveal the αἰτία or explanation through the adduction of the middle term in the syllogism. Only in this way will drawing the conclusion from the demonstrative premisses guarantee the acquisition of knowledge in the unqualified sense, or ἐπιστήμη. Among the few examples that Aristotle gives of such explanation are those contained in the *Posterior Analytics B* 10 and 11. Why something is (διὰ τί), such as why thunder is, is explained by the proposition "Because fire is quenched in the clouds." What something is (τί ἐστι) or its essential definition, expressed in the case of thunder by the proposition "The noise of the fire being quenched in the clouds."[34] Aristotle goes on to claim that knowledge of the αἰτία is a precondition of our thinking that we have scientific knowledge. He gives four different possible types of αἰτία, which are usually loosely correlated with the four causes that make up the doctrine Aristotle expounds directly in the *Metaphysics* and other works. For example, we might use the following syllogism to demonstrate the efficient cause of why the Athenians fought a war against the Persians led by Datis:

> Unprovoked raiding belongs to the Athenians.
> War belongs to unprovoked raiding (i.e., men make war on the unjust aggressor).
> So war belongs to the Athenians (i.e., war is waged upon them).

In a nutshell, the Athenians antagonized the Persians by accompanying the Eretrians in a raid on Sardis. The order of the terms will be slightly different where the final cause is to be demonstrated (Aristotle uses the example of the after-dinner walk as an explanation of health). It should be noted that such syllogisms as the above are not apodeictic, since the constitutive propositions are neither universal nor necessary.

---

[34]   *An. Post.* 94ª3–9.

The example above of an αἰτία that explains the outbreak of one of the Persian wars shows an interesting feature of Aristotle's system that has been little remarked upon. The αἰτία is not just a middle term in the demonstrative syllogism in the sense of being one word or classificatory expression. As shown by Aristotle's several examples of the Persian war, the twinkling stars and the non-twinkling planets, thunder, eclipses, deciduousness, and the post-prandial stroll, the αἰτία given in each is essentially elliptical for an entire proposition. Possibly we would say that it stands for what would amount to a theory (rather than just an "initial condition," as philosophers of science use that phrase). The explanation of "being near" is really a statement of relation between the earth and the planets that is attempted to be stated and used as one element in a broader categorical proposition. The teacher, in laying out the αἰτία, might have to call upon a background understanding by the learner that makes sense of what is being presented as the middle term. Even then, the teacher's proffered explanation will be incomplete if it is ascertained that the phenomenon being explained has a better explanation; that is, if the non-twinkling of the planets in the night sky, for example, is explained not just by their proximity to the earth but also by the refraction of light penetrating the earth's atmosphere. The relation between unprovoked raiding and the typical retaliatory attitude of the country of the victims might be a causal explanation of what final event touched off the hostilities between two armies. The problem is that an understanding of what explains the situation in which this efficient cause operates may be a matter of some dispute among historians long after the events in question occur. We learn from our historical studies not to rush to conclusions about the inevitability of certain effects from alleged causes. For example, we might ask why the middle term in the syllogism about the Persian wars does not apply equally to the aftermath of the sinking of the Lusitania in 1915. So long as Aristotle sees teachers as capable of conveying to their students the necessary connections between historical events, the more he would be surprised at the continuing controversy about what are *the* explanations of what happened in history.

There are, as well, many types of explanations that are used in educational settings that are not differentiated on Aristotle's account.

For example, there are explanations in the form of clarifications of what a word or expression means, in the form of justifications and of causes, in the form of invoking a law or a principle, or in the form of a teacher giving the function of a natural or artificial object or of an institution in society.[35] In each science there have grown up, and sometimes been discarded or modified, models and criteria for deciding whether an explanation is relevant and fruitful. The role of laws and statistical generalizations in the physical sciences are not always analogous to, let alone the same as, the role of those same things in the social sciences or history.[36] Aristotle's account fails to allow the possibility that each science, besides having its own set of first principles and objects for study, also works within its own framework of what is to count as an adequate scientific explanation.

What value lies in requiring, as Aristotle does, that knowledge of the explanation shall be a criterion of scientific knowledge? Aristotle's theory of explanation, although it might appear crude because some of the examples he cites do not appear to us to go to the bottom of the phenomenon in question, is at least a significant forerunner of how in modern science laws and theories are used to account for what we claim to observe. Just as science is interested in answering the question why, so is a considerable part of a teacher's day occupied, directly or indirectly, with providing answers or materials by which the students may answer that same question. The scientist does not rest satisfied with collecting unrelated facts for their own sake, but rather seeks to put her observations and experimental results (when he can control and modify the conditions of observation) into relation with a theory, law, or principle that has explanatory power. This is why some philosophers of science depreciate what they call mere "natural history."[37] Teachers are also

---

[35]   See Martin, *supra* n. 8, pp. 45–46, and Robert H. Ennis, *Logic in Teaching* (Englewood Cliffs, N.J.: Prentice-Hall, 1969), pp. 255–60.

[36]   See Ernest Nagel, *The Structure of Science* (New York: Harcourt, Brace and World, 1961), pp. 459 *et seq.*, 503 *et seq.*

[37]   For example, Toulmin, *supra* n. 2, p. 45. writes as follows:
       But so long as one remains within natural history there is little scope for *explaining* anything: "Chi-chi is black, because Chi-chi is a raven and all ravens are black" is hardly the kind of thing a scientist calls an

imputed with this insatiable curiosity, though not at the level necessarily of making discoveries. It is enough that they are supposed to keep up the currency of their knowledge of what

explanation. Indeed, among scientists, to say that a newly fledged subject is still in the "natural-history stage" is a way of depreciating it: natural history and the like are felt to lack many of the essential features of a full-grown science, and to be entitled to the name of sciences only conditionally and out of courtesy.

It is noteworthy that Toulmin selects as an example of a naturalist's reasoning the type of syllogism that has traditionally been found wanting by critics of syllogism, and which was discussed at length in Chapter Five above. It was there shown to be quite uncharacteristic of what Aristotle meant by a demonstrative syllogism that contains an explanation in its premises. Against Toulmin's rather perfunctory dismissal of what sort of facts a naturalist deals with and of what he tries to explain, we may cite, first, a discussion such as Gould's explanation of the matricidal habits of the cecidomyian gall midge. The reason for such behaviour appears to lie in the population ecology of the swarm, so that when the flies are in a short-lived, favourable environment they tend to reproduce early and in great fecundity. Parthenogenesis occurs with the interesting twist that the mother reproduces while still a larva and she supplies the offspring with nutrient in the form of her own body. For a description of this process, see Stephen Jay Gould, *Ever Since Darwin: Reflections in Natural History* (New York: W. W. Norton, 1977), pp. 91–96. Secondly, we should not be misled into thinking that Aristotle was the first in a long line of gentlemen-naturalists, who collect facts like jackdaws and for their own sake. There is an enlightening discussion on how the physical sciences, such as chemistry, were at one time considered "no proper avocation for a gentleman" in D'Arcy W. Thompson, *Science and the Classics* (London: Oxford University Press, 1940), pp. 46–47. By natural history, Toulmin seems to mean something like the leisurely collection of curiosities; to this extent, he is speaking at cross purposes with those who see natural history as an important forerunner of modern zoology and botany, which included many explanations which had to be rediscovered, in the case of Aristotle's work on fishes, two thousand years later. His work on classification is neither easy nor without value for contemporary philosophers of natural science. Despite numerous crucial differences in principle between Aristotelian biology and its modern counterpart, some things Aristotle has to say about function, τέλος, and the relation of εἶδος both to ὕλη (matter) and to γένος (species) are illuminating. See Marjorie Grene, "Aristotle and Modern Biology" (1972) 33 Journal of the History of Ideas 395–424, reprinted in Robert S. Cohen and Marx W. Wartofsky (eds.), *Boston Studies in the Philosophy of Science*, vol. 23: *The Understanding of Nature* (Boston and Dordrecht: D. Reidel, 1974), pp. 74–107.

working scientists have discovered or speculated, and be competent to bring such knowledge to bear in the classroom or school laboratory. At the least, it is not strange to us that Aristotle would claim that teaching involves explanation, though as we shall see below, it is odd to think that the teacher's sole activity should be to give explanations.[38]

The covering law, or deductive-nomological, model of scientific explanation is a direct descendant of Aristotle's theory of demonstration.[39] In such a model, an attempt is made to account for the explanandum phenomenon (encompassed in the proposition we have elsewhere called the demonstrandum of an apodeictic syllogism) by giving other propositions as premises from which the explanandum proposition logically follows. These other propositions may be general laws, such as Newton's laws of motion or of gravitation, or more empirical laws such as those formulated by Galileo. The premises may also be singular propositions that disclose the initial conditions, as they are called, of the explanandum.[40] The explanation will be successful and be counted a scientific explanation if the premises contain the antecedent grounds that permit the conclusion to be drawn. The explanandum will thereby be proven. The rules of deduction used in modern science are not, of course, limited to the valid syllogistic forms acknowledged by Aristotle. Moreover, what proposition in general

---

[38]   See Martin, *supra* n. 8, where he notes at p. 65:
> The teacher engages in this activity, but not all of the teacher's activity is explanatory and not all discourse used by the teacher is explanatory discourse.

[39]   Credit for being the first to analyze the structure of a finished science as deductive and explanatory is generally accorded to Aristotle: see Nagel, *supra* n. 36, p. 29. Aristotle, of course, only discussed first principles (ἀρχαί) as the starting points of demonstration, rather than what subsequent scientists call "laws of nature" or, in Greek, νόμοι. Hence the second part of the hyphenated expression, deductive-nomological, is not characteristic of Aristotle's programme. It is tempting to coin a parallel phrase for describing that programme, but this results in "deductive-archaeological," which will hardly do.

[40]   See Nagel, *supra* n. 36, p. 31, and Carl G. Hempel, *Philosophy of Natural Science* (Englewood Cliffs, N.J.: Prentice-Hall, 1966), pp. 49–54.

form is to count as a law is a matter, in part, of the scientific theories that are accepted as authoritative at any given time. What were formerly thought of as laws can be challenged and have their status usurped by more accurate generalizations (for example, Kepler's laws of planetary motion were replaced by Newton's laws). Or a law may be affected by the discovery of more comprehensive generalizations which show that the former law holds only in a limited range of circumstances (for example, as Newtonian dynamics have been affected by theoretical developments in subatomic physics). What was once accepted as a plausible theory by which to explain events studied by physicists or chemists may be completely discarded when a superior theory is developed. Thus, the explanation of combustion by postulating a substance called phlogiston was debunked by Lavoisier. Likewise, the explanation of the behaviour of light by movements in the luminiferous ether, and of the behaviour of heat by the existence of a caloric fluid have been consigned to the archives of science, as electrodynamic and thermodynamic theories, respectively, have become more sophisticated.[41] Such changes and displacements, repeated more rapidly in recent history it seems, entitle us to doubt what a finished science would look like. And if we cannot envision how the fundamental laws would cover all particular instances and how those laws would interrelate, then we cannot yet envision how such scientific knowledge would be taught as well. From Aristotle to Newton and beyond there has been this ideal of making a complete inventory of nature and exposing her lineaments in a logical fashion. The problem with such a vision, in at least one respect, is that current teaching cannot be founded on the unreached ideal; nor, as we have said, would we know how to teach the science until we can know the structure and logical relationships between its different levels of propositions.

This is not to say that scientific activity is in such constant ferment that the results obtained by working scientists and the theories that

---

[41]　The value of guiding students through the archival history of science is not to be discounted altogether as a teaching technique, since it may be one way of helping them to gain an understanding of how an explanation is to be judged for inclusion or not in the prevailing body of theory.

they adhere to from time to time cannot be pinned down for the purpose of conveying them to science students. The fact that those scientists are continually setting new problems for themselves and trying to investigate them in novel ways, taking into account both current theory and alternatives thereto, is an important feature, however, of science itself. It means that a teacher cannot rest satisfied with presenting explanations without reference to what theory is presupposed by those explanations, nor can a learner advance very far in scientific understanding if she operates under the apprehension that the body of knowledge and protocol of techniques she is studying amounts to a closed system that will permit no modification or addition. It would be a gross misrepresentation if the sciences were now taught as if the laws and theories that currently hold sway were immune from change. This ideal, foreign as it may seem to us, is part of the ideal conception that forms the background for Aristotle's pedagogic scheme in the *Posterior Analytics*. To this extent, as a philosophy of science that would have some value in articulating what science teachers should strive for in their classrooms, the *Posterior Analytics* is now antiquated and probably has been since Galileo developed his theory of mechanics by measuring the events occurring in his experiments.

Nor does the theory of demonstration seem appropriate for other school subjects. History was not, for Aristotle, a theoretical science, partly because it does not deal with universals.[42] Indeed, Aristotle evinces more of an interest in history as a species of literature (and one that is inferior to poetry, at that). Even if it were a science, it would be difficult to imagine historical knowledge being comprised in propositions that can be marshalled into the premises necessary for achieving demonstration (compare the problems we had with understanding the middle term in Aristotle's example above of the efficient cause of the Persian conflict). The problems that beset the science teacher, on Aristotle's account, would also affect the teaching of history. Indeed, such problems may be felt with more pungency in the latter discipline because so few historians' theories ever aspire

---

[42]   See *Poet.* 51^{b}6–10.

to the status of universal laws.[43] Nowadays there is something hubristic about an historian making such a claim.

We might find it illustrative of the weaknesses of Aristotle's position to consider an actual attempt to organize a field of study, viz. politics, into an axiomatic science. A pattern of propositions is laid out that would reveal by a deductive form all of the essential knowledge encompassed in the science. James Mill, in his *Essay on Government*, published in the early nineteenth century, purported to do just that.[44] The conclusion of his deductions from the basic laws of human nature, as postulated by him, is that a representative system of government is the best form for all times and places. He calls this the "grand discovery of modern times."[45] Macaulay made his name in replying to Mill's essay, and apparently owed the beginnings of his political career to his critique's notoriety. Leaving aside Macaulay's penchant for hyperbole and his astonishing arguments *ad hominem*, we may note that some of his criticisms are applicable to any attempt to rear a science when the materials at hand are still inadequate. Mill, he claims, is guilty of a priori reasoning in setting forth certain propensities of human nature, and any deduction therefrom is synthetic, that is, artificial. Such notions as power, happiness, misery, pleasure, and motives are not susceptible to the same kind of precise definition as the primitive terms in Euclid's system of geometry, such as lines and numbers.[46] Mill's maxims, if they are true necessarily and tautologically, are undeniable, but then they do not allow us to advance in practical knowledge. Where those maxims are false or ambiguous, they constitute "verbal sophisms" and:

---

[43]   See Michael Scriven, "Truisms as the Grounds for Historical Explanations" in Patrick Gardiner (ed.), *Theories of History* (New York: Free Press, 1959), pp. 443–75.

[44]   The text of Mill's essay, originally published in 1820 in the Supplement to the fifth edition of the *Encyclopedia Britannica*, is reproduced, along with Macaulay's first critical review in respect of it, in Jack Lively and John Rees (eds.), *Utilitarian Logic and Politics* (Oxford: Clarendon Press, 1978).

[45]   *Ibid.*, p. 73.

[46]   *Ibid.*, p. 107.

> There is no proposition so monstrously untrue in morals and politics that we will not undertake to prove it, by something that shall sound like a logical demonstration, from admitted principles.[47]

This is the kind of response to which premature claims that fresh knowledge can be deduced and conveyed by demonstration are prone. Such a system requires substantial agreement over what are to count as the first principles, and such assent is more likely to be obtained by a Euclid or even a Newton than a student of politics.[48] On many fronts there has been a distinct movement away from according to deductive methods in teaching a body of achieved knowledge, and towards a so-called inductive method. The latter is not really a single, specifiable method but instead, its meaning is related to the context and content of the science for which its use is pleaded.[49]

We may also wonder whether, because of our current rather benighted state in respect of what Aristotle would call the essential natures of things, the teacher would use definitions strictly in the way supposed by Aristotle. Again, as emphasized throughout this chapter, the discourse in which the teacher participates is richer than Aristotle's model presupposes. The demands of the curriculum and of the students may lead the teacher to formulate many different

---

[47]   *Ibid.*

[48]   See R. Harré, *An Introduction to the Logic of the Sciences* (London: Macmillan and Co. Ltd., 1963), p. 74, for a description of comparable attempts to apply deductive and classificatory analyses, inspired by Aristotle's system, to knowledge of human affairs, particularly politics.

[49]   For example, see James Bryant Conant, *Two Modes of Thought* (New York: Trident Press, 1964). Conant distinguishes between the "empirical-inductive" and the "theoretical-deductive" methods of Inquiry. He draws a rather hard and fast line between these. The latter of the two, he contends, has been overrated. To Conant we owe the programme of teaching science by having students examine "case histories." One precedent for such a design of learning, which Conant speaks highly of in this book, is Christopher C. Langdell's installation of the case method of studying law at Harvard in the 1870s. This pedagogy, claims Conant, has had a profound effect on American business and politics, since so many lawyers have ended up as executives rather than practising law. See *ibid.*, ch. 3.

kinds of statements in an attempt to provide a definition. This will be true not only for the teacher but for the writer of a textbook as well. Among the types of statements that may be loosely grouped together under the rubric of definition are the giving of a synonym, a classification, an equivalent expression, or an operation on the basis of which something else is said to hold.[50] For Aristotle the process of definition in teaching (though not necessarily in scientific inquiry) is invariably linked with disclosing both what is the thing in question and what is its essence. This is an extremely narrow and rigorous standard for teachers to achieve. About some things in science they are agnostics. Learning does take place notwithstanding that a teacher's locutions often fall short of meeting such a standard. What is important and sufficient for educational purposes is that the teacher be in a position to give an illuminating or functional answer to the question of what something is, and not always how something is placed in a hierarchy of classes and sub-classes. On occasion, the teacher may justifiably use *ad hoc* definitions, for example, in trying to teach young children something about the relation between heat and molecular activity. It may not be reasonable or good practice on such an occasion to go into a technical exposition of what kinetic energy means.

In the foregoing paragraphs I have criticized Aristotle's theory by which he sets forth the criteria that will guarantee the acquisition of ἐπιστήμη or scientific knowledge through being taught. It remains for us to discuss in this part how his assumption that all knowledge worth teaching is expressible in a type of proposition, composed of a subject and a predicate, and in the indicative mood. Such knowledge is propositional and thus forms one group of the "epistemological darlings" referred to by Ryle.[51] The premises and the conclusion of a demonstrative syllogism are each a πρότασις or proposition. Presumably the learner takes note of these, while they are set forth by the teacher, by literally writing them out on a tablet or pad. She can then perhaps rehearse them to herself and recall

---

50   This list of types of definition, which is partial only, is taken from Ennis, *supra* n. 35, pp. 191–243.

51   Gilbert Ryle, *The Concept of Mind* (Harmondsworth: Penguin Books, 1963), p. 177.

them when tested or when she herself, as in a monitorial type of setting, is required to teach them to another, less advanced, learner. The picture that emerges is that a person cannot be said to have knowledge of Y unless she can give an account of Y in conformity with the criteria set forth in the *Posterior Analytics*. This is a broad claim and gives, not just a primacy to propositional knowledge as against other forms of knowledge, but also an incorrigible privilege to the knower of such propositions, because she alone deserves to claim to have unqualified knowledge.

This emphasis on propositional knowledge tends to ignore whole other dimensions of knowledge and learning, which may have as important an educational value as Aristotle's preferred type. His emphasis on definition and the knowledge of the essential nature of an object may conjure up an image such as the Dickensian portrait of Mr. Gradgrind interrogating Sissy Jupe on the question of what is a horse. She is unable to give a response, notwithstanding that her father works with horses every day and she may be presumed to have a first hand knowledge of them. Bitzer, when called upon, formulates the definition of a horse according to the Gradgrind canon, namely, "Quadriped, Graminivorous, Forty teeth, namely twenty-four grinders, four eye-teeth, and twelve incisive," and so on.[52]

We might say that a learner such as Sissy Jupe grasps Y even though she has never formulated Y to herself and has never had Y told to her in any didactic setting. Nevertheless, she could point out a horse when she comes across one and perhaps tell us very many interesting things about it. Knowledge may be implicit, or as it has been also called, tacit, in respect of the learner, when she may not be able to make it explicit or to tell it on command, even if she tries to. Polanyi gives as an example the knowledge of a person's face that allows us to recognize it but which cannot be put into words.[53] Or, to cite another type of implicit knowledge, we might consider the case of the aging hockey player, who we and the sports journalists agree, knows that his career is finished even though he has not

---

[52]   Charles Dickens, *Hard Times*, ed. David Craig (Harmondsworth: Penguin Books Ltd., 1969), pp. 48–50.

[53]   Polanyi, *supra* n. 18, pp. 4–5.

expressed this to himself. He nevertheless goes to training camp laden with his sticks and equipment despite the adjurations and warnings from his spouse and his doctor. The same problem of unexpressed knowledge, in a less mundane context, leads St. Anselm to try to explain how the fool, as the Psalmist portrays him, could say in his heart that there is no God.[54] Unless the fool is totally dull, Anselm finds some knowledge implicit in him that contradicts what he professes even to himself.

A second dimension of knowledge unaccounted for by Aristotle's standard way of thinking about knowledge claims solely in the form of propositions is "knowing how." This is to be contrasted with "knowing that."[55] Aristotle's interest in teaching and demonstration is confined to the latter. This is so in spite of our recognition that to demonstrate something in a classroom or in a laboratory or on a playing field involves the teacher often in showing how, for example, something is to be performed. This may be anything from how to mix certain basic colours of paint to obtain a desired shade, to tracing through in front of the class, using the blackboard, a geometric theorem. It may also involve a field trip, for example, to illustrate a principle by duplicating Torricelli's experiment regarding the effect of the earth's atmospheric pressure using a mercury barometer. Any account of teaching that ignores the knowledge of how to do something, and concentrates instead on knowledge of what something is in its essential nature is hardly accurate as a description of that which teaching as a whole consists in.[56] This is because, in

---

[54] St. Anselm, *Proslogium*, in *Basic Writings*, ed. and trans. S. N. Deane, 2nd ed. (La Salle, Ill.: Open Court Publishing Company, 1962), ch. 4.

[55] See Ryle, *supra* n. 51, ch. 2 and *passim*.

[56] Such a programme is also liable to the charge that what learning is cultivated is mere "verbalism," or the learning of words rather than things. This specification of a dengenerate form of learning is a common refrain in a philosopher's critique of the current practises he surveys. So we read in Comenius, *supra* n. 16, p. 68, the following:

In the Latin School boys were allowed to spend some years in learning words without any reference to objects.

He recommends, instead of this, at *ibid.*, p. 86 that:

Words, therefore, should always be taught and learned in combination with things, just as wine is bought and sold together with the cask that

Ryle's words:

> Theorists have been so preoccupied with the task of investigating the nature, the source, and the credentials of the theories that we adopt that they have for the most part ignored the question of what it is for someone to know how to perform tasks. In ordinary life, on the contrary, as well as in the special business of teaching, we are much more concerned with people's competence than with their cognitive repertoires, with the operations than with the truths that they learn. Indeed even when we are concerned with their intellectual excellences and deficiencies, we are less interested in the stocks of truths that they acquire and retain than in their capacities to find out truths for themselves and their ability to organize and exploit them, when discovered.[57]

Of all the philosophers who have studied problems of knowledge,

---

> contains it . . . For what are words but the husks and coverings of things? Dewey, who is very sensitive to apparent antitheses (and is keen on reconciling them by discovering a higher, more accurate conception of what each limb means for educational practices), notes two senses of learning, the first of which is relevant to Aristotle's method of demonstration:
>
>> Another antithesis is suggested by the two senses of the word "learning." On the one hand, learning is the sum total of what is known, as that is handed down by books and learned men. It is something external, an accumulation of cognitions as one ight store material commodities in a warehouse . . . On the other hand, learning means something which the individual does when he studies. It is an active, personally conducted affair.
>
> John Dewey, *Democracy and Education* (New York: Free Press, 1966), p. 335. Dewey sees an educational evil springing from such opposition and, we might say, bases his commendations on a concept of learning and teaching that will make such different senses of learning continuous. In his philosophical work on the foundations of education, the student is shown to need something more than a guided tour through the current stock of achieved knowledge.

[57] Ryle, *supra* n. 51, pp. 28–29. A roughly similar type of knowledge is included in Bloom's taxonomy under the heading "intellectual abilities or skills" and is contrasted with information. This is by no means congruous with Ryle's account, since information is deemed synonymous with knowledge, and is used in combination with a skill. See Benjamin S. Bloom (ed.), *Taxonomy of Educational Objectives*, vol. 1: *Cognitive Domain* (New York and London: Longman, 1956, reprinted, 1981), p. 38.

Aristotle in many ways shows the most acute understanding of Ryle's distinction between the aforementioned types of knowledge. His *Nicomachean Ethics* contains a full discussion of how a person learns to become virtuous, not by an intellectual grasp of propositions that might be expounded by a preceptor, but through performing certain types of acts and a process of habituation.[58] His account may not be right in every respect, but it definitely reveals Aristotle's sensitivity in that context to different kinds of knowledge. Virtue becomes a knowledge of how to do something rather than a knowledge that is expressible in propositions. This knowledge that underlies a performance rather than a statement is even subject to some assistance by a teacher of sorts in its acquisition. But it remains true that, for Aristotle, scientific knowledge, which only teaching can convey, strictly is a matter of general propositions. The resultant role of the teacher of the sciences is lecturing and telling, not showing how something is done and arranging for students to try to do it themselves. Demonstration is the method of transmitting knowledge codified in the theoretical, not the practical, sciences.

We might justifiably wonder if Aristotle's method of demonstration is designed only for students who are studying a terminal course in the subject in question, rather than being taught as one step in the preparation for eventually becoming researchers themselves. That is, the method seems inappropriate for those science students who aspire to pass through the required stages in order to become working scientists in their own right. There is no requirement in the *Posterior Analytics* that learners should struggle to find the explanation of a phenomenon; they are instead to imbibe the one given to them by the teacher. Such explanations are sanctified by their being the explanations discovered by a finished science which has no gaps and leaves no room for doubt or further research. Such a suggestion would not be uncongenial to the spirit in which Aristotle conceives of a science in the *Posterior Analytics*. His model of teaching looks forward to the day when the sciences are finally erected and the notion of further scientific progress is obsolete. The

---

[58]　See *supra*, n. 32. Also see William K. Frankena, *Three Historical Philosophies of Education* (Chicago: Scott, Foresman and Company, 1965), pp. 54–57.

teaching of science by demonstration is not to train students in how scientific explanations are hypothesized and confirmed or refuted, but to instruct them in what are the authoritative explanations. In so far as this conception of what scientists have accomplished and can accomplish in the future is quite foreign to what we understand is the tireless quest for better (that is, more general and more accurate) laws and theories, Aristotle's programme is based on, quite possibly, a vain hope. It might be better used for training catechists in a dogma, or the disciples of Lysenko in the science of genetics, than for teaching postulant scientists or those learners who wish to acquire just a basic understanding of a scientific subject. One of the lessons of the history of science since Aristotle's day is that, in teaching about prevalent theories and received knowledge, there is a proper balance struck between, on the one hand, the respect of authority as tested by objective criteria, and, on the other hand, the maintenance of an open mind. In this the teacher must be an exemplar as well as a preacher.

Demonstration as the sole method of teaching

One point stressed in modern philosophy of education is how wrong it is to see in the concept of teaching just one, single-track, nuclear activity that can be isolated independently of any context in which it might occur.[59] Teaching has been compared to gardening, for instance, to illustrate how many different sorts of activities can possibly be tried to achieve an overall purpose.[60] A teacher, in carrying out the business of having students learn something, may lay down general laws, present an hypothesis, ask questions, review the previous day's class, answer inquiries, summarize her current

---

[59]   For example, see Ryle, *supra* n. 51, p. 292. Also, note the following cautionary advice by Passmore, *supra* n. 6, p. 28:

> If the teacher-trainer remembers the triadic character of teaching, this will help him, in particular, to avoid the temptation—so widespread in the last part of the nineteenth century when teachers of education were commonly known as "masters of method"—to suppose that there must be some single method, *the* method of teaching, which is applicable in the teaching of any subject to any pupil.

[60]   Hirst and Peters, *supra* n. 7, p. 74.

lecture, demonstrate the application of a formula, have a student attempt such an application, correct a student's response to a question, discipline or admonish a student, give hints, commendations and directions, feign ignorance as a strategy for making students curious, examine verbally and by written papers what the learner knows, and so on. All of these things, and the list of them could be very long, are activities associated with the teacher's job of promoting learning. The wide variety of subjects taught in elementary and secondary schools, in vocational and technical centres, in university undergraduate and graduate faculties, and in professional schools and continuing education programmes should alert us to the danger of generalizing about a single method appropriate for teaching all of these subjects to anyone at any time. To an increasing degree, teachers have seen their training become more specialized by the offering of courses in curriculum and instruction in specific subject areas, or by programmes in the training of teachers for students with special needs or abilities.

To hold, as Aristotle does, that the individual activities listed in the preceding paragraph may be forsworn by the teacher in favour of the single activity of demonstrating a conclusion by means of syllogism is a prescription that differs greatly from what we observe teachers doing in fact. Barnes is probably correct in wondering how even the erotetic syllogism would find a place in the classroom Aristotle envisions. As we have interpreted it, Aristotle's scheme is backed up by an achieved fund of knowledge that will not suffer modification. The Preacher's homily about there being nothing new under the sun will be extended beyond the solar system. The rational presentation of such knowledge will be accomplished by following the logical ordering of its elements, and the assimilation by the learners will be guaranteed as long as they have normal human capacities. Learning is not only possible (and so Aristotle puts the skeptic's doubts to rest), but it is inevitable, so long as the method of demonstration is employed.

One of the crucial differences between what Aristotle recommends and what everyday teachers in fact strive for, and between what Aristotelian science is meant to convey and what modern curricula are geared towards, is what different things are meant in each case by understanding and explanation. For Aristotle, the understanding of the αἰτία is conveyed by its inclusion and disclosure in the course of syllogizing. Grasping the conclusion just is the learning of scientific knowledge. The αἰτία is discovered by the learner in the sense that it is revealed to her by the demonstration. The validity of the explanation is guaranteed by the fact that the theoretical science and its practitioners have adopted it as the correct explanation, and secondly, in so far as the explanation occurs in the major premiss as the middle term, its truth will be a matter of immediate knowledge to the learner. For Aristotle, objects or events may have more than one explanation only because there are different sorts of αἰτία that reflect whether we are trying to expose to view the efficient or the final cause, and so forth. There are not different explanations that reflect competing theories or principles or schools of thought on an issue. For modern science, its practitioners and its teachers, the emphasis is not on giving the explanation of a phenomenon to a learner in the form of an accomplished fact, but rather in equipping the learner to go on as much as possible by her own lights and to figure out the explanation in a way that shows both an understanding of what she has been taught and her capacity for learning new things as a result of his achieved understanding. This goal of equipping the student is what involves so many different activities on the part of the teacher and makes the discourse between teacher and student proceed along such a multitude of lines, no one of which we would call teaching in a focal sense.

Thus we introduce students to such activities as generating and testing hypotheses, seeing what criteria might be used for confirming or refuting a hypothesis, and using auxiliary hypotheses in developing explanations. We may also wish that learners would become, as a result of their current learning, able to conceive how future data might tend to refute theories which now command assent. These goals would be outworn by the time Aristotle's programme could be used. The quick-witted person would be exceptional when taught by demonstration because it would be easier for her to grasp the stock of human knowledge, not because she would have anything to contribute to the sciences once they were completed.

The degree of the variety of teaching discourse may be illustrated by charting and analyzing the different types of acts that are performed by both the student and the teacher in an educational setting. We might imagine an anthropologist, or some other analyst trained in observing and recording human behaviour, compiling long lists of acts undertaken by the teacher in trying to convey the essentials of a subject, and then showing us how such acts differ from subject to subject, and from grade to grade and school to school. The lecture as the paradigm of instruction may play only a small role in what a teacher does, and may be nearly nonexistent at a certain level of schooling. For many subjects and students it may not be a particularly appropriate or efficient means of teaching. Even within the teaching of philosophy, the activity of lecturing from prepared notes and publishing these as continuous treatises thereafter is not without its competitors among forms of philosophical discourse. There is, for example, the models of teaching that have come down to us in the form of a written dialogue between master and student or between philosophic equals. Besides the best-known example of Plato, we have the productions of Augustine, Anselm, Aquinas, Berkeley and Hume. Even some of Descartes's arguments were stimulated by and organized in reaction to an opponent or correspondent. The use of an imaginary dialogue is not confined to philosophy. Galileo, for instance, gives a masterful exposition of then prevailing scientific views on fundamental topics in the sciences.[61] The exchanges in his dialogue can even be quite humorous. The dialogue has the advantage over the pure lecture that the learner

---

[61]   Galileo Galilei, *Dialogue Concerning the Two Chief World Systems—Ptolemaic and Copernican*, trans. Stillman Drake, 2nd ed. (Berkeley: University of California Press, 1967). An amusing example of the participants in the discussion attempting to develop a syllogistic proof of the earth's motionlessness is contained at pp. 139–41. Galileo's dialogue was part of a significant literary genre. In such dialogues, the parties were often expressly named Master and Scholar: see, for example, Marie Boas, *The Scientific Renaissance 1450–1630* (New York: Harper & Brothers, 1962), pp. 94–95 for a discussion of a dialogue by Robert Recorde, who was inclined towards Copernicanism. Part of Galileo's purpose is using the dialogue as an "indirect" means of discussing his cosmological ideas, of course, was to circumvent the censorship of the Inquisition. In this, he was unsuccessful. Galileo's dialogue was banned by religious authoritles soon after its publication and its author summoned to Rome.

reading it is initiated directly into the debate and the intellectual achievements it comprises, such as making and confuting assumptions, challenging purported evidence, construing ambiguous expressions, setting dilemmas and escaping them, and recognizing or debunking alleged proofs. These activities are common to different subjects taught to learners; they are not the exclusive domain of the logician. Our need for learning them has not noticeably atrophied just because we think that progress has been made in the scientific understanding of our world. It continues to form a necessary balance to the imparting of knowledge by the teacher speaking *ex cathedra*, or by the authority of a textbook certified for use by the relevant governmental authority. In the process of rejecting Plato's proposed solution to the dilemma posed by Meno, Aristotle also rejects many significant means of teaching, one of the most evident of which is the use of dialogue, both between the teacher and student or between students, but also as a model for how controversy and rational debate proceeds. This is ironic, because the model that Aristotle himself uses to develop his formal logic, if we have stated what is near the truth in Chapter Two, is the dialectical exercise that Aristotle would likely have engaged in as a student combatant.

There may even be a justifiable use of an aporetic technique by the teacher, wherein he poses a problem that has no known solution. This may be attempted on the ground, *inter alia*, of inculcating intellectual humility; but it should not be done as if this were the sole means of teaching or of introducing a subject. Passmore notes in this regard:

> But at the same time a teacher will not want his pupils to be *merely* bewildered; he will hope to teach them in what way the questions which puzzle them ought to be discussed, what sort of evidence is relevant to their solution.[62]

Socratic questioning has its place, but it has its use in the furtherance of the learner's understanding. The ἔλεγχος in an educational setting should be a prelude to a fresh attempt to tackle

---

62   Passmore, *supra* n. 6, p. 179.

the subject. Both Plato and Aristotle may have overrated the student's curiosity after he has run into an *impasse*. The teacher cannot presume that every student will have Aristotle's boundless and resilient curiosity.

A further difficulty with using syllogism as the single mode for all teaching is that it depends for its effectiveness on the learner being able to follow the steps in the deductive pattern and being able, as well, to grasp the relatively sophisticated first principles without the teacher's help. Psychologists who have studied the reasoning processes of children at different stages of development have given us descriptions and theories that may well make us wonder whether the deductive pattern of the demonstrative syllogism would not be beyond the understanding of most learners until they are well into their school years. For example, Piaget has characterized the child at the preoperational stage as typically reasoning by transduction, in that he proceeds from particular to particular and generally lacks a conception of a hierarchy of categories.[63] The ability to reason in and to follow the pattern of deductions from general principles would, on Piaget's account, be expected only when a child was approaching or had reached the formal operations stage of development. Only at this stage also would a child have the experience and the "construction of reality" that allow her to formulate, to follow, and to test hypotheses. It may be adolescence or beyond before the learner will grasp the form of a syllogism as the clue to an argument's validity, rather than focussing on the content of the argument.

The point of this excursion into what has been suggested by some

---

[63]   The summary below is based on Barbel Inhelder and Jean Piaget, *The Growth of Logical Thinking from Childhood to Adolescence*, trans. Anne Parsons and Stanley Milgram (New York: Basic Books, Inc., 1958). See also Jean Piaget, *Judgment and Reasoning in the Child*, trans. Marjorie Worden (New York: Harcourt, Brace & World, 1928). There is even no guarantee that after a certain age all students may be presumed to have grasped the form of a syllogism, as attested by an experiment in the 1940s with a sample group of college students. In John L. Phillips, Jr., *The Origins of Intellect: Piaget's Theory* (San Francisco: W. H. Freeman and Company, 1969), p. 103, an article entitled "The Distortion of Syllogistic Reasoning Produced by Personal Convictions" is cited for a vivid illustration of lack of understanding of syllogistic form long after the formal operations stage should have been reached.

psychologists is that the method of demonstration would seem, at best, to be useful only long after the learner is first put under the tutelage of another. Furthermore, the learner's grasp of categories and class relationships and what Aristotle calls universals cannot be taken for granted at the start of a child's learning. If Piaget is correct in even the general thrust of his conclusions, and if the growth of logical abilities is maturational, then the teacher will have an important task in bringing the learner along to the point where a demonstration may be tried and understood. Much non-demonstrative, which is not to say illogical, teaching will have to precede this achievement however.

The point made by Piaget is not offered here as if its truth were self-evident. It is cited to show that we may have good grounds for doubting whether a six-year-old, for example, could grasp a deductive proof. With respect to the general claim that all understanding proceeds in a definite order, we may note Hamlyn's following remark:

> I certainly do not believe that it is possible to lay down any general law of development which the child must follow in acquiring concepts and coming to see the relationships between them. I would, however, point to the fact that concepts vary in complexity and abstractness, and that this determines certain general priorities.[64]

The didactic lecture, in which the universal terms and definitions are used as starting points and explanations are adduced in the proper order, and the student is moved by the force of the valid form of the demonstration to assent to the conclusion, makes up, we might say, a highly stylized form of teaching. It would be appropriate only if the content of human knowledge were finally settled in its boundaries and shown to bear an intrinsic order that the normal mind could grasp. That is, the logical order of the sciences could

---

64   D. W. Hamlyn, "Logical and Psychological Aspects of Learning" in R. S. Peters (ed.), *The Concept of Teaching* (London: Routledge and Kegan Paul, 1967), pp. 34–35.

determine the logical cultivation of the mind.[65] Unfortunately, the textbooks used in schools are not in their final editions and scientific discovery proceeds apace. Moreover, we can as yet not say whether this is an accidental and problematic feature that will be surmounted with time and energy, or whether it will remain a permanent feature of what we mean by doing science. Either way, so long as our knowledge remains incomplete, the teaching of science will be conditioned by such a fact. Teaching science will continue to involve trying to convey an understanding of the scientific method (or scientific methods, as some would prefer to have it.) Such a method or methods are at the opposite pole from Aristotle's prescribed

---

[65] There is some similarity between the view advanced by Aristotle and the "logical" as opposed to a "psychological" method of teaching science that was decried by Dewey. See his *Democracy and Education, supra* n. 56, ch. 17. He characterizes the situation as follows at *ibid.*, p. 219:

> Logical order is not a form imposed upon what is known; it is the proper form of knowledge as perfected. For it means that the statement of subject matter is of a nature to exhibit to one who understands it the premises from which it follows and the conclusions to which it points.

Therefore, he contends at *ibid.*, p. 220:

> From the standpoint of the learner scientific form is an ideal to be achieved, not a starting point from which to set out. It is, nevertheless, a frequent practice to start in instruction with the rudiments of science somewhat simplified. The necessary consequence is an isolation of science from significant experience.

He goes on to argue why the psychological method is preferable to the logical method, since the former will ensure that the scientific training received by learners will allow them to apply their own intelligence in a way conducive to social progress. Throughout his work, Dewey reveals a close acquaintance with Aristotle's logic of science teaching. Dewey's criticism differs from what follows in our argument, in that scientific progress is here not taken to be logically synonymous with social progress. Secondly, there may be a valuable role for the technique of setting out definitions and basic principles as the propaedeutic to the study of a science. This does not mean that they should, in such a context, be presented as essential definitions or indubitable principles, but part of the initiation into seeing what scientists do and, perhaps, later emulating them, is learning the vocabulary of a science and going on from there, revising one's original conceptions as more is learned. On this dualism in possible methods, see the fruitful discussion in Paul H. Hirst, "Logical and Psychological Aspects of Teaching" in R. S. Peters (ed.), *The Concept of Education* (London: Routledge and Kegan Paul, 1967), pp. 44–60.

method of demonstration in teaching. This does not mean that they are disorganized or illogical. Different methods of teaching have been developed, for which their proponents claim specific virtues and advantages. The illusion created by Aristotle's programme, and which is shattered by our examining how teachers actually go about their tasks with a congeries of aids, activities, and intermediate and long-range goals, is that there is but one method of teaching; that it can be followed mechanically; and that by itself it will guarantee scientific understanding. The logic of teaching, developed by Aristotle as part and parcel of his fundamentally important work in organizing the first system of formal inference, is remarkable for its compendiousness and its ambitiousness. It presents, with considerable philosophic rigour, an impressive vision of axiomatized knowledge and a certified method for conveying that knowledge to a subsequent generation of learners. It may, as we have argued, rest on some questionable presuppositions in Aristotle's argument. There is no denying, however, that much can be learned about learning by our having to compare our modern assumptions about education with Aristotle's thorough analysis. In the matter of seeing teaching as a rational enterprise, he remains, indeed, the master.

Index

New Perspectives
in Philosophical Scholarship:
Texts and Issues

This series features innovations in philosophical scholarship on texts and issues in both Eastern and Western philosophy. The books in this series either will present more comprehensive scholarly and philosophical perspectives on their subjects than usually presented or will deal with their subjects from novel perspectives. Most books in this series either will be editions or translations of important texts in the history of Eastern or Western philosophy, along with philosophical commentaries, or will be studies of a philosophical issue in contemporary Eastern or Western philosophy or in the history of Eastern or Western philosophy.

The general editor is Professor James Duerlinger, Philosophy Department, University of Iowa, Iowa City, IA 52242.